The logs herewith are the first translations into English, and read like many modern adventure stories such as *Around the World in 80 Days*. It also contains essays by Adolph Caso and Marco Giacomelli.

Caso takes on the polemics surrounding the persona of Columbus--especially the issues of Lief Ericson--with the forged Vinland Map; of Columbus' *Jewishness*-- with the claims that Columbus secretly worked for his Jewish brothers to find and to create for them a Jewish state in the new world; and whether America should have a Columbus Day. Giacomelli, on the other hand, tells the story of how America got its name.

In grateful recognition of

Naples · Fort Myers
Greyhound Track

for support of

Edison Community College

through

The Campaign for Edison

1991

TO AMERICA
AND AROUND
THE WORLD

**The Logs of
Christopher Columbus
And
Ferdinand Magellan**

Branden Publishing Company
Boston

Library of Congress Cataloging-in-Publication Data

To America and around the world : the logs of Christopher Columbus
and Ferdinand Magellan.
    p. cm.
Includes bibliographical references and index.
ISBN 0-8283-1992-8 : $19.95
    1. Columbus, Christopher--Diaries.
    2. Magalhães, Fernão de, d. 1521--Diaries.
    3. Columbus, Christopher--Birth.
    4. America--Name.
    5. Voyages around the world.
    6. America--Discovery and exploration--Spanish.
    7. Explorers--America--Biography.
    8. Explorers--Spain--Biography.
E118.T6 1990
970.01'6--dc20   90-38850
                                                          CIP

Branden Publishing Company, Inc.
17 Station Street
Box 843, Brookline Village
Boston, MA 02147

Contents

In appreciation of

JOSEPH BANKS

and *in memory of*

EDMUND R. BROWN

and

SAMUEL ELIOT MORISON

Coat of Arms of Columbus

Foreword

The accounts of Columbus and of Magellan read--today, still--as great adventure stories, fresh in narrative, luxuriant in descriptions, and epic in extent. For this reason, the transcriptions of these stories are void of footnotes and of other details.

This volume includes the original logs (journals) of Christopher Columbus' first voyage to the *New World* while in search of a western route to the Orient--India and China. The present English translation, done by Clements R. Markham, was printed in England in 1893 by the Hakluyt Society, and is considered one of the first translations from the Spanish into English.

The volume also includes the original daily logs of Ferdinand Magellan (as written by Antonio Pigafetta), in his voyage around the world, to prove that the earth was *finally* round. The present English translation (of John Pinkerton), was printed in England in 1812, and is considered one of the first translations from the Italian into English.

7--To America and Around the World

The above translations are faithfully transcribed into modern English orthography for easy reading. No attempt was made to edit or to change any part of the originals--the goal being to give the modern reader the closest rendition of the original manuscripts. Generally speaking, the first works (or translations), though having rough edges, are closer to the original thoughts and renditions of their authors.

Of the two famous voyagers and explorers, the most controversial is Christopher Columbus--both as a man and as a sailor. He is also either the most beloved or the most maligned. The essays point out a multifarious polemic involving the Scandinavian, Italian, Portuguese, Spanish, French, and their American counterparts, with a major portion devoted to the question of Columbus' *Jewish* origin.

Of particular interest is the essay on how America got its name.

Birthplace of Columbus, near Genoa, Italy

Columbus with an astrolabe
(Thevet's Portrait, 1584)

9--To America and Around the World

To Francis Parkman, LL.D.,
The Historian of New France.

Dear Mr. Parkman:

You and I have not followed the maritime peoples of western Europe in planting and defending their flags on the American shores without observing the strange fortunes of the Italians, in that they have provided pioneers for those Atlantic nations without having once secured in the New World a foothold for themselves.

When Venice gave her Cabot to England and Florence bestowed Verrazano upon France, these explorers established the territorial claims of their respective and foster motherlands, leading to those contrasts and conflicts which it has been your fortune to illustrate as no one else has.

When Genoa gave Columbus to Spain and Florence accredited her Vespucius to Portugal, these adjacent powers, whom the Bull of Demarcation would have kept asunder in the new hemisphere, established their rival races in middle and southern America, neighboring as in the Old World: but their contrasts and conflicts have never had so worthy a historian as you have been for those of the north.

The beginnings of their commingled history I have tried to relate in the present work, and I turn naturally to associate in it the name of the brilliant historian of France and England in North America with that of your obliged friend.

Justin Winsor
Cambridge, June 1893

Columbus taking leave of Ferdinand and Isabella
at Palos in 1492 (Teodore de Bry, 1594)

Caravels in port
(Teodore de Bry, 1594)

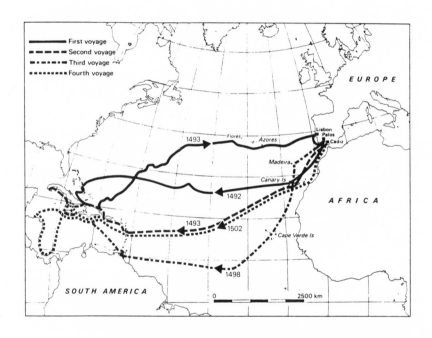

The four voyages of Columbus
(by C. Fisher)

The Journal
of the
First Voyage of
Christopher Columbus

translated
by
Clements S. Markham, C.B., F.R.S.

London
Printed for the Hakluyt Society
Lincoln's Inn Fields, W.C. 1893

14--To America and Around the World

This is the first voyage and the routes and direction taken by the Admiral Don Cristobal Colon when he discovered the Indies, summarized; except the prologue made for the Sovereigns, which is given word for word and commences in this manner.

In the name of our Lord Jesus Christ.

Because, O most Christian, and very high, very excellent, and puissant Princes, King and Queen of the Spains and of the islands of the Sea, our Lords, in this present year of 1492, after your Highness had given an end to the war with the Moors who reigned in Europe, and had finished it in the very great city of Granada, where in this present year, on the second day of the month of January, by force of arms, I saw the royal banners of your Highness placed on the towers of Alhambra, which is the fortress of that city, I saw the Moorish King come forth from the gates of the city and kiss the royal hands of your Highness, and of the Prince My Lord, and presently in that same month, acting on the information that I had given to your Highness touching the lands of India, and respecting a Prince who is called Gran Can, which means in our language, King of Kings, how he and his ancestors had sent to Rome many times to ask for learned men of our holy faith to teach him, and how the Holy Father had never complied, insomuch that many people believing in idolatries were lost by receiving doctrine of perdition: Your Highness, as Catholic Christians and Princes who love the holy Christian faith, and the propagation of it, and who are enemies to the sect of Mahomet and to all idolatries and heresies, resolved to send me, Cristobal Colon, to the said parts of India to see the said princes, and the cities and lands, and their disposition, with a view that they might be converted to our holy faith; and ordered that I should not go by land to the eastward, as had been customary, but that I should go by way of the west, whither up to this day, we do not know for certain that any one has gone.

Thus, after having turned out all the Jews from all your kingdoms and lordships, in the same month of January, your Highness gave orders to me that with a sufficient fleet I should go to the said parts of India, and for this they made great concessions to me, and ennobled me, so that henceforward I should be called Don, and should be Chief Admiral of the Ocean Sea, perpetual Viceroy and Governor of all the islands and continents that I should discover and gain, and that I might hereafter discover and gain in the Ocean Sea, and that my eldest son should succeed, and so on from generation to generation for ever.

I left the city of Granada on the 12th day of May in the same year of 1492, being Saturday, and came to the town of Palos, which is a seaport; where I equipped three vessels well suited for such service; and departed from that port, well supplied with provisions and with many sailors, on the 3rd day of August of the same year, being Friday, half an hour before sunrise, taking the route to the islands of Canaria, belonging to your Highness, which are in the said Ocean Sea, that I might thence take my departure for navigating until I should arrive at the Indies, and give the letters of your Highness to those princes, so as to comply with my orders. As part of my duty I thought it well to write an account of all the voyage very punctually, noting from day to day all that I should do and see, and that should happen, as will be seen further on. Also, Lords Princes, I resolved to describe each night what passed in the day, and to note each day how I navigated at night. I propose to construct a new chart for navigating, on which I shall delineate all the sea and lands of the Ocean in their proper positions under their bearings; and further, I propose to prepare a book, and to put down all as it were in a picture, by latitude from the equator, and western longitude. Above all, I shall have accomplished much, for I shall forget sleep, and shall work at the business of navigation, that so the service may be performed; all which will entail great labor.

Friday, 3rd of August.
We departed on Friday, the 3rd of August, in the year 1492, from the bar of Saltes, at 8 o'clock, and proceeded with a strong sea breeze until sunset, towards the south, for 60 miles, equal to 15 leagues; afterwards S.W. and W.S.W., which was the course for the Canaries.

16--To America and Around the World

Saturday, 4th of August.
They steered S.W. 1\4 S.

Sunday, 5th of August.
They continued their course day and night more than 40 leagues.

Monday, 6th of August.
The rudder of the caravel Pinta became unshipped, and Martin Alonso Pinzon, who was in command, believed or suspected that it was by contrivance of Gomes Rascon and Cristobal Quintero, to whom the caravel belonged, for they dreaded to go on that voyage. The Admiral says that, before they sailed, these men had been displaying a certain backwardness, so to speak. The Admiral was much disturbed at not being able to help the said caravel without danger, and he says that he was eased of some anxiety when he reflected that Martin Alonso Pinzon was a man of energy and ingenuity. They made, during the day and night, 29 leagues.

Tuesday, 7th of August.
The rudder of the Pinta was shipped and secured, and they proceeded on a course for the island of Lanzarote, one of the Canaries. They made, during the day and night, 25 leagues.

Wednesday, 8th of August.
Opinions respecting their position varied among the pilots of the three caravels; but that of the Admiral proved to be nearer the truth. He wished to go to Gran Canaria, to leave the caravel Pinta, because she was disabled by the faulty hanging of her rudder, and was taking water. He intended to obtain another there if one could be found. They could not reach the place that day.

Thursday, 9th of August.
The Admiral was not able to reach Gomera until the night of Sunday, while Martin Alonso remained on that coast of Gran Canaria by order of the Admiral, because his vessel could not be navigated. Afterwards the Admiral took her to Canaria, and they repaired the Pinta very thoroughly through the pains and labor of the Admiral, of Martin Alonso, and of the rest. Finally they came to Gomera. They saw a great fire issue from the mountain of the island of Tenerife,

17--To America and Around the World

which is of great height. They rigged the Pinta with square sails, for she was lateen rigged; and the Admiral reached Gomera on Sunday, the 2nd of September, with the Pinta repaired.

The Admiral says that many honorable Spanish gentlemen who were at Gomera with Dona Ines Peraza, mother of Guillem Peraza (who was afterwards the first Count of Gomera), and who were natives of the island of Hierro, declared that every year they saw land to the west of the Canaries; and others, natives of Gomera, affirmed the same on oath. The Admiral here says that he remembers, when in Portugal in the year 1484, a man came to the King from the island of Madeira, to beg for a caravel to go to this land that was seen, who swore that it could be seen every year, and always in the same way. He also says that he recollects the same thing being affirmed in the islands of the Azores; and all these lands were described as in the same direction, and as being like each other, and of the same size. Having taken in water, and meat, and all else that the men had who were left at Gomera by the Admiral when he went to the island of Canaria to repair the caravel Pinta, he finally made sail from the said island of Gomera, with his three caravels, on Thursday, the 6th of September.

Thursday, 6th of September.

He departed on that day from the port of Gomera in the morning, and shaped a course to go on his voyage; having received tidings from a caravel that came from the island of Hierro that three Portuguese caravels were off that island with the object of taking him. (This must have been the result of the King's annoyance that Colon should have gone to Castile.) There was a calm all that day and night, and in the morning he found himself between Gomera and Tenerife.

Friday, 7th of September.

The calm continued all Friday and Saturday, until the third hour of the night.

Saturday, 8th of September.

At the third hour of Saturday night it began to blow from the N.E., and the Admiral shaped a course to the west. He took in much sea over the bows, which retarded progress, and 9 leagues were made in that day and night.

18–To America and Around the World

Sunday, 9th of September.

This day the Admiral made 19 leagues, and he arranged to reckon less than the number run, because if the voyage was of long duration, the people would not be so terrified and disheartened. In the night he made 120 miles, at the rate of 12 miles an hour, which are 30 leagues. The sailors steered badly, letting the ship fall off to N.E., and even more, respecting which the Admiral complained many times.

Monday, 10th of September.

In this day and night he made 60 leagues, at the rate of 10 miles an hour, which are 2 1\2 leagues; but he only counted 48 leagues, that the people might not be alarmed if the voyage should be long.

Tuesday, 11th of September.

That day they sailed on their course, which was west, and made 20 leagues and more. They saw a large piece of the mast of a ship of 120 tons, but were unable to get it. In the night they made nearly 20 leagues, but only counted 16, for the reason already given.

Wednesday, 12th of September.

That day, steering their course, they made 33 leagues during the day and night, counting less.

Thursday, 13th of September.

That day and night, steering their course, which was west, they made 33 leagues, counting 3 or 4 less. The currents were against them. On this day, at the commencement of the night, the needles turned a half point to north-west, and in the morning they turned somewhat more north-west.

Friday, 14th of September.

That day they navigated, on their westerly course, day and night 20 leagues, counting a little less. Here those of the caravel Nina reported that they had seen a tern and a boatswain bird, and these birds never go more than 25 leagues from the land.

Saturday, 15th of September.

That day and night they made 27 leagues and rather more on their west course; and in the early part of the night there fell from heaven into the sea a marvelous flame of fire, at a distance of about 4 or 5 leagues from them.

Sunday, 16th of September.
That day and night they steered their course west, making 39 leagues, but the Admiral only counted 36. There were some clouds and small rain. The Admiral says that on that day, and ever afterwards, they met with very temperate breezes, so that there was great pleasure in enjoying the mornings, nothing being wanted but the song of nightingales. He says that the weather was like April in Andalusia. Here they began to see many tufts of grass which were very green, and appeared to have been quite recently torn from the land. From this they judged that they were near some island, but not the main land, according to the Admiral, "because", as he says, "I make the main land to be more distant."

Monday, 17th of September.
They proceeded on their west course, and made over 50 leagues in the day and night, but the Admiral only counted 47. They were aided by the current. They saw much very fine grass and herbs from rocks, which came from the west. They, therefore, considered that they were near land. The pilots observed the north point, and found that the needles turned a full point to the west of north. So the mariners were alarmed and dejected, and did not give their reason. But the Admiral knew, and ordered that the north should be again observed at dawn. They then found that the needles were true. The cause was that the star makes the movement, and not the needles. At dawn, on that Monday, they saw much more weed appearing, like herbs from rivers, in which they found a live crab, which the Admiral kept. He says that these crabs are certain signs of land. The sea-water was found to be less than it had been since leaving the Canaries. The breezes were always soft. Everyone was pleased, and the best sailors went ahead to sight the first land. They saw many tunny-fish, and the crew of the Nina killed one. The Admiral here says that these signs of land came from the west, "in which direction I trust in that high God in whose hands are all victories that very soon we shall sight land." In that morning he says that a white bird was seen which has not the habit of sleeping on the sea called *rabo de junco* (boatswain-bird).

Tuesday, 18th of September.

20–To America and Around the World

This day and night they made over 44 leagues, the Admiral only counting 38. In all these days the sea was very smooth, like the river at Seville. This day Martin Alonso, with the Pinta, which was a fast sailer, did not wait, for he said to the Admiral, from his caravel, that he had seen a great multitude of birds flying westward, that he hoped to see land that night, and that he therefore pressed onward. A great cloud appeared in the north, which is a sign of the proximity of land.

Wednesday, 17th of September.
The Admiral continued on his course, and during the day and night he made but 25 leagues because it was calm. He counted 22. This day, at 10 o'clock, a booby came to the ship, and in the afternoon another arrived, these birds not generally going more than 20 leagues from the land. There was also some drizzling rain without wind, which is a sure sign of land. The Admiral did not wish to cause delay by beating to windward to ascertain whether land was near, but he considered it certain that there were islands both to the north and south of his position, (as indeed there were, and was passing through the middle of them). For his desire was to press onwards to the Indies, the weather being fine. For on his return, God willing, he could see all. These are his words. Here the pilots found their positions. He of the Nina made the Canaries 440 leagues distant, the Pinta 420. The pilot of The Admiral's ship made the distance exactly 400 leagues.

Thursday, 20th of September.
This day the course was W.b.N., and as her head was all round the compass owing to the calm that prevailed, the ships made only 7 or 8 leagues. Two boobies came to the ship, and afterwards another, a sign of proximity of land. They saw much weed, although none was seen on the previous day. They caught a bird with the hand, which was like a tern. But it was a river-bird, not a sea-bird, the feet being like those of a gull. At dawn two or three land-birds came singing to the ship, and they disappeared before sunset. Afterwards a booby came from W.N.W., and flew to the S.W., which was a sign that it left land in the W.N.W.; for these birds sleep on shore, and go to sea in the mornings in search of food, not extending their flight more than two leagues from the land.

Friday, 21st of September.

21--To America and Around the World

Most of the day it was calm, and later there was a little wind. During the day and night they did not make good more than 13 leagues. At dawn they saw so much weed that the sea appeared to be covered with it, and it came from the west. A booby was seen. The sea was very smooth, like a river, and the air the best in the world. They saw a whale, which is a sign that they were near land, because they always keep near the shore.

Saturday, 22nd of September.
They shaped a course W.N.W. more or less, her head turning from one to the other point, and made 30 leagues. Scarcely any weed was seen. They saw some sandpipers and another bird. Here the Admiral says: "This contrary wind was very necessary for me, because my people were much excited at the thought that in these seas no wind ever blew in the direction of Spain." Part of the day there was no weed, and later it was very thick.

Sunday, 23rd of September.
They shaped a course N.W., and at times more northerly; occasionally they were on their course, which was west, and they made about 22 leagues. They saw a dove and a booby, another river-bird, and some white birds. There was a great deal of weed, and they found crabs in it. The sea being smooth and calm, the crew began to murmur, saying that here there was no great sea, and that the wind would never blow so that they could return to Spain. Afterwards the sea rose very much, without wind, which astonished them. The Admiral here says: "Thus the high sea was very necessary to me, such as had not appeared but in the time of the Jews when they went out of Egypt and murmured against Moses, who delivered them out of captivity."

Monday, 24th of September.
The Admiral went on his west course all day and night, making 14 leagues. He counted 12. A booby came to the ship, and many sandpipers.

Tuesday, 25th of September.
This day began with a calm, and afterwards there was wind. They were on their west course until night. The Admiral conversed with Martin Alonso Pinzon, captain of the other caravel Pinta, respecting a chart which he had sent to the caravel three days before,

on which, as it would appear, the Admiral had certain islands depicted in that sea. Martin Alonso said that the ships were in the position on which the islands were placed, and the Admiral replied that so it appeared to him: but it might be that they had not fallen in with them, owing to the currents which had always set the ships to the N.E., and that they had not made so much as the pilots reported. The Admiral then asked for the chart to be returned, and it was sent back on a line. The Admiral then began to plot the position on it, with the pilot and mariners. At sunset Martin Alonso went up on the poop of his ship, and with much joy called to the Admiral, claiming the reward as he had sighted land. When the Admiral heard this positively declared, he says that he gave thanks to the Lord on his knees, while Martin Alonso said the *Gloria in excelsis* with his people. The Admiral's crew did the same. Those of the Nina all went up on the mast and into the rigging, and declared that it was land. It so seemed to the Admiral, and that it was distant 25 leagues. They all continued to declare it was land until night. The Admiral ordered the course to be altered from W. to S.W., in which direction the land had appeared. That day they made 4 leagues on a west course, and 17 S.W. during the night, in all 21; but the people were told that 13 was the distance made good: for it was always feigned to them that the distances were less, so that the voyage might not appear so long. Thus two reckonings were kept on this voyage, the shorter being feigned, and the longer being the true one. The sea was very smooth, so that many sailors bathed alongside. They saw many *dorados* and other fish.

Saturday, 29th of September.

The course was west, and they made 24 leagues, counting 21 for the people. Owing to calms, the distance made good during day and night was not much. They saw a bird called *rabiforcado* (man-o'-war bird), which makes the boobies vomit what they have swallowed, and eats it, maintaining itself on nothing else. It is a sea-bird, but does not sleep on the sea, and does not go more than 20 leagues from the land. There are many of them at the Cape Verde Islands. Afterwards they saw two boobies. The air was very mild and agreeable, and the Admiral says that nothing was wanting but to hear the nightingale. The sea smooth as a river. Later, three boobies and a man-o'-war bird were seen three times. There was much weed.

Sunday, 30th of September.

23--To America and Around the World

The western course was steered, and during the day and night, owing to calms, only 14 leagues were made, 11 being counted. Four boatswain-birds came to the ship, which is a great sign of land, for so many birds of this kind together is a sign that they are not straying or lost. They also twice saw four boobies. There was much weed. *Note* that the stars which are called *las guardias* (The Pointers), when night comes on, are near the western point, and when dawn breaks they are near the N.E. point; so that, during the whole night, they do not appear to move more than three lines or 9 hours, and this on each night. The Admiral says this, and also that at nightfall the needles vary a point westerly, while at dawn they agree exactly with the star. From this it would appear that the north star has a movement like the other stars, while the needles always point correctly.

Monday, 1st of October.
Course west, and 25 leagues made good, counted for the crew as 20 leagues. There was a heavy shower of rain. At dawn the Admiral's pilot made the distance from Hierro 578 leagues to the west. The reduced reckoning which the Admiral showed to the crew is 484 leagues; but the truth which the Admiral observed and kept secret was 707.

Tuesday, 2nd of October.
Course west, and during the day and night 39 leagues were made good, counted for the crew as 30. The sea always smooth. Many thanks be given to God, says the Admiral, that the weed is coming from east to west, contrary to its usual course. Many fish were seen, and one was killed. A white bird was also seen that appeared to be a gull.

Wednesday, 3rd of October.
They navigated on the usual course, and made good 47 leagues, counted 40. Sandpipers appeared, and much week, some of it very old and some quite fresh and having fruit. They say no birds. The Admiral, therefore, thought that they had left the islands behind them which were depicted on the charts. The Admiral here says that he did not wish to keep the ships beating about during the last week, and in the last few days when there were so many signs of land, although he had information of certain islands in the region. For he wished to

avoid delay, his object being to reach the Indies. He says that to delay would not be wise.

Thursday, 4th of October.
Course west, and 63 leagues made good during the day and night, counted as 46. More than forty sandpipers came to the ship in a flock, and two boobies, and a ship's boy hit one with a stone. There also came a man-o'-war bird and a white bird like a gull.

Friday, 5th of October.
The Admiral steered his course, going 11 miles an hour, and during the day and night they made good 57 leagues, as the wind increased somewhat during the night: 45 were counted. The sea was smooth and quiet. "To God", he says, "be many thanks given, the air being pleasant and temperate, with no weed, many sandpipers, and flying-fish coming on the deck in numbers.

Saturday, 6th of October.
The Admiral continued his west course, and during day and night they made good 40 leagues, 33 being counted. This night Martin Alonso said that it would be well to steer south of west, and it appeared to the Admiral that Martin Alonso did not say this with respect to the island of Cipango. He saw that if an error was made the land would not be reached so quickly, and that consequently it would be better to go at once to the continent and afterwards to the islands.

Sunday, 7th of October.
The west course was continued: for two hours they went at the rate of 12 miles an hour, and afterwards 8 miles an hour. They made good 23 leagues, counting 18 for the people. This day, at sunrise, the caravel Nina, which went ahead, being the best sailer, and pushed forward as much as possible to sight the land first, so as to enjoy the reward which the Sovereigns had promised to whoever should see it first, hoisted a flag at the mast-head and fired a gun, as a signal that she had sighted land, for such was the Admiral's order. He had also ordered that, at sunrise and sunset, all the ships should join him; because those two times are most proper for seeing the greatest distance, the haze clearing away. No land was seen during the afternoon, as reported by the caravel Nina, and they passed a great number of birds flying from N. to S.W. This gave rise to the belief

25--To America and Around the World

that the birds were either going to sleep on land, or were flying from the winter which might be supposed to be near in the land whence they were coming. The Admiral was aware that most of the islands held by the Portuguese were discovered by the flight of birds. For this reason he resolved to give up the west course, and to shape a course W.S.W. for the two following days. He began the new course one hour before sunset. They made good, during the night, about 5 leagues, and 23 in the day, altogether 28 leagues.

Monday, 8th of October
The course was W.S.W., and 11 1\2 or 12 leagues were made good in the day and night; and at times it appears that they went at the rate of 15 miles an hour during the night (if the handwriting is not deceptive). The sea was like the river at Seville. "Thanks be to God", says the Admiral, "the air is very soft like the April at Seville; and it is a pleasure to be here, so balmy are the breezes." The weed seemed to be very fresh. There were many land-birds, and they took one that was flying to the S.W. Terns, ducks, and a booby were also seen.

Tuesday, 9th of October
The course was S.W., and they made 5 leagues. The wind then changed, and the Admiral steered W. by N. 4 leagues. Altogether, in day and night, they made 11 leagues by day and 20 1\2 leagues by night; counted as 17 leagues altogether. Throughout the night birds were heard passing.

Wednesday, 10th of October.
The course was W.S.W., and they went at the rate of 10 miles an hour, occasionally 12 miles, and sometimes 7. During the day and night they made 59 leagues, counted as no more than 44. Here the people could endure no longer. They complained of the length of the voyage. But the Admiral cheered them up in the best way he could, giving them good hopes of the advantages they might gain from it. He added that, however much they might complain, he had to go to the Indies, and that he would go on until he found them, with the help of the Lord.

Thursday, 11th of October.
The course was W.S.W., and there was more sea than there had been during the whole of the voyage. They saw sandpipers, and a

26--To America and Around the World

green reed near the ship. Those of the caravel Pinta saw a cane and a pole, and they took up another small pole which appeared to have been worked with iron; also another bit of cane, a land-plant, and a small board. The crew of the caravel Nina also saw signs of land, and a small branch covered with berries. Everyone breathed afresh and rejoiced at these signs. The run until sunset was 26 leagues.

After sunset the Admiral returned to his original west course, and they went along at the rate of 12 miles an hour. Up to two hours after midnight they had gone 90 miles, equal to 22 1\2 leagues. As the caravel Pinta was a better sailer, and went ahead of the Admiral, she found the land, and made the signals ordered by the Admiral. The land was first seen by a sailor named Rodrigo de Triana. But the Admiral, at ten in the previous night, being on the castle of the poop, saw a light, though it was so uncertain that he could not affirm it was land. He called Pedro Gutierrez, a gentleman of the King's bed chamber, and said that there seemed to be a light, and that he should look at it. He did so, and saw it. The Admiral said the same to Rodrigo Sanchez of Segovia, whom the King and Queen had sent with the fleet as inspector, but he could see nothing, because he was not in a place whence anything could be seen. After the Admiral had spoken he saw the light once or twice, and it was like a wax candle rising and falling. It seemed too few to be an indication of land; but the Admiral made certain that land was close. When they said the *Salve*, which all the sailors were accustomed to sing in their way, the Admiral asked and admonished the men to keep a good look-out on the forecastle, and to watch well for land; and to him who should first cry out that he saw land, he would give a silk doublet, besides the other rewards promised by the Sovereigns, which were 10,000 maravedis to him who should first see it. At two hours after midnight the land was sighted at a distance of two leagues. They shortened sail, and lay by under the mainsail without the bonnets. The vessels were hove to, waiting for daylight; and on Friday they arrived at a small island of the Lucayos, called, in the language of the Indians, *Guanahani*. Presently they saw naked people. The Admiral went on shore in the armed boat, and Martin Alonso Pinzon, and Vicente Yanez, his brother, who was captain of the Nina. The Admiral took the royal standard, and the captains went with two banners of the green cross, which the Admiral took in all the ships as a sign, with an F and a Y and a crown over each letter, one on one side of the cross and the other on the other. Having landed, they saw trees very green, and much water, and fruits of diverse kinds. The

27--To America and Around the World

Admiral called to the two captains, and to the others who leaped on shore, and to Rodrigo Escovedo, secretary of the whole fleet, and to Rodrigo Sanchez of Segovia, and said that they should bear faithful testimony that he, in presence of all, had taken, as he now took, possession of the said island for the King and for the Queen, his Lords making the declarations that are required, as is more largely set forth in the testimonies which were then made in writing.

Presently, many inhabitants of the island assembled. What follows is in the actual of the Admiral in his book of the first navigation and discovery of the Indies.

"I," he says, "that we might form great friendship, for I knew that they were a people who could be more easily freed and converted to our holy faith by love than by force, gave to some of them red caps, and glass beads to put round their necks, and many other things of little value, which gave them great pleasure, and made them so much our friends that it was a marvel to see. They afterwards came to the ship's boats where we were, swimming and bringing us parrots, cotton threads in skeins, darts, and many other things; and we exchanged them for other things that we gave them such as glass beads and small bells. In fine, they took all, and gave what they had with good will. It appeared to me to be a race of people very poor in everything. They go as naked as when their mothers bore them, and so do the women, although I did not see more than one young girl. All I saw were youths, none more than thirty years of age. They are very well made, with very handsome bodies, and very good countenances. Their hair is short and coarse, almost like the hairs of a horse's tail. They wear the hairs brought down to the eyebrows, except a few locks behind, which they wear long and never cut. They paint themselves black, and they are the color of the Canarians, neither black nor white. Some paint themselves white, others red, and others of what color they find. Some paint their faces, others the whole body, some only round the eyes, others only on the nose. They neither carry nor know anything of arms, for I showed them swords, and they took them by the blade and cut themselves through ignorance. They have no iron, their darts being wands without iron, some of them having a fish's tooth at the end, and other being pointed in various ways. They are all of fair stature and size, with good faces, and well made. I saw some with marks of wounds on their bodies, and I made signs to ask what it was, and they gave me to understand that people from other adjacent islands came with the intention of seizing them, and that they defended themselves.

I believed, and still believe, that they come here from the mainland to take them prisoners. They should be good servants and intelligent, for I observed that they quickly took in what was said to them, and I believe that they would easily be made Christians, as it appeared to me that they had no religion. I, our Lord being pleased, will take hence, at the time of my departure, six natives for your Highness, that they may learn to speak. I saw no beast of any kind except parrots, on this island."

The above is in the words of the Admiral.

Saturday, 13th of October.

"As soon as dawn broke many of these people came to the beach, all youths, as I have said, and all of good stature, a very handsome people. Their hair is not curly, but loose and coarse, like horse hair. In all the forehead is broad, more so than in any other people I have hitherto seen. Their eyes are very beautiful and not small, and themselves far from black, but the color of the Canarians. Nor should anything else be expected, as this island is in a line east and west from the island of Hierro in the Canaries. Their legs are very straight, all in one line, and no belly, but very well formed. They came to the ship in small canoes, made out of the trunk of a tree like a long boat, and all of one piece, and wonderfully worked, considering the country. They are large, some of them holding 40 to 45 men, others smaller, and some only large enough to hold one man. They are propelled with a paddle like a baker's shovel, and go at a marvelous rate. If the canoe capsizes they all promptly begin to swim, and to bale it out with calabashes that they take with them. They brought skeins of cotton thread, parrots, darts, and other small things which it would be tedious to recount, and they give all in exchange for anything that may be given to them. I was attentive, and took trouble to ascertain if there was gold. I saw that some of them had a small piece fastened in a hole they have in the nose, and by signs I was able to make out that to the south, or going from the island to the south, there was a king who had great cups full, and who possessed a great quantity. I tried to get them to go there, but afterwards I saw that they had no inclination. I resolved to wait until tomorrow in the afternoon and then to depart, shaping a course to the S.W., for, according to what many of them told me, there was land to the S., to the S.W., and N.W., and that the natives from the N.W. often came to attack them, and went on to the S.W. in search of gold and precious stones.

29--To America and Around the World

 "This island is rather large and very flat, with bright green trees, much water, and a very large lake in the center, without any mountain, and the whole land so green that it is a pleasure to look on it. The people are very docile, and for the longing to possess our things, and not having anything to give in return, they take what they can get, and presently swim away.   Still, they give away all they have got, for whatever may be given to them, down to broken bits of crockery and glass.   I saw one give 16 skeins of cotton for three *ceotis* of Portugal, equal to one *blanca* of Spain, the skeins being as much as an *arroba* of cotton thread.   I shall keep it, and shall allow no one to take it, preserving it all for your Highnesses, for it may be obtained in abundance. It is grown in this island, though the short time did not admit of my ascertaining this for a certainty.   Here also is found the gold they wear fastened in their noses.   But, in order not to lose time, I intend to go and see if I can find the island of Cipango.   Now, as it is night, all the natives have gone on shore with their canoes."

Sunday, 14th of October.
"At dawn I ordered the ship's boat and the boats of the caravels to be got ready, and I went along the coast of the island to the N.N.E., to see the other side, which was on the other side to the east, and also to see the villages.   Presently I saw two or three, and the people all came to the shore, calling out and giving thanks to God.   Some of them brought us water, others came with food, and when they saw that I did not want to land, they got into the sea, and came swimming to us.   We understood that they asked us if we had come from heaven. One old man came into the boat, and others cried out, in loud voices, to all the men and women, to come and see the men who had come from heaven, and to bring them to eat and drink.   Many came, including women, each bringing something, giving thanks to God, throwing themselves on the ground and shouting to us to come on shore.   But I was afraid to land, seeing an extensive reef of rocks which surrounded the island, with deep water between it and the shore forming a port large enough for as many ships as there are in Christendom, but with a very narrow entrance.   It is true that within this reef there are some sunken rocks, but the sea has no more motion than the water in a well.   In order to see all this I went this morning, that I might be able to give a full account to your Highness, and also where a fortress might be established.   I saw a piece of land which appeared like an island, although it is not one, and on it there were six

houses. It might be converted into an island in two days, though I do not see that it would be necessary, for these people are very simple as regards the use of arms, as your Highnesses will see from the seven that I caused to be taken, to bring home and learn our language and return; unless your Highnesses should order them all to be brought to Castile, or to be kept as captives on the same island; for with fifty men they can all be subjugated and made to do what is required of them. Close to the above peninsula there are gardens of the most beautiful trees I ever saw, and with leaves as green as those of Castile in the month of April and May, and much water. I examined all that port, and afterwards I returned to the ship and made sail. I saw so many islands that I hardly knew how to determine to which I should go first. Those natives I had with me said, by signs, that there were so many that they could not be numbered, and they gave the names of more than a hundred. At last I looked out for the largest, and resolved to shape a course for it, and so I did. It will be distant five leagues from this of San Salvador, and the others some more, or less. All are very flat, and all are inhabited. The natives make war on each other, although these are very simple-minded and handsomely-formed people."

Monday, 15th of October.
"I had laid by during the night, with the fear of reaching the land to anchor before daylight, not knowing whether the coast was clear of rocks, and at dawn I made sail. As the island was more than 5 leagues distant and nearer 7, and the tide checked my way, it was noon when we arrived at the said island. I found that side facing towards the island of San Salvador trended north and south with a length of 5 leagues, and the other which I followed ran east and west for more than 10 leagues. As from this island I saw another larger one to the west, I clued up the sails, after having run all that day until night, otherwise I could not have reached the western cape. I gave the name of *Santa Maria de la Concepcion* to the island, and almost as the sun set I anchored near the said cape to ascertain if it contained gold. For the people I had taken from the island of San Salvador told me that here they wore very large rings of gold on their arms and legs. I really believed that all they said was nonsense, invented that they might escape. My desire was not to pass any island without taking possession, so that, one having been taken, the same may be said of all. I anchored, and remained until today, Tuesday, when I went to the shore with the boats armed, and landed. The people, who were numerous,

went naked, and were like those of the other island of San Salvador. They let us go over the island, and gave us what we required. As the wind changed to the S.E., I did not like to stay, and returned to the ship. A large canoe was alongside the Nina, and one of the men of the island of San Salvador, who was on board, jumped into the sea and got into the canoe. In the middle of the night before, another swam away behind the canoe, which fled, for there never was a boat that could have overtaken her, seeing that in speed they have a great advantage. So they reached the land and left the canoe. Some of my people went on shore in chase of them, but they all fled like fowls, and the canoe they had left was brought alongside the caravel Nina, whither, from another direction, another small canoe came, with a man who wished to barter with skeins of cotton. Some sailors jumped into the sea, because he would not come on board the caravel, and seized him. I was on the poop of my ship, and saw everything. So I sent for the man, gave him a red cap, some small beads of green glass, which I put on his arms, and small bells, which I put in his ears, and ordered his canoe, which was also on board, to be returned to home. I sent him on shore, and presently made sail to go to the other large island which was in sight to the westward. I also ordered the other large canoe, which the caravel Nina was towing astern, to be cast adrift; and I soon saw that it reached the land at the same time as the man to whom I had given the above things. I had not wished to take the skein of cotton that he offered me. All the others came round him and seemed astonished, for it appeared clear to them that we were good people. The other man who had fled might do us some harm, because we had carried him off, and for that reason I ordered this man to be set free and gave him the above things, that he might think well of us, otherwise, when your Highnesses again send an expedition, they might not be friendly. All the presents I gave were not worth four maravedis. At 10 we departed with the wind S.W., and made for the south, to reach that other island, which is very large, and respecting which all the men that I bring from San Salvador make signs that there is much gold, and that they wear it as bracelets on the arms, on the legs, in the ears and nose, and round the neck. The distance of this island from that of Santa Maria is 9 leagues on a course east to west. All this part of the island trends N.W. and S.E., and it appeared that this coast must have a length of 28 leagues. It is very flat, without any mountain, like San Salvador and Santa Maria, all being beach without rocks, except that there are some sunken rocks near the land, whence it is necessary to keep a good lookout when it is desired to anchor, and not to come to very near the land; but the water is always very clear, and the bottom is visible. At a distance of two shots of a lombard, there is, off all these islands, such a depth that the bottom cannot be reached. These islands are very green and fertile, the climate very mild. They may contain many things of which I have no knowledge, for I do not wish to stop, in discovering and visiting many islands, to find gold. These people make signs that it is worn on the arms and legs; and it must be gold, for they point to some pieces that I have. I cannot err, with the help of our Lord, in finding out where this gold has its origin. Being in the middle of the channel between these two islands, that is to say, that of Santa Maria and this large one, to which I give the name of *Fernandina*, I came upon a man alone in a canoe going from Santa Maria to Fernandina. He had little of their bread, about the size of a fist, a calabash of water, a piece of brown earth powdered and then kneaded, and some dried leaves, which must be a thing highly valued by them, for they bartered with it at San Salvador. He also had with him a native basket with a string of glass beads, and two *blanca*, by which I knew that he had come from the island of San Salvador, and had been to Santa Maria, and thence to Fernandina. He came alongside the ship, and I made him come on board as he desired, also getting the canoe inboard, and taking care of all his property. I ordered him to be given to eat bread and treacle, and also to drink: and so I shall take him on to Fernandina, where I shall return everything to him, in order that he may give a good account of us, that, our Lord pleasing, when your Highnesses shall send here, those who come may receive honor, and that the natives may give them all they require."

Tuesday, 16th of October.
"I sailed from the island of Santa Maria de la Conception at about noon, to go to Fernandina island, which appeared very large to the westward, and I navigated all that day with light winds. I could not arrive in time to be able to see the bottom, so as to drop the anchor on a clear place, for it is necessary to be very careful not to lose the anchors. So I stood off and on all that night until day, when I came to an inhabited place where I anchored, and whence that man had come that I found yesterday in the canoe in mid channel. He had given such a good report of us that there was no want of canoes alongside the ship all that night, which brought us water and what they

had to offer. I ordered each one to be given something, such as a few beads, ten or twelve of those made of glass on a thread, some timbrels made of brass such as are worth a maravedi in Spain, and some straps, all of which they looked upon as most excellent. I also ordered them to be given treacle to eat when they came on board. At three o'clock I sent the shop's boat on shore for water, and the natives with good will showed my people where the water was, and they themselves brought the full casks down to the boat, and did all they could to please us.

"This island is very large, and I have determined to sail around it, because, so far as I can understand, there is a mine in or near it. The island is eight leagues from Santa Maria, nearly east and west; and this point I had reached, as well as all the coast, trends N.N.W. and S.S.E. I saw at least 20 leagues of it, and then it had not ended. Now, as I am writing this, I made sail with the wind at the south, to sail round the island, and to navigate until I find *Samaot*, which is the island or city where there is gold, as all the natives say who are on board, and as those of San Salvador and Santa Maria told us. These people resemble those of the said islands, with the same language and customs, except that these appear to me a rather more domestic and tractable people, yet also more subtle. For I observed that those who brought cotton and other trifles to the ship, knew better than the others how to make a bargain. In this island I saw cotton cloths made like mantles. The people were better disposed, and the women wore in front of their bodies a small piece of cotton which scarcely covered them.

"It is a very green island, level and very fertile, and I have no doubt that they sow and gather corn all the year round, as well as other things. I saw many trees very unlike those of our country. Many of them have their branches growing in different ways and all from one trunk, and one twig is one form, and another in a different shape, and so unlike that it is the greatest wonder in the world to see the great diversity; thus one branch has leaves like those of a cane, and others like those of a mastick, tree: and on a single tree there are five or six different kinds. Nor are these grafted, for it may be said that grafting is unknown, the trees being wild, and untended by these people. They do not know any religion, and I believe they could easily be converted to Christianity, for they are very intelligent. Here the fish are so unlike ours that it is wonderful. Some are the shape of dories, and of the finest colors in the world, blue, yellow, red, and other tints, all painted in various ways, and the colors are so bright that there is not a man who would not be astonished, and would not take great delight in seeing them. There are also whales. I saw no beasts on the land of any kind, except parrots and lizards. A boy told me that he saw a large serpent. I saw neither sheep, nor goats, nor any other quadruped. It is true I have been here a short time, since noon, yet I could not have failed to see some if there had been any. I will write respecting the circuit of this island after I have been round it."

Wednesday, 17th of October.

"At noon I departed from the village off which I was anchored, and where I took in water, to sail round this island of Fernandina. The wind was S.W. and South. My wish was to follow the coast of this island to the S.E., from where I was, the whole coast trending N.N.W. and S.S.E.; because all the Indians I bring with me, and others, made signs to this southern quarter, as the direction of the island they call Samoet, where the gold is. Martin Alonso Pinzon, captain of the caravel Pinta, on board of which I had three of the Indians, came to me and said that one of them had given him to understand very positively that the island might be sailed round much quicker by shaping a N.N.W. course. I saw that the wind would not help me to take the course I desired, and that it was fair for the other, so I made sail to the N.N.W. When I was two leagues from the cape on the island, I discovered a very wonderful harbour. It has one mouth, or, rather, it may be said to have two, for there is an islet in the middle. Both are very narrow, and within it is wide enough for a hundred ships, if there was depth and a clean bottom, and the entrance was deep enough. It seemed desirable to explore it and take soundings, so I anchored outside, and went in with all the shop's boats, when we saw there was insufficient depth. As I thought, when I first saw it, that it was the mouth of some river, I ordered the water-casks to be brought. On shore I found eight or ten men, who presently came to us and showed us the village, whither I sent the people for water, some with arms, and others with casks: and, as it was some little distance, I waited two hours for them.

"During that time I walked among the trees, which was the most beautiful thing I had ever seen, beholding as much verdure as in the month of May in Andalusia. The trees are as unlike ours as night from day, as are the fruits, the herbs, the stones, and everything. It is true that some of the trees bore some resemblance to those in Castile, but most of them are very different, and some were so unlike that no one could compare them to anything in Castile. The people were all like those already mentioned: like them naked, and the same size. They give what they possess in exchange for anything that may be given to them. I here saw some of the ship's boys bartering broken bits of glass and crockery for darts. The men who went for water told me that they had been in the houses of the natives, and that they were very plain and clean inside. Their beds and bags for holding things were like nets of cotton. The houses are like booths, and very high, with good chimneys. But, among many villages that I saw, there was none that consisted of more than from twelve to fifteen houses. Here they found that the married women wore clouts of cotton, but not the young girls, except a few who were over eighteen years of age. They had dogs, mastiffs and hounds; and here they found a man who had a piece of gold in his nose, the size of half a *castellano*, on which they saw letters. I quarrelled with these people because they would not exchange or give what was required; as I wished to see what and whose this money was; and they replied that they were not accustomed to barter.

"After the water was taken I returned to the ship, made sail, and shaped a course N.W., until I had discovered all the part of the coast of the island which trends east to west. Then all the Indians turned round and said that this island was smaller than Samoet, and that it would be well to return back so as to reach it sooner. The wind presently went down, and then sprang up from W.N.W., which was contrary for us to continue on the previous course. So I turned back, and navigated all that night to E.S.E., sometimes to east and to S.E. This course was steered to keep me clear of the land, for there were very heavy clouds and thick weather, which did not admit of my approaching the land to anchor. On that night it rained very heavily from midnight until nearly dawn, and even afterwards the clouds threatened rain. We found ourselves at the S.W. end of the island, where I hoped to anchor until it cleared up, so as to see the other island whither I have to go. On all these days, since I arrived in these Indies, it has rained more or less. Your Highnesses may believe that this land is the best and most fertile, and with a good climate, level, and as good as there is in the world."

Thursday, 18th of October.

"After it had cleared up I went before the wind, approaching the island as near as I could, and anchored when it was no longer light enough to keep under sail But I did not go on shore, and made sail at dawn...".

Friday, 19th of October.

"I weighed the anchors at daylight, sending the caravel Pinta on an E.S.E. course, the caravel Nina S.S.E., while I shaped a S.E. course, giving orders that these courses were to be steered until noon, and that then the two caravels should alter course so as to join company with me. Before we had sailed for three hours we saw an island to the east, for which we steered, and all three vessels arrived at the north point before noon. Here there is an islet, and a reef of rock to seaward of it, besides one between the islet and the large island. The men of San Salvador, whom I bring with me, called it *Saomete*, and I gave it the name of *Isabella*. The wind was north, and the said islet bore from the island of Fernandina, whence I had taken my departure, east and west. Afterwards we ran along the coast of the island, westward from the islet, and found its length to be 12 leagues as far as a cape, which I named *Cabo Hermoso*, at the western end. The island is beautiful, and the coast very deep, without sunken rocks off it. Outside the shore is rocky, but further in there is a sandy beach, and here I anchored on that Friday night until morning. This coast and the part of the island I saw is almost flat, and the island is very beautiful; for if the other islands are lovely, this is more so. It has many very green trees, which are very large. The land is higher than in the other islands, and in it there are some hills, which cannot be called mountains; and it appears that there is much water inland. From this point to the N.E. the coast makes a great angle, and there are many thick and extensive groves. I wanted to go and anchor there, so as to go on shore and see so much beauty; but the water was shallow, and we could only anchor at a distance from the land. The wind also was fair for going to this cape, where I am now anchored, to which I gave the name of *Cabo Hermoso*, because it is so. Thus it was that I do not anchor in that angle, but as I saw this cape so green and so beautiful, like all the other lands of these islands, I scarcely knew which to visit first: for I can never tire my eyes in looking at such lovely vegetation, so different from ours. I believe that there are many herbs and many trees that are worth much in Europe for dyes and for medicines; but I do not know, and this causes me great sorrow. Arriving at this cape, I found the smell of the trees and flowers so delicious that it seemed the pleasantest thing in the world. Tomorrow, before I leave this place, I shall go on shore to see what there is at this cape. There are no people, but three are villages in the interior, where, the Indians I bring with me say, there is a king who has much gold. Tomorrow I intend to go so far inland as to find the village, and see and have some speech with this king, who, according to the signs they make, rules over all the neighboring islands, goes about clothed, and wears much gold on his person. I do not give much faith to what they say, as well because I do not understand them as because they are so poor in gold that even a little that this king may have would appear much to them. This cape, to which I have given the name of Cabo Hermoso, is, I believe, on an island separated from Saometo, and there is another small islet between them. I did not try to examine them in detail because it could not be done in 50 years. For my desire is to see and discover as much as I can before returning to your Highnesses, our Lord willing, in April. It is true that in the event of finding places where there is gold or spices in quantity I should stop until I had collected as much as I could. I, therefore, proceed in the hope of coming across such places."

Saturday, 20th of October.

"Today, at sunrise, I weighed the anchors from where I was with the ship and anchored off the S.W. point of the island of Saometo, to which I gave the name of *Cabo de la Laguna*, and to the island *Isabella*. My intention was to navigate to the north-east and east from the southeast and south, where, I understood from the Indians I brought with me, was the village of the king. I found the sea so shallow that I could not enter nor navigate in it, and I saw that to follow a route by the south-east would be a great round. So I determined to return by the route that I had taken from the N.N.E. to the western part, and to sail round this island to...".

"I had so little wind that I never could sail along the coast, except during the night. As it was dangerous to anchor off these islands except in the day, when one can see where to let go the anchor: for the bottom is all in patches, some clear and some rocky: I lay to all this Sunday night. The caravels anchored because they found themselves near the shore, and they thought that, owing to the signals that they were in the habit of making, I would come to anchor, but I did not wish to do so."

Sunday, 21st of October.

38--To America and Around the World

"At ten o'clock I arrived here, off this islet, and anchored, as well as the caravels. After breakfast I went on shore, and found only one house, in which there was no one, and I supposed they had fled from fear, because all their property was left in the house. I would not allow anything to be touched, but set out with the captains and people to explore the island. If the others already seen are very beautiful, green, and very fertile, this is much more so, with large trees and very green. Here there are large lagoons with wonderful vegetation on their banks. Throughout the island all is green, and the herbage like April in Andalusia. The songs of the birds were so pleasant that it seemed as if a man could never wish to leave the place. The flocks of parrots concealed the sun; and the birds were so numerous, and of so many different kinds, that it was wonderful. There are trees of a thousand sorts, and all have their several fruits; and I feel the most unhappy man in the world not to know them, for I am well assured that they are all valuable. I bring home specimens of them, and also of the land. Thus walking along round one of the lakes I saw a serpent, which we killed, and I bring home the skin for your Highnesses. As soon as it saw us it went into the lagoon, and we followed, as the water was not very deep, until we killed it with lances. It is 7 *palmos* long, and I believe that there are many like it in these lagoons. Here I came upon some aloes, and I have determined to take ten quintals on board tomorrow, for they tell me that they are worth a good deal. Also, while in search of good water, we came to a village about half a league from our anchorage. The people, as soon as they heard us, all fled and left their houses, hiding their property in the wood. I would not allow a thing to be touched, even the value of a pin. Presently some men among them came to us, and one came quite close. I gave him some bells and glass beads, which made him very content and happy. That our friendship might be further increased, I resolved to ask him for something; I requested him to get some water. After I had gone on board, the natives came to the beach with calabashes full of water, and they delighted much in giving it to us. I ordered another string of glass beads to be presented to them and they said they would come again tomorrow. I wished to fill up all the ships with water at this place, and, if there should be time, I intended to search the island until I had speech with the king, and seen whether he had the gold of which I had heard. I shall then shape a course for another much larger island, which I believe to be Cipango, judging from the signs made by the Indians I bring with me. They call it *Cuba*, and they say that there are ships and many skilful sailors there. Beyond this island there is another called *Bosio*, which they also say is very large, and others we shall see as we pass, lying between. According as I obtain tidings of gold or spices I shall settle what should be done. I am still resolved to go to the mainland and the city of Guisay, and to deliver the letters of your Highnesses to the Gran Can, requesting a reply and returning with it."

Monday, 22nd of October.
"All last night and today I was here, waiting to see if the king or other person would bring gold or anything of value. Many of these people came, like those of the other islands, equally naked, and equally painted, some white, some red, some black, and others in many ways. They brought darts and skeins of cotton to barter, which they exchanged with the sailors for bits of glass, broken crockery, and pieces of earthenware. Some of them had pieces of gold fastened in their noses, which they willingly gave for a hawk's bell and glass beads. But there was so little that it counts for nothing. It is true that they looked upon any little thing that I gave them as a wonder, and they held our arrival to be a great marvel, believing that we came from heaven. We got water for the ships from a lagoon which is near the Cabo del Isleo, as we named it. In the said lagoon Martin Alonso Pinzon, captain of the Pinta, killed another serpent 7 *palmos* long, like the one we got yesterday. I made them gather here as much of the aloe as they could find."

Tuesday, 23rd of October.
"I desired to set out today for the island of Cuba, which I think must be Cipango, according to the signs these people make, indicative of its size and riches, and I did not delay any more here... round this island to the residence of the King or Lord, and have speech with him, as I had intended. This would cause me much delay, and I see that there is no gold mine here. To sail round would need several winds, for it does not blow here as men may wish. It is better to go where there is great entertainment, so I say that it is not reasonable to wait, but rather to continue the voyage and inspect much land, until some very profitable country is reached, my belief being that it will be rich in spices. That I have no personal knowledge of these products causes me the greatest sorrow in the world, for I see a thousand kinds of trees, each one with its own special fruit, all green now as in Spain

during the months of May and June, as well as a thousand kinds of herbs with the flowers; yet I know none of them except this aloe, of which I ordered a quantity to be brought on board to bring to your Highnesses. I have not made sail for Cuba because there is no wind, but a dead calm with much rain. It rained a great deal yesterday without causing any cold. On the contrary, the days are hot and the nights cool, like May in Andalusia."

Wednesday, 24th of October.

"At midnight I weighed the anchors and left the anchorage at Cabo del Isleo, in the island of Isabella. From the northern side, where I was, I intended to go to the island of Cuba, where I heard of the people who were very great, and had gold, spices, merchandise, and large ships. They showed me that the course thither would be W.S.W., and so I hold. For I believe that it is so, as all the Indians of these islands, as well as those I brought with me in the ships, told me by signs. I cannot understand their language, but I believe that it is of the island of Cipango that they recount these wonders. On the spheres I saw, and on the delineations of the map of the world, Cipango is in this region. So I shaped a course W.S.W. until daylight, but at dawn it fell calm and began to rain, and went on nearly all night. I remained thus, with little wind, until the afternoon, when it began to blow fresh. I set all the sails in the ship, the mainsail with two bonnets, the foresail, spritsail, mizen, main topsail, and the boat's sail on the poop. So I proceeded until nightfall, when the Cabo Verde of the island of Fernandina, which is at the S.W. end, bore N.W. distant 7 leagues. As it was now blowing hard, and I did not know how far it was to this island of Cuba, I resolved not to go in search of it during the night; all these islands being very steep-to, with no bottom round them for a distance of two shots of a lombard. The bottom is all in patches, one bit of sand and another of rock, and for this reason it is not safe to anchor without inspection with the eye. So I determined to take in all the sails except the foresail, and to go on under that reduced canvas. Soon the wind increased, while the route was doubtful, and there was very thick weather, with rain. I ordered the foresail to be furled, and we did not make two leagues during that night."

Thursday, 25th of October.

"I steered W.S.W. from after sunset until 9 o'clock, making 5 leagues. Afterwards I altered course to west, and went 8 miles an hour until one in the afternoon; and from that time until three made good 44 miles. Then land was sighted, consisting of 7 or 8 islands, the group running north and south, distant from us 5 leagues."

Friday, 26th of October.
"This ship was on the south side of the islands, which were all low, distant 5 or 6 leagues. I anchored there. The Indians on board said that thence to Cuba was a voyage in their canoes of a day and a half; these being small dug-outs without a sail. Such are their canoes. I departed thence for Cuba, for by the signs the Indians made of its greatness, and of its gold and pearls, I thought that it must be Cipango."

Saturday, 27th of October.
"I weighed from these islands at sunrise, and gave them the name of *Las Islas de Arena*, owing to the little depth the sea had for a distance of 6 leagues to the southward of them. We went 8 miles an hour S.S.W. course until one o'clock, having made 40 miles. Until night we had run 28 miles on the same course, and before dark the land was sighted. At night there was much rain. The vessels, on Saturday until sunset, made 17 leagues on a S.S.W. course."

Sunday, 28th of October.
"I went thence in search of the island of Cuba on a S.S.W. coast, making for the nearest point of it, and entered a very beautiful river without danger of sunken rocks or other impediments. All the coast was clear of dangers up to the shore. The mouth of the river was 12 *brazos* across, and it is wide enough for a vessel to beat in. I anchored about a lombard-shot inside."

The Admiral says that "he never beheld such a beautiful place, with trees bordering the river, handsome, green, and different from ours, having fruits and flowers each one according to its nature. There are many birds, which sing very sweetly. There are a great number of palm trees of a different kind from those in Guinea and from ours, of a middling height, the trunks without that covering, and the leaves very large, with which they thatch their houses. The country is very level."

The Admiral jumped into his boat and went ashore. He came to two houses, which he believed to belong to fishermen who had fled from fear. In one of them he found a kind of dog that never barks, and in both there were nets of palm-fibre and cordage, as well as horn fish-hooks, bone harpoons, and other apparatus "for fishing, and several hearths. He believed that many people lived together in one house. He gave orders that nothing in the houses should be touched, and so it was done."

The herbage was as thick as in Andalusia during April and May. He found much purslane and wild amaranth. He returned to the boat and went up the river for some distance, and he says it was great pleasure to see the bright verdure, and the birds, which he could not leave to go back. He says that this island is the most beautiful that eyes have seen full of good harbors and deep rivers, and the sea appeared as if it never rose; for the herbage on the beach nearly reached the waves, which does not happen where the sea is rough. He says that the island is full of very beautiful mountains, although they are not very extensive as regards length, but high; and all the country is like Sicily. It is abundantly supplied with water, as they gathered from the Indians they had taken with them from the island of Guanahani. These said by signs that there are ten great rivers, and that they cannot go round the island in twenty days. When they came near land with the ships, two canoes came out; and, when they saw the sailors get into a boat and row about to find the depth of the river where they could anchor, the canoes fled. The Indians say that in this island there are gold mines and pearls, and the Admiral saw a likely place for them and mussel-shells, which are signs of them. He understood that large ships of the Gran Can came here, and that from here to the mainland was a voyage of ten days. The Admiral called this river and harbour *San Salvador.*

Monday, 29th of October.

The Admiral weighed anchor from this port and sailed to the westward, to go to the city, where, as it seemed, the Indians said that there was a king. They doubled a point six leagues to the N.W., and then another point, then east ten leagues. After another league he saw a river with no very large entrance, to which he gave the name of *Rio de la Luna.* He went on until the hour of Vespers. He saw another river much larger than the others, as the Indians told him by signs, and near he saw goodly villages of houses. He called the river *Rio de Mares.* He sent two boats on shore to a village to communicate, and one of the Indians he had brought with him, for now they understood a little, and show themselves content with Christians. All the men, women, and children fled, abandoning their houses with all they contained. The Admiral gave orders that nothing should be touched. The houses were better than those he had seen before, and he believed that the houses would improve as he approached the mainland. They were made like booths, very large, and looking like tents in a camp without regular streets, but one here and another there. Within they were clean and well swept, with the furniture well made. All are of palm branches beautifully constructed. They found many images in the shape of women, and many heads like masks, very well carved. It was not known whether these were used as ornaments, or to be worshipped. They had dogs which never bark, and wild birds tamed in their houses. There was a wonderful supply of nets and other fishing implements, but nothing was touched. He believed that all the people on the coast were fishermen, who took the firs inland, for this island is very large, and so beautiful, that he is never tired of praising it. He says that he found trees and fruits of very marvelous taste; and adds that they must have cows or other cattle, for he saw skulls which were like those of cows. The songs of the birds and the chirping of crickets throughout the night lulled everyone to rest, while the air was soft and healthy, and the nights neither hot nor cold. On the voyage through the other islands there was great heat, but here it is tempered like the month of May. He attributed the heat of the other islands to their flatness, and to the wind coming from the east, which is hot. The water of the rivers was salt at the mouth, and they did not know whence the natives got their drinking water, though they have sweet water in their houses. Ships are able to turn in this river, both entering and coming out, and there are very good leading marks. He says that all this sea appears to be constantly smooth, like the river at Seville, and the water suitable for the growth of pearls. He found large shell unlike those of Spain. Remarking on the position of the river and port, to which he gave the name of San Salvador, he describes its mountains as lofty and beautiful, like the Pena de las Enamoradas, and one of them has another little hill on its summit, like a graceful mosque. The other river and port, in which he now was, has two round mountains to the S.W., and a fine low cape running out to the W.S.W.

Tuesday, 30th of October.

He left the Rio de Mares and steered N.W., seeing a cape covered with palm trees, to which he gave the name of *Cabo de Palmas*, after having made good 15 leagues. The Indians on board the caravel Pinta said that beyond that cape there was a river, and that from the river to Cuba it was four days' journey. The captain of the Pinta reported that he understood from that, that this Cuba was a city, and that the land was a great continent trending far to the north. The king of that country, he gathered, was at war with the Gran Can, whom they called *Cami*, and his land or city *Fava*, with many other names. The Admiral resolved to proceed to that river, and to send a present, with the letter of the Sovereigns, to the king of that land. For this service there was a sailor who had been to Guinea, and some of the Indians of Guanahani wished to go with him, and afterwards to return to their homes. The Admiral calculated that he was forty two degrees to the north of the equinoctial line. He says that he must attempt to reach the Gran Can, who he thought was here or at the city of Cathay, which belongs to him, and is very grand, as he was informed before leaving Spain. All this land, he adds, is low and beautiful, and the sea deep.

Wednesday, 31st of October.

All Tuesday night he was beating to windward, and he saw a river, but could not enter it because the entrance was narrow. The Indians fancied that the ships could enter wherever their canoes go. Navigating onwards, he came to a cape running out very far, and surrounded by sunken rocks, and he saw a bay where small vessels might take shelter. He could not proceed because the wind had come round to the north, and all the coast runs N.W. and S.W. Another cape further on ran out still more. For these reasons, and because the sky showed signs of a gale, he had to return to the Rio de Mares.

Thursday, November the 1st.

At sunrise the Admiral sent the boats on shore to the houses that were there, and they found that all the people had fled. After some time a man made his appearance. The Admiral ordered that he should be left to himself, and the sailors returned to the boats. After dinner, one of the Indians on board was sent on shore. He called out from a distance that there was nothing to fear, because the strangers were good people and would do no harm to anyone, nor were they people of the Gran Can, but they had given away their things in many islands where they had been. The Indian then swam on shore, and two of the natives took him by the arms and brought him to a house, where they heard what he had to say. When they were certain that no harm would be done to them they were reassured, and presently more than sixteen canoes came to the ships with cotton thread and other trifles. The Admiral ordered that nothing should be taken from them, that they might understand that he sought for nothing but gold, which they call *nucay*. Thus they went to and fro between the ships and the shore all day, and they came to the Christians on shore with confidence. The Admiral saw no gold whatever among them, but he says that he saw one of them with a piece of worked silver fastened to his nose. They said, by signs, that within three days many merchants from inland would come to buy the things brought by the Christians, and would give information respecting the king of that land. So far as could be understood from their signs, he resided at a distance of four days' journey. They had sent many messengers in all directions, with news of the arrival of the Admiral.

"These people", says the Admiral, "are of the same appearance and have the same customs as those of the other islands, without any religion so far as I know, for up to this day I have never seen the Indians on board say any prayer; though they repeat the *Salve* and *Ave Maria* with their hands raised to heaven, and they make the sign of the cross. The language is also the same, and they are all friends; but I believe that all these islands are at war with the Gran Can, whom they called *Cavila*, and his province *Bafan*. They all go naked like the others." This is what the Admiral says. "The river", he adds, "is very deep, and the ships can enter the mouth, going close to the shore. The sweet water does not come within a league of the mouth. It is certain," says the Admiral, "that this is the mainland, and that I am in front of *Zayto* and *Guinsay*, a hundred leagues, a little more or less, distant the one from the other. It is very clear that no one before has been so far as this by sea. Yesterday, with wind from the N.W., I found it cold."

Friday, 2nd of November.

The Admiral decided upon sending two Spaniards, one name Rodrigo de Jerez, who lived in Ayamonte, and the other Luis de Torres, who had served in the household of the Adelantado of Murcia, and had been a Jew, knowing Hebrew, Chaldee, and even some Arabic. With these men he sent two Indians, one from among those he had brought from Guanahani, and another a native of the houses by the river side. He gave them strings of beads with which to buy food if they should be in need, and ordered them to return in six days. He gave them specimens of spices, to see if any were to be found. Their instructions were to ask for the king of that land, and they were told what to say on the part of the Sovereigns of Castile, how they had sent the Admiral with letters and a present, to inquire after his health and establish friendship, favoring him in what he might desire from them. They were to collect information respecting certain provinces, ports, and rivers of which the Admiral had notice, and to ascertain their distances from where he was.

This night the Admiral took an altitude with a quadrant, and found that the distance from the equinoctial line was 42 degrees. He says that, by his reckoning, he finds that he has gone over 1,142 leagues from the island of Hierro. He still believes that he has reached the mainland.

Saturday, 3rd of November.

In the morning the Admiral got into the boat, and, as the river is like a great lake at the mouth, forming a very excellent port, very deep, and clear of rocks, with a good beach for careening ships, and plenty of fuel, he explored it until he came to fresh water at a distance of two leagues from the mouth. He ascended a small mountain to obtain a view of the surrounding country, but could see nothing, owing to the dense foliage of the trees, which were very fresh and odoriferous, so that he felt no doubt that there were aromatic herbs among them. He said that all he saw was so beautiful that his eyes could never tire of gazing upon such loveliness, nor his ears of listening to the songs of birds. That day many canoes came to the ships, to barter with cotton threads and with the nets in which they sleep, called *hamacas*.

Sunday, 4th of November.

At sunrise the Admiral again went away in the boat, and landed to hunt the birds he had seen the day before. After a time, Martin Alonso Pinzon came to him with two pieces of cinnamon, and said that a Portuguese, who was one of his crew, had seen an Indian carrying two very large bundles of it; but he had not bartered for it, because of the penalty imposed by the Admiral on anyone who bartered. He further said that this Indian carried some brown things like nutmeg. The master of the Pinta said that he had found the cinnamon trees. The Admiral showed the Indians some specimens of cinnamon and pepper he had brought from Castile, and they knew it, and said, by signs, that there was plenty in the vicinity, pointing to the S.E. He also showed them gold and pearls, on which certain old men said that there was an infinite quantity in a place called *Bohio*, and that the people wore it on their necks, ears, arms, and legs, as well as pearls. He further understood them to say that there were great ships and much merchandise, all to the S.E. He also understood that, far away, there were men with one eye and others with dogs' noses who were cannibals, and that when they captured an enemy they beheaded him and drank his blood.

The Admiral then determined to return to the ship and wait for the return of the two men he had sent, intending to depart and seek for those lands, if his envoys brought some good news touching what he desired. The Admiral further says:

"These people are very gentle and timid; they go naked, as I have said, without arms and without law. The country is very fertile. The people have plenty of roots called *zanahorias* (yams), with a smell like chestnuts; and they have beans of kinds very different from ours. They also have much cotton, which they do not sow, as it is wild in the mountains, and I believe they collect it throughout the year, because I saw pods empty, others full, and flowers all on one tree. There are a thousand other kinds of fruits which it is impossible for me to write about, and all must be profitable." All this the Admiral says.

Monday, 5th of November.

This morning the Admiral ordered the ship to be careened, afterwards the other vessels, but not all at the same time. Two were always to be at the anchorage, as a precaution; although he says that these people were very safe, and that without fear all the vessels might have been careened at the same time. Things being in this state, the master of the Nina came to claim a reward from the Admiral because he had found mastick, but he did not bring the specimen, as he had dropped it. The Admiral promised him a reward, and sent Rodrigo Sanchez and master Diego to the trees. They collected some, which was kept to present to the Sovereigns, as well as the tree. The Admiral says that he knew it was mastick, though it ought to be gathered at the proper season. There is enough in that district for a yield of 1,000 *quintals* every year. The Admiral also found here a great deal of the plant called aloe. He further says that the Puerto de Mares is the best in the world, with the finest climate and the most gentle people. As it has a high, rocky cape, a fortress might be built, so that, in the event of the place becoming rich and important, the merchants would be safe from any other nations. He adds:

"The Lord, in whose hands are all victories, will ordain all things for his service. An Indian said by signs that the mastick was good for pains in the stomach."

Tuesday, 6th of November.
"Yesterday, at night", says the Admiral, "the two men came back who had been sent to explore the interior. They said that after walking 12 leagues they came to a village of 50 houses, where there were a thousand inhabitants, for many live in one house. These houses are like very large booths. They said that they were received with great solemnity, according to custom, and all, both men and women, came out to see them. They were lodged in the best houses, and the people touched them, kissing their hands and feet, marvelling and believing that they came from heaven, and so they gave them to understand. They gave them to eat of what they had. When they arrived, the chief people conducted them by the arms to the principal houses, gave them two chairs on which to sit and all the natives sat around them on the ground. The Indian who came with them described the manner of living of the Christians, and said that they were good people. Presently the men went out, and the women came sitting round them in the same way, kissing their hands and feet, and looking to see if they were of flesh and bones like themselves. They begged the Spaniards to remain with them at least five days,"

The Spaniards showed the natives specimens of cinnamon, pepper, and other spices which the Admiral had given them, and they said, by signs, that there was plenty at a short distance from thence to S.E., but that there they did not know whether there was any. Finding that they had no information respecting cities, the Spaniards returned; and if they had desired to take those who wished to accompany them, more than 500 men and women would have come, because they thought the Spaniards were returning to heaven. There came, however, a principal man of the village and his son, with a servant. The Admiral conversed with them, and showed them much honor. They made signs respecting many lands and islands in those parts. The Admiral thought of bringing them to the Sovereigns. He says that he knew not what fancy took them; either from fear, or owing to the dark night, they wanted to land. The ship was at the time high and dry, but, not wishing to make them angry, he let them go on their saying that they would return at dawn, but they never came back. The two Christians met with many people on the road going home, men and women with a half-burnt weed in their hands, being the herbs they are accustomed to smoke. They did not find villages on the road of more than five houses, all receiving them with the same reverence. They saw many kinds of trees, herbs, and sweet-smelling flowers; and birds of many different kinds, unlike those of Spain, except the partridges, geese, of which there are many, and singing nightingales. They saw no quadrupeds except the dogs that do not bark. The land is very fertile, and is cultivated with yams and several kinds of beans different from ours, as well as corn. There were great quantities of cotton gathered, spun, and worked up. In a single house they saw more than 500 *arrobas*, and as much as 4,000 *quintals* could be yielded every year.

The Admiral said that "it did not appear to be cultivated, and that it bore all the year round. It is very fine, and has a large boll. All that was possessed by these people they gave at a very low price, and a great bundle of cotton was exchanged for the point of a needle or other trifle. They are a people," says the Admiral, "guileless and unwarlike. Men and women go as naked as when their mothers bore them. It is true that the women wear a very small rag of cotton-cloth, and they are of very good appearance, not very dark, less so than the Canarians. I hold, most serene Princes, that if devout religious persons were here, knowing the language, they would all turn Christians. I trust in our Lord that your Highnesses will resolve upon this with much diligence, to bring so many great nations within the Church, and to convert them; as you have destroyed those who would not confess the Father, the Son, and the Holy Ghost. And after your days, all of us being mortal, may your kingdoms remain in peace, and free from heresy and evil, and may your be well received before the eternal Creator, to whom I pray that you may have long life and great increase of kingdoms and lordships, with the will and disposition to increase the holy Christian religion as you have done hitherto. Amen!"

"Today I got the ship afloat, and prepared to depart on Thursday, in the name of God, and to steer S.E. in search of gold and spices, and to discover land."

These are the words of the Admiral, who intended to depart on Thursday, but, the wind being contrary, he could not go until the 12th of November.

Monday, 12th of November.

The Admiral left the port and river of Mares before dawn to visit the island called *Babeque*, so much talked of by the Indians on board, where, according to their signs, the people gather the gold on the beach at night with candles, and afterwards beat it into bars with hammers. To go thither it was necessary to shape a course E.b.S. After having made 8 leagues the coast, a river was sighted, and another 4 leagues brought them to another river, which appeared to be of great volume, and larger than any they had yet seen. The Admiral did not wish to stop nor to enter any of these rivers, for two reasons: the first and principal one being that wind and weather were favorable for going in search of the said island of Babeque; the other, that, if there was a populous and famous city near the sea, it would be visible, while, to go up the rivers, small vessels are necessary, which those of the expedition were not. Much time would thus be lost; moreover, the exploration of such rivers is a separate enterprise. All that coast was peopled near the river, to which the name of *Rio del Sol* was given.

The Admiral says that, on the previous Sunday, the 11th of November, it seemed good to take some persons from amongst those at Rio de Mares, to bring to the Sovereigns, that they might learn our language, so as to be able to tell us what there is in their lands. Returning, they would be the mouthpieces of the Christians, and would adopt our customs and the things of the faith.

"I saw and knew that these people are without any religion, not idolaters, but very gentle, not knowing what is evil, nor the sins of murder and theft, being without arms, and so timid that a hundred would fly before one Spaniard, although they joke with them. They, however, believe and know that there is a God in heaven, and say that we have come from heaven. At any prayer that we say, they repeat, and make the sign of the cross. Thus your Highnesses should resolve to make them Christians, for I believe that, if the work was begun, in a little time a multitude of nations would be converted to our faith, with the acquisition of great lordships, peoples, and riches for Spain. Without doubt, there is in these lands a vast quantity of gold, and the Indians I have on board do not speak without reason when they say that in these islands there are places where they dig out gold, and wear it on their necks, ears, arms, and legs, the rings being very large. There are also precious stones, pearls, and an infinity of spices. In this river of Mares, whence we departed tonight, there is undoubtedly a great quantity of mastick, and much more could be raised, because the trees may be planted, and will yield abundantly. The leaf and fruit are like the mastick, but the tree and leaf are larger. As Pliny describes it, I have seen it on the island of Chios in the Archipelago. I ordered many of these trees to be tapped, to see if any of them would yield resin; but, as it rained all the time I was in that river, I could not get any, except a very little, which I am bringing to your Highnesses. It may not be the right season for tapping, which is, I believe, when the trees come forth after winter and begin to flower. But when I was there the fruit was nearly ripe. Here also there is a great quantity of cotton, and I believe it would have a good sale here without sending it to Spain, but to the great cities of the Gran Can, which will be discovered without doubt, and many others ruled over by other lords, who will be pleased to serve your Highnesses, and whither will be brought other commodities of Spain and of the Eastern lands; but these are to the west as regards us. There is also here a great yield of aloes, though this is not a commodity that will yield great profit. The mastick, however, is important, for it is only obtained from the said island of Chios, and I believe the harvest is worth 50,000 ducats, if I remember right. There is here, in the mouth of the river, the best port I have seen up to this time, wide, deep, and clear of rocks. It is an excellent site for a town and fort, for any ship could come close up to the walls; the land is high, with temperate climate, and very good water.

"Yesterday a canoe came alongside the ship, with six youths in it. Five came on board, and I ordered them to be detained. They are now here. I afterwards sent to a house on the western side of the river, and seized seven women, old and young, and three children. I did this because the men would behave better in Spain if they had women of their own land, than without them. For on many occasions the men of Guinea have been brought to learn the languages of Portugal, and afterwards, when they returned, and it was expected that they would be useful in their land, owing to the good company they had enjoyed and the gifts they had received, they never appeared after arriving. Others may not act thus. But, having women, they have the wish to perform what they are required to do; besides, the women would teach our people their language, which is the same in all these island so that those who make voyages in their canoes are understood everywhere. On the other hand, there are a thousand different languages in Guinea, and one native does not understand another.

"The same night the husband of one of the women came alongside in a canoe, who was father of the three children--one boy and two girls. He asked me to let him come with them, and besought me much. They are now all consoled at being with one who is a relation of them all. He is a man of about 45 years old." All these are the words of the Admiral.

He also says that he had felt some cold, and that it would not be wise to continue discoveries in a northerly direction in the winter. On this Monday, until sunset, he steered a course E.b.S., making 18 leagues, and reaching a cape, to which he gave the name of *Cabo de Cuba*.

Tuesday, 13th of November.

This night the ships were on a bowline, as the sailors say, beating to windward without making any progress. At sunset they began to see an opening in the mountains, where two very high peaks were visible. It appeared that here was the division between the land of Cuba and that of Bohio, and this was affirmed by signs, by the Indians who were on board. As soon as they day had dawned, the Admiral made sail towards the land, passing a point which appeared at night to be distant two leagues. He then entered a large gulf, 5 leagues to the S.S.E., and there remained 5 more, to arrive at the point where, between two great mountains, there appeared to be an opening; but it could not be made out whether it was an inlet of the sea. As he desired to go to the island called Babeque, where, according to the information he had received, there was much gold; and as it bore east, and as no large town was insight, the wind freshening more than ever, he resolved to put out to sea, and work to the east with a northerly wind. The ship made 8 miles an hour, and from ten in the forenoon, when that course was taken, until sunset, 56 miles, which is 14 leagues to the eastward from the Cabo de Cuba. The other land of Bohio was left to leeward. Commencing from the cape of the said gulf, he discovered, according to his reckoning, 80 miles, equal to 20 leagues, all that coast running E.S.E and W.N.W.

Wednesday, 14th of November.

All last night the Admiral was beating to windward (he said that it would be unreasonable to navigate among those islands during the night, until they had been explored), for the Indians said yesterday that it would take three days to go from Rio de Mares to the island of Babeque, by which should be understood days' journeys in their canoes equal to about 7 leagues. The wind fell, and, the course being east, she could not lay her course nearer than S.E., and, owing to other mischances, he was detained until morning. At sunrise he determined to go in search of a port, because the wind had shifted from north to N.E., and, if a port could not be found, it would be necessary to go back to the ports in the island of Cuba, whence they came. The Admiral approached the shore, having gone over 28 miles E.S.E. that night. He steered south...miles to the land, where he saw many islets and openings. As the wind was high and the sea rough, he did not dare to risk an attempt to enter, but ran along the coast W.N.W., looking out for a port and saw many but none very clear of rocks. After having proceeded for 64 miles, he found a very deep opening, a quarter of a mile wide, with a good port and river. He ran in with her head S.S.W., afterwards south to S.E. The port was spacious and very deep, and he saw so many islands that he could not count them all, with very high land covered with trees of many kinds, and an infinite number of palms. He was much astonished to see so many lofty islands; and assured the Sovereigns that the mountains and isles he had seen since yesterday seemed to him to be second to none in the world; so high and clear of clouds and snow, with the sea at their bases so deep. He believed that these islands are those innumerable ones that are depicted on the maps of the world in the Far East. He believed that they yielded very great riches in precious stones and spices, and that they extend much further to the south, widening out in all directions. He gave the name of *La Mar de Nuestra Senora*, and to the haven, which is near the mouth of the entrance to these island, *Puerto del Principe*. He did not enter it, but examined it from outside, until another time, on Saturday of the next week, as will there appear. He speaks highly of the fertility, beauty, and height of the islands which he found in this gulf, and he tells the Sovereigns not to wonder at his praise of them, for that he has not told them the hundredth part. Some of them seemed to reach to heaven, running up into peaks like diamonds. Others have a flat top like a table. At their bases the sea is of a great depth, with enough water for a very large carrack. All are covered with foliage and without rocks.

Thursday, 15th of November.

The Admiral went to examine these islands in the ships' boats, and speaks marvels of them, how he found mastick, and aloes without end. Some of them were cultivated with the roots of which the Indians make bread; and he found that fires had been lighted in several places. He saw no fresh water. There were some natives, but they fled. In all parts of the sea where the vessels were navigated he found a depth of

15 or 16 fathoms, and all *basa*, by which he means that the ground is sand, and not rocks; a thing much desired by sailors, for the rocks cut their anchor cables.

Friday, 16th of November.

As in all parts, whether islands or mainlands, that he visited, the Admiral always left a cross; so, on this occasion, he went in a boat to the entrances of these havens, and found two very large trees on a point of land, one longer than the other. One being placed over the other, made a cross, and he said that a carpenter could not have made it better. He ordered a very large and high cross to be made out of these timbers. He found canes on the beach, and did not know where they had grown, but thought they must have been brought down by some river, and washed up on the beach (in which opinion he had reason). He went to a creek on the south-east side of the entrance to the port. Here, under a height of rock and stone like a cape, there was depth enough for the largest carrack in the world close in shore, and there was a corner where six ships might lie without anchors as in a room. It seemed to the Admiral that a fortress might be built here at small cost, if at any time any famous trade should arise in that sea of islands.

Returning to the ship, he found that the Indians who were on board had fished up very large shells found in those seas. He made the people examine them, to see if there was mother-o'-pearl, which is in the shells where pearls grow. They found a great deal, but no pearls, and their absence was attributed to its not being the season, which is May and June. The sailors found an animal which seemed to be a *taso*, or *taxo*. They also fished with nets, and, among many others, caught a fish which was exactly like a pig, not like a tunny, but all covered with a very hard shell, without a soft place except the eyes. It was ordered to be salted, to bring home for the Sovereigns to see.

Saturday, 17th of November.

The Admiral got into the boat, and went to visit the islands he had not yet seen to the S.W. He saw many more very fertile and pleasant islands, with a great depth between them. Some of them had springs of fresh water, and he believed that the water of those streams came from some sources at the summits of the mountains. He went on, and found a beach bordering on very sweet water, which was very cold. There was a beautiful meadow, and many very tall palms. They found a large nut of the kind belonging to India, great rats, and enormous crabs. He saw many birds, and there was a strong smell of musk, which made him think it must be there. This day the two eldest of the six youths brought from the Rio de Mares, who were on board the caravel Nina, made their escape.

Sunday, 18th of November.

The Admiral again went away with the boats, accompanied by many of the sailors, to set up the cross which he had ordered to be made out of the two large trees at the entrance to the Puerto del Principe, on a fair site cleared of trees, whence there was an extensive and very beautiful view. He says that there is a greater rise and fall there than in any other port he has seen, and that this is no marvel, considering the numerous islands. The tide is the reverse of ours, because here, when the moon is S.S.W., it is low water in the port. He did not get under weigh, because it was Sunday.

Monday, 19th of November.

The Admiral got under weigh before sunrise, in a calm. In the afternoon there was some wind from the east, and he shaped a N.N.E. course. At sunset the Puerto del Principe bore S.S.W. 7 leagues. He saw the island of Babeque bearing due east about 60 miles. He steered N.E. all that night, making 60 miles, and up to ten o'clock of Tuesday another dozen; altogether 18 leagues N.E.b.W.

Tuesday, 20th of November.

They left Babeque, or the islands of Babeque, to the E.S.E., the wind being contrary; and, seeing that no progress was being made, and the sea was getting rough, the Admiral determined to return to the Puerto del Principe, whence he had started, which was 25 leagues distant. He did not wish to go to the island he had called Isabella, which was 12 leagues off, and where he might have anchored that night, for two reasons: one was that he had seen two islands to the south which he wished to explore; the other, because the Indians he brought with him, whom he had taken at the island of Guanahani, which he named San Salvador, 8 leagues from Isabella, might get away, and he said that he wanted to take them to Spain. They thought that, when the Admiral had found gold, he would let them return to their homes. He came near the Puerto del Principe, but could not reach it, because it was night, and because the current drifted them to the N.W. He turned her head to N.E. with a light wind. At three o'clock in the morning the wind changed, and a course was shaped E.N.E., the wind being S.S.W., and changing at dawn to south and S.E. At sunset Puerto del Principe bore nearly S.W. by W. 48 miles, which are 12 leagues.

Wednesday, 21st of November.

At sunrise the Admiral steered east, with a southerly wind, but made little progress, owing to a contrary sea. At vespers he had gone 24 miles. Afterwards the wind changed to east, and he steered S.b.E., at sunset having gone 12 miles. Here he found himself 42 degrees north of the equinoctial line, as in the port of Mares, but he says that he kept the result from the quadrant in suspense until he reached the shore, that it might be adjusted (as it would seem that he thought this distance was too great, and he had reason, it not being possible, as these islands are only in... degrees).

This day Martin Alonso Pinzon parted company with the caravel Pinta, in disobedience to and against the wish of the Admiral, and out of avarice, thinking that an Indian who had been put on board his caravel could show him where there was much gold. So he parted company, not owing to bad weather, but because he chose. Here the Admiral says:

"He had done and said many other things to me."

Thursday, 22nd of November.

On Wednesday night the Admiral steered S.S.E., with the wind east, but it was nearly calm. At 3 it began to blow from N.N.E.; and he continued to steer south to see the land he had seen in that quarter. When the sun rose he was as far off as the day before, owing to adverse currents, the land being 40 miles off. This night Martin Alonso shaped a course to the east, to go to the island of Babeque, where the Indians say there is much gold. He did this in sight of the Admiral, from whom he was distant 16 miles. The Admiral stood towards the land all night. He shortened sail, and showed a lantern, because Pinzon would thus have an opportunity of joining him, the night being very clear, and the wind fair to come, if he had wished to do so.

Friday, 23rd of November.

The Admiral stood towards the land all day, always steering south with little wind, but the current would never let them reach it, being as far off at sunset as in the morning. The wind was E.N.E., and they could shape a southerly course, but there was little of it. Beyond this cape there stretched out another land or cape, also trending east, which the Indians on board called Bohio. They said that it was very large, and that there were people in it who had one eye in their foreheads, and others who were cannibals, and of whom they were much afraid. When they saw that this course was taken, they said that they could not talk to these people because they would be eaten, and that they were very well armed. The Admiral says that he well believes that there were such people, and that if they are armed they must have some ability. He thought that they may have captured some of the Indians, and because they did not return to their homes, the others believed that they had been eaten. They thought the same of the Christians and of the Admiral when some of them first saw the strangers.

Saturday, 24th of November.
They navigated all night, and at 3 they reached the island at the very same point they had come to the week before, when they started for the island of Babeque. At first the Admiral did not dare to approach the shore, because it seemed that there would be a great surf in that mountain-girded bay. Finally he reached the sea of *Nuestra Senora*, where there are many islands, and entered a port near the mouth of the opening to the islands. He says that if he had known of this port before he need not have occupied himself in exploring the islands, and it would not have been necessary to go back. He, however, considered that the time was well spent in examining the islands. On nearing the land he sent in the boat to sound; finding a good sandy bottom in 6 to 20 fathoms. He entered the haven, pointing the ship's head S.W. and then west, the flat island bearing north. This, with another island near it, forms a harbour which would hold all the ships of Spain sage from all winds. This entrance on the S.W. side is passed by steering S.S.W., the outlet being to the west very deep and wide. Thus a vessel can pass amidst these islands, and he who approaches from the north, with a knowledge of them, can pass along the coast. These islands are at the foot of a great mountain-chain running east and west, which is longer and higher than any others on this coast, where there are many. A reef of rocks outside runs parallel with the said mountains, like a bench, extending to the entrance. On the side of the flat island, and also to the S.E., there is another small reef, but

between them there is great width and depth. Within the port, near the S.E. side of the entrance, they saw a large and very fine river, with more volume than any they had yet met with, and fresh water could be taken from it as far as the sea. At the entrance there is a bar, but within it is very deep, 19 fathoms. The banks are lined with palms and many other trees.

Sunday, 25th of November.

Before sunrise the Admiral got into the boat, and went to see a cape or point of land to the S.E. of the flat island, about a league and a half distant, because there appeared to be a good river there. Presently, near to S.E. side of the cape, at a distance of two cross-bow shots, he saw a large stream of beautiful water falling from the mountains above, with a loud noise. He went to it, and saw some stones shining in its bed like gold. He remembered that in the river Tejo, near its junction with the sea, there was gold; so it seemed to him that this should contain gold, and he ordered some of these stones to be collected, to be brought to the Sovereigns. Just then the sailor boys called out that they had found large pines. The Admiral looked up the hill, and saw that they were so wonderfully large that he could not exaggerate their height and straightness, like stout yet fine spindles. He perceived that here there was material for great store of planks and masts for the largest ships in Spain. He saw oaks and arbutus trees, with a good river, and the means of making water-power. The climate was temperate, owing to the height of the mountains. On the beach he saw many other stones of the color of iron, and others that some said were like silver ore, all brought down by the river. Here he obtained a new mast and yard for the mizen of the caravel Nina. He came to the mouth of the river, and entered a creek which was deep and wide, at the foot of that S.E. part of the cape, which would accommodate a hundred ships without any anchor or hawsers. Eyes never beheld a better harbor. The mountains are very high, whence descend many limpid streams, and all the hills are covered with pines, and an infinity of diverse and beautiful trees. Two or three other rivers were not visited.

The Admiral describes all this, in much detail, to the Sovereigns, and declared that he had derived unspeakable joy and pleasure at seeing it, more especially the pines, because they enable as many ships as is desired to be built here, bringing out the rigging, but finding here abundant supplies of wood and provisions. He affirms that he has not enumerated a hundredth part of what there is here, and that it pleased our Lord always to show him one thing better than another, as well on the ground and among the trees, herbs, fruits, and flowers, as in the people, and always something different in each place. It had been the same as regards the havens and the waters. Finally, he says that if it caused him who saw it so much wonder, how much more will it affect those who hear about it; yet no one can believe until he sees it.

Monday, 26th of November.

At sunrise the Admiral weighed the anchors in the haven of Santa Catalina, where he was behind the flat island, and steered along the coast in the direction of Cabo del Pico, which was S.E. He reached the cape late, because the wind failed, and then saw another cape, S.E.b. 60 miles, which, when 20 miles off, was named *Cabo de Campana*, but it could not be reached that day. They made good 32 miles during the day, which is 8 leagues. During this time the Admiral noted 9 remarkable ports, which all the sailors thought wonderfully good, and 5 large rivers; for they sailed close along the land, so as to see everything. All along the coast there are very high and beautiful mountains, not arid or rocky, but all accessible, and very lovely. The valleys, like the mountains, were full of tall and fine trees, so that it was a glory to look upon them, and there seemed to be many pines. Also, beyond the said Cabo del Pico to the S.E. thee are two islets, each about two leagues round, and inside them three excellent havens and two large rivers. Along the whole coast no inhabited places were visible from the sea. There may have been some, and there were indications of them, for, when the men landed, they found signs of people and numerous remains of fires. The Admiral conjectured that the land he saw today S.E. of the Cabo de Campana was the island called by the Indians Bohio: it looked as if this cape was separated from the mainland. The Admiral says that all the people he has hitherto met with have very great fear of those of *Caniba* or *Canima*. They affirm that they live in the island of Bohio, which must be very large, according to all accounts. The Admiral understood that those of Caniba come to take people from their homes, they being very cowardly, and without knowledge of arms. For this cause it appears that these Indians do not settle on the sea coast, owing to being near the land of Caniba. When the natives who were on board saw a course shaped for that land, they feared to speak, thinking they were going to be eaten; nor could they rid themselves of their fear. They decided that the Canibas had only one eye and dogs' faces. The Admiral thought they lied, and was inclined to believe that it was people from the dominions of the Gran Can who took them into captivity.

Tuesday, 27th of November.

Yesterday, at sunset, they arrived near a cape named *Campana* by the Admiral; and, as the sky was clear and the wind light, he did not wish to run in close to the land and anchor, although he had 5 or 6 singularly good havens under his lee. The Admiral was attracted on the one hand by the longing and delight he felt to gaze upon the beauty and freshness of those lands, and on the other by a desire to complete the work he had undertaken. For these reasons he remained close hauled, and stood off and on during the night. But, as the currents had set him more than 5 or 6 leagues to the S.E. beyond where he had been at nightfall, passing the land of Campana, he came in sight of a great opening beyond that cape, which seemed to divide one land from another, leaving an island between them. He decided to go back, with the wind S.E., steering to the point where the opening had appeared, where he found that it was only a large bay; and at the end of it, on the S.E. side, there was a point of land on which was a high and square-cut hill, which had looked like an island. A breeze sprang up from the north, and the Admiral continued on a S.E. course, to explore the coast and discover all that was there. Presently he saw, at the foot of the Cabo de Campana, a wonderfully good port, and a large river, and, a quarter of a league on, another river, and a third, and a fourth to a seventh at similar distances, from the furthest one to Cabo de Campana being 20 miles S.E. Most of these rivers have wide and deep mouths, with excellent havens for large ships, without sandbanks or sunken rocks. Proceeding onwards from the last of these rivers, on a S.E. course, they came to the largest inhabited place they had yet seen and a vast concourse of people came down to the beach with loud shouts, all naked, with their darts in their hands. The Admiral desired to have speech with them, so he furled sails and anchored. The boats of the ship and the caravel were sent on shore, with orders to do no harm whatever to the Indians, but to give them presents. The Indians made as if they would resist the landing, but, seeing that the boats of the Spaniards continued to advance without fear, they retired from the beach. Thinking that they would not be terrified if only 2 or 3 landed, 3 Christians were put on shore, who told them not to be afraid, in their own language, for they had been able to learn a little from the natives who were on board. But all ran away, neither great nor small remaining. The Christians went to the houses, which were of straw, and built like the others they had seen, but found no one in any of them. They returned to the ships, and made sail at noon in the direction of a fine cape to the eastward, about 8 leagues distant. Having gone about half a league, the Admiral saw, on the south side of the same bay, a very remarkable harbour, and to the S.E. some wonderfully beautiful country like a valley among the mountains, whence much smoke arose, indicating a large population, with signs of much cultivation. So he resolved to stop at this port, and see if he could have any speech or intercourse with the inhabitants. It was so that, if the Admiral had praised the other havens, he must praise this still more for its lands, climate, and people. He tells marvels of the beauty of the country and of the trees, there being palms and pine trees; and also of the great valley, which is not flat, but diversified by hill and dale, the most lovely scene in the world. Many streams flow from it, which fall from the mountains.

As soon as the ship was at anchor the Admiral jumped into the boat, to get soundings in the port, which is the shape of a hammer. When he was facing the entrance he found the mouth of a river on the south side of sufficient width for a galley to enter it, but so concealed that it is not visible until close to. Entering it for the length of the boat, there was a depth of from 5 to 8 fathoms. In passing by it, the freshness and beauty of the trees, the clearness of the water, and the birds, made it all so delightful that he wished never to leave them. He said to the men who were with him that to give a true relation to the Sovereigns of the things they had seen a thousand tongues would not suffice, nor his hand to write it, for that it was like a scene of enchantment. He desired that many other prudent and credible witnesses might see it, and he was sure that they would be as unable to exaggerate the scene as he was.

The Admiral also says:

"How great the benefit that is to be derived from this country would be, I cannot say. It is certain that where there are such lands there must be an infinite number of things that would be profitable. But I did not remain long in one port, because I wished to see as much of the country as possible, in order to make a report upon it to your Highnesses; and besides, I do not know the language, and these people neither understand me nor any other in my company; while the Indians I have on board often misunderstand. Moreover, I have not been able to see much of the natives, because they often take to flight. But now, if our Lord pleases, I will see as much as possible, and will proceed by little and little, learning and comprehending; and I will make some of my followers learn the language. For I have perceived that there is only one language up to this point. After they understand the advantages, I shall labor to make all these people Christians. They will become so readily, because they have no religion nor idolatry, and your Highnesses will send orders to build a city and fortress, and to convert the people. I assure your Highnesses that it does not appear to me that there can be a more fertile country nor a better climate under the sun, with abundant supplies of water. This is not like the rivers of Guinea, which are all pestilential. I thank our Lord that, up to this time, there has not been a person of my company who has so much as had a headache, or been in bed from illness, except an old man who has suffered from the stone all his life, and he was well again in two days. I speak of all three vessels. If it will please God that your Highnesses should send learned men out here, they will see the truth of all I have said. I have related already how good a place Rio de Mares would be for a town and fortress, and this is perfectly true; but it bears no comparison with this place, nor with the Mar de Nuestra Senora. For here there must be a large population, and very valuable productions, which I hope to discover before I return to Castile. I say that if Christendom will find profit among these people, how much more will Spain, to whom the whole country should be subject. Your Highnesses ought not to consent that any stranger should trade here, or put his foot in the country, except Catholic Christians, for this was the beginning and end of the undertaking; namely, the increase and glory of the Christian religion, and that no one should come to these parts who was not a good Christian."

All the above are the Admiral's words. He ascended the river for some distance, examined some branches of it, and, returning to the mouth, he found some pleasant groves of trees, like a delightful orchard. Here he came upon a canoe, dug out of one tree, as big as a galley of 12 benches, fastened under a boat-house made of wood, and thatched with palm leaves, so that it could be neither injured by the sun nor by the water. He says that here would be the proper side for a town and fort, by reason of the good port, good water, good land, and abundance of fuel.

Wednesday, 28th of November.

63--To America and Around the World

The Admiral remained during this day, in consequence of the rain and thick weather, though he might have run along the coast, the wind being S.W., but he did not weigh, because he was unacquainted with the coast beyond, and did not know what danger there might be for the vessels. The sailors of the two vessels went on shore to wash their clothes, and some of them walked inland for a short distance. They found indications of a large population, but the houses were empty, everyone having fled. They returned by the banks of another river, larger than that which they knew of, at the port.

Thursday, 27th of November.
The rain and thick weather continuing, the Admiral did not get under weigh. Some of the Christians went to another village to the N.W., but found no one, and nothing in the houses. On the road they met an old man who could not run away, and caught him. They told him they did not wish to do him any harm, gave him a few presents, and let him go. The Admiral would have liked to have had speech with him, for he was exceedingly satisfied with the delights of that land, and wished that a settlement might be formed there, judging that it must support a large population. In one house they found a cake of wax, which was taken to the Sovereigns, the Admiral saying that where there was wax there was also a thousand other good things. The sailors also found, in one house, the head of a man in a basket, covered with another basket, and fastened to a post of the house. They found the same things in another village. The Admiral believed that they must be the heads of some founder, or principal ancestor of a lineage, for the houses are built to contain a great number of people in each; and these should be relations, and descendants of a common ancestor.

Friday, 30th of November.
They could not get under weigh today because the wind was east, and dead against them. The Admiral sent 8 men well armed, accompanied by two of the Indians he had on board, to examine the villages inland, and get speech with the people. They came to many houses, but found no one and nothing, all having fled. They saw four youths who were digging in their fields, but, as soon as they saw the Christians, they ran away, and could not be overtaken. They marched a long distance, and saw many villages and a most fertile land, with much cultivation and many streams of water. Near one river they saw

a canoe dug out of a single tree, 95 palmos long, and capable of carrying 150 persons.

Saturday, 1st of December.

They did not depart, because there was still a foul wind, with much rain. The Admiral set up a cross at the entrance of this port, which he called *Puerto Santo*, on some bare rocks. The point is that which is on the S.E. side of the entrance; but he who has to enter should make more over to the N.W.; for at the foot of both, near the rock, there are 12 fathoms and a very clean bottom. At the entrance of the port towards the S.E. point, there is a reef of rocks above water, sufficiently far from the shore to be able to pass between if it is necessary; for both on the side of the rock and the shore there is a depth of 12 to 15 fathoms; and, on entering, a ship's head should be turned S.W.

Sunday, 2nd of December.

The wind was still contrary, and they could not depart. Every night the wind blows on the land, but no vessel need be alarmed at all the gales in the world, for they cannot blow home by reason of a reef of rocks at the opening to the haven. A sailor boy found, at the mouth of the river, some stones which looked as if they contained gold; so they were taken to the shown to the Sovereigns.
The Admiral says that thee are great rivers at the distance of a lombard shot.

Monday, 3rd of December.

By reason of the continuance of an easterly wind the Admiral did not leave this port. He arranged to visit a very beautiful headland a quarter of a league to the S.E. of the anchorage. He went with the boats and some armed men. At the foot of the cape there was the mouth of a fair river, and on entering it they found the width to be a hundred paces, with a depth of one fathom. Inside they found 12, 5, 4, and 2 fathoms, so that it would hold all the ships there are in Spain. Leaving the river, they came to a cove in which were 5 very large canoes, so well constructed that it was a pleasure to look at them. They were under spreading trees, and a path led from them to a very well-built boat house, so thatched that neither sun nor rain could do any harm. Within it there was another canoe made out of a single tree like the others, like a galley with 17 benches. It was a pleasant sight to look upon such goodly work. The Admiral ascended a mountain, and afterwards found the country level, and cultivated with many things of that land, including such calabashes, as it was a glory to look upon them. In the middle there was a large village, and they came upon the people suddenly; but, as soon as they were seen, men and women took to flight. The Indians from on board, who was with the Admiral, cried out to them that they need not be afraid, as the strangers were good people. The Admiral made him give them bells, copper ornaments, and glass beads, green and yellow, with which they were well content. He saw that they had no gold nor any other precious thing, and that it would suffice to leave them in peace. The whole district was well peopled, the rest having fled from fear. The Admiral assures the Sovereigns that 10,000 of these men would run from ten, so cowardly and timid are they. No arms are carried by them, except wands, on the point of which a short piece of wood is fixed, hardened by fire, and these they are very ready to exchange. Returning to where he had left the boats, he sent back some men up the hill, because he fancied he had seen a large apiary. Before those he had sent could return, they were joined by many Indians, and they went to the boats, where the Admiral was waiting with all his people. One of the natives advanced into the river near the stern of the boat, and made a long speech, which the Admiral did not understand. At intervals the other Indians raised their hands to heaven, and shouted. The Admiral thought he was assuring him that he was pleased at his arrival; but he saw the Indian who came from the ship change the color of his face, and turn as yellow as wax, trembling much, and letting the Admiral know by signs that he should leave the river, as they were going to kill him. He pointed to a cross-bow which one of the Spaniards had, and showed it to the Indians, and the Admiral let it be understood that they would all be slain, because that cross-bow carried far and killed people. He also took a sword and drew it out of the sheaf, showing it to them, and saying the same, which, when they had heard, they all took to flight; while the Indian from the ship still trembled from cowardice, though he was a tall, strong man. The Admiral did not want to leave the river, but pulled towards the place where the natives had assembled in great numbers, all painted, and as naked as when their mothers bore them. Some had tufts of feathers on their heads, and all had their bundles of darts.

The Admiral says:

""I came to them, and gave them some mouthfuls of bread, asking for the darts, for which I gave in exchange copper ornaments, bells, and glass beads. This made them peaceable, so that they came to the boats again, and gave us what they had. The sailors had killed a turtle, and the shell was in the boat in pieces. The sailor boys gave them some in exchange for a bundle of darts. These are like the other people we have seen, and with the same belief that we came from heaven. They are ready to give whatever thing they have in exchange for any trifle without saying it is little; and I believe they would do the same with gold and spices if they had any. I saw a fine house, not very large, and with 2 doors, as all the rest have. On entering, I saw a marvelous work, there being rooms made in a peculiar way, that I scarcely know how to describe it. Shells and other things were fastened to the ceiling. I thought it was a temple, and I called them and asked, by signs, whether prayers were offered up there. They said that they were not, and one of them climbed up and offered me all the things that were there, of which I took some."

Tuesday, 4th of December.
The Admiral made sail with little wind, and left that port, which he called Puerto Santo. After going two leagues, he saw the great river of which he spoke yesterday. Passing along the land, and beating to windward on S.E. and W.N.W. courses, they reached Cabo Lindo, which is E.S.E. 5 leagues from Cabo del Monte. A league and a half from Cabo del Monte there is an important but rather narrow river, which seemed to have a good entrance, and to be deep. Three-quarters of a league further on, the Admiral saw another very large river and he thought it must have its source at a great distance. It had a hundred paces at its mouth, and no bar, with a depth of 8 fathoms. The Admiral sent the boat in, to take soundings, and they found the water fresh until it enters the sea.
The river had great volume, and must have a large population on its banks. Beyond Cabo Lindo there is a great bay, which would be open for navigation to E.N.E. and S.E. and S.S.W.

Wednesday, 5th of December.
All this night they were beating to windward off Cape Lindo, to reach the land to the east, and at sunrise the Admiral sighted another cape, 2 1\2 leagues to the east. Having passed it, he saw that the land trended S. and S.W., and presently saw a fine high cape in

that direction, 7 leagues distant. He would have wished to go there, but his object was to reach the island of Babeque, which, according to the Indians, bore N.E.; so he gave up the intentions. He could not go to Babeque either, because the wind was N.E. Looking to the S.E., he saw land, which was a very large island, according to the information of the Indians, well peopled, and called by them Bohio. The Admiral says that the inhabitants of Cuba, or Juana, and of all the other islands, are much afraid of the inhabitants of Bohio, because they say that they eat people. The Indians relate other things, by signs, which are very wonderful; but the Admiral did not believe them. He only inferred that those of Bohio must have more cleverness and cunning to be able to capture the others, who, however, are very poor spirited. The wind veered from N.E. to North, so the Admiral determined to leave Cuba, or Juana, which, up to this time, he had supposed to be the mainland, on account of its size, having coasted along it for 120 leagues. He shaped a course S.E.b.E., the land he had sighted bearing S.E.; taking this precaution because the wind always veered from N. to N.E. again, and thence to east and S.E. The wind increased, and he made all sail, the current helping them; so that they were making 8 miles an hour from the morning until one in the afternoon (which is barely 6 hours, for they say that the nights were nearly 15 hours). Afterwards they went 10 miles an hour, making good 88 miles by sunset, equal to 22 leagues, all to the S.E. As night was coming on, the Admiral ordered the caravel Nina, being a good sailer, to proceed ahead, so as to sight a harbor at daylight. Arriving at the entrance of a port which was like the Bay of Cadiz, while it was still dark, a boat was sent in to take soundings, which showed a light from a lantern. Before the Admiral could beat up to where the caravel was, hoping that the boat wold show a leading mark for entering the port, the candle in the lantern went out. The caravel, not seeing the light, showed a light to the Admiral, and, running down to him, related what had happened. The boat's crew then showed another light, and the caravel made for it; but the Admiral could not do so, and was standing off and on all night.

Thursday, 6th of December.
When daylight arrived the Admiral found himself 4 leagues from the port, to which he gave the name *Puerto Maria*, and to a fine cape bearing S.S.W. he gave the name of *Cabo del Estrella*. It seemed to be the furthest point of the island towards the south, appeared about 40 miles to the east. To another fine point, 54 miles to the east, he have

the name of *Cabo del Elefante*, and he called another, 28 miles to the S.E., *Cabo di Cinquin*. There was a great opening or bay, which might be the mouth of a river, distant 20 miles. It seemed that between Cabo Elefante and that of Cinquin there was a great opening, and some of the sailors said that it formed an island, to which the name of *Isla de la Tortuga* was given. The island appeared to be very high land, not closed in with mountains, but with beautiful valleys, well cultivated, the crops appearing like the wheat on the plain of Cordova in May. That night they saw many fires, and much smoke, as if from workshops, in the day time; it appeared to be a signal made by people who were at war. All the coast of this land trends to the east.

At the hour of vespers the Admiral reached this port, to which he gave the name of *Puerto de Dan Nicolas*, in honor of St. Nicholas, whose day it was; and on entering it he was astonished at its beauty and excellence. Although he had given great praise to the ports of Cuba, he had no doubt that this one not only equalled, but excelled them, and none of them are like it. At the entrance of it is a league and a half wide, and a vessel's head should be turned S.S.E., though, owing to the great width, she may be steered on any bearing that is convenient; proceeding on this course for 2 leagues. On the south side of the entrance the coast forms a cape, and thence the course is almost the same as far as a point where there is a fine beach, and a plain covered with fruit-bearing trees of many kinds; so that the Admiral thought there must be nutmeg and other spices among them, but he did not know them, and they were not ripe. There is a river falling into the harbor, near the middle of the beach. The depth of this port is surprising, for, until reaching the land, for a distance of... the lead did not reach the bottom at 40 fathoms; and up to this length there are 15 fathoms with a very clean bottom. Throughout the port there is a depth of 15 fathoms, with a clean bottom, at a short distance from the shore; and all along the coast there are soundings with clean bottom, and not a single sunken rock. Inside, at the length of a boat's oar from the land, there are 5 fathoms. Beyond the limit of the port to the S.S.E. a thousand carracks could beat up. One branch of the port to the N.E. runs into the land for a long half league, and always the same width, as if it had been measured with a cord. Being in this creek, which is 25 paces wide, the principal entrance to the harbor is not in sight, so that it appears land-locked. The depth of this creek is 11 fathoms throughout, all with clean bottom; and close to the land, where one might put the gangboards on the grass, there are 8 fathoms.

The whole port is open to the air, and clear of tress. All the island appeared to be more rocky than any that had been discovered. The trees are smaller, and many of them of the same kinds as are found in Spain, such as the ilex, the arbutus, and others, and it is the same with the herbs. It is a very high country, all open and clear, with a very fine air, and no such cold has been met with elsewhere, though it cannot be called cold except by comparison. Towards the front of the haven there is a beautiful valley, watered by a river; and in that district there must be many inhabitants, judging from the number of large canoes, like galleys, with 15 benches. All the natives fled as soon as they saw the ships. The Indians who were on board had such a longing to return to their homes that the Admiral considered whether he should not take them back when he should depart from here. They were already suspicious, because he did not shape a course towards their country; whence he neither believed what they said, nor could understand them, nor they him, properly. The Indians on board had the greatest fear in the world of the people of this island. In order to get speech of the people it would be necessary to remain some days in harbor; but the Admiral did not do so, because he had to continue his discoveries, and because he could not tell how long he might be detained. He trusted in our Lord that the Indians he brought with him would understand the language of the people of this island; and afterwards he would communicate with them, trusting that it might please God's Majesty that he might find trade in gold before he returned.

Friday, 7th of December.

At daybreak the Admiral got under weigh, made sail, and left the port of St. Nicholas. He went on with the wind in the west for two leagues, until he reached the point which forms the *Carenero*, when the angle in the coast bore S.E., and the Cabo de la Estrella was 24 miles to the S.W. Thence he steered along the coast eastward to Cabo Cinquin about 48 miles, 20 of them being on an E.N.E. coast. All the coast is very high, with a deep sea. Close in shore there are 20 to 30 fathoms, and at the distance of a lombard shot there is no bottom; all which the Admiral discovered that day, as he sailed along the coast with the wind S.W., much to his satisfaction. The cape, which runs out in the port of St. Nicholas the length of a shot from a lombard, could be made an island by cutting across it, while to sail round it is a circuit of 3 or 4 miles. All that land is very high, not clothed with very high trees, but with ilex, arbutus, and others proper to the land of Castile. Before reaching Cape Cinquin by two leagues, the Admiral discovered an opening in the mountains, through which he could see a very large valley, covered with crops like barley, and he therefore judged that it must sustain a large population. Behind there was a high range of mountains. On reaching Cabo Cinquin, the Cabo de la Tortuga bore N.E. 32 miles. Off Cabo Cinquin, at the distance of a lombard shot, there is a high rock, which is a good landmark. The Admiral being there, he took the bearing of Cabo del Elefante, which was E.S.E. about 70 miles, the intervening land being very high. At a distance of 6 leagues there was a conspicuous cape, and he saw many large valleys and plains, and high mountains inland, all reminding him of Spain. After 8 leagues he came to a very deep but narrow river, though a carrack might easily enter it, and the mouth without bar or rocks. After 16 miles there was a wide and deep harbor, with no bottom at the entrance, nor, at 3 paces from the shore, less than 15 fathoms; and it runs inland a quarter of a league. It being yet very early, only one o'clock in the afternoon, and the wind being aft and blowing fresh, yet, as the sky threatened much rain, and it was very thick, which is dangerous even on a known coast, how much more in an unknown country, the Admiral resolved to enter the port, which he called *Puerto de la Concepcion*. He landed near a small river at the point of the haven, flowing from valleys and plains, the beauty of which was a marvel to behold. He took fishing nets with him; and, before he landed, a skate, like those of Spain, jumped into the boat, this being the first time they had seen fish resembling the fist of Castile. The sailors caught and killed others. Walking a short distance inland, the Admiral found much land under cultivation, and heard the singing of nightingales and other birds of Castile. Five men were seen, but they would not stop, running away. The Admiral found myrtles and other Spanish plants, while land and mountains were like those of Castile.

Saturday, 8th of December.

In this port there was heavy rain, with a fresh breeze from the north. The harbor is protected from all winds except the north; but even this can do no harm whatever, because there is a great surf outside, which prevents such a sea within the river as would make a ship work on her cables. After midnight the wind veered to N.E., and then to East, from which winds this port is well sheltered by the island of Tortuga, distant 36 miles.

Sunday, 9th of December.

Today it rained, and the weather was wintry, like October in Castile. No habitants had been seen except a very beautiful house in the Puerto de S. Nicolas, which was better built than any that had been in other parts.

"The island is very large," says the Admiral: "it would not be much if it has a circumference of 200 leagues. All the parts he had seen were well cultivated. He believed that the villages must be at a distance from the sea, whither they went when the ships arrived; for they all took to flight, taking everything with them, and they made smoke signals, like a people at war."

This port has a width of a 1000 paces at its entrance, equal to a quarter of a league. There is neither bank nor reef within, and there are scarcely soundings close in shore. Its length, running inland, is 3,000 paces, all clean, and with a sandy bottom; so that any ship may anchor in it without fear, and enter it without precaution. At the upper end there are the mouths of two rivers, with the most beautiful campaign country, almost like the lands of Spain: these even have the advantage; for which reason the Admiral gave the name of the said island *Isla Espanola.*

Monday, 10th of December.

It blew hard from the N.E., which made them drag their anchors half a cable's length. This surprised the Admiral, who had seen that the anchors had taken good hold of the ground. As he saw that the wind was foul for the direction in which he wanted to steer, he sent six men on shore, well armed, to go 2 or 3 leagues inland, and endeavour to open communications with the natives. They came and returned without having seen either people of houses. But they found some hovels, wide roads, and some places where many fires had been made. They saw excellent lands, and many mastick trees, some specimens of which they took; but this is not the time for collecting it, as it does not coagulate.

Tuesday, 11th of December.

The Admiral did not depart, because the wind was still east and S.E. In front of this port, as has been said, is the island of La Tortuga. It appears to be a large island, with the coast almost like that of Espanola, and the distance between them is about 10 leagues. It is well to know that from the Cabo de Cinquin, opposite Tortuga, the coast trends to the south. The Admiral had a great desire to see that channel between these two islands, and to examine the island of Espanola, which is the most beautiful thing in the world. According to what the Indians said who were on board, he would have to go to the island of Babeque. They declared that it was very large, with great mountains, rivers, and valleys; and that the island of Bohio was large than Juana, which they call Cuba, and that it is not surrounded by water. They seem to imply that there is mainland behind Espanola, and they call it *Caritaba*, and say it is of vast extent. They have reason in saying that the inhabitants are a clever race, for all the people of these islands are in great fear of those of Caniba. So the Admiral repeats, what he has said before, that Caniba is nothing else but the Gran Can, who ought now to be very near. He sends ships to capture the islander; and as they do not return, their countrymen believe that they have been eaten. Each day we understand better what the Indians say, and they us, so that very often we are intelligible to each other. The Admiral sent people on shore, who found a great deal of mastick, but did not gather it. He says that the rains make it, and that in Chios they collect it in March. In these lands, being warmer, they might take it in January. They caught many fish like those of Castile--dace, salmon, hake, dory, gilt heads, skates, *corbinas*, shrimp, and they saw sardines. The found many aloes.

Wednesday, 12th of December.

The Admiral did not leave the port today, for the same reason: a contrary wind. He set up a great cross on the west side of the entrance, on a very picturesque height, "in sign", "that your Highnesses hold this land for your own, but chiefly as a sign of our Lord Jesus Christ."

This being done, 3 sailors strolled into the woods to see the trees and bushes. Suddenly they came upon a crowd of people, all naked like the rest. They called to them, and went towards them, but they ran away. At last they caught a woman; for I had ordered that some should be caught, that they might be treated well, and made to lose their fear. This would be a useful event, for it could scarcely be otherwise, considering the beauty of the country. So they took the woman, who was very young and beautiful, to the ship, where she talked to the Indians on board; for they all speak the same language. The Admiral caused her to be dressed, and gave her glass beads, hawks' bells, and brass ornaments; then he sent her back to the shore very courteously, according to his custom. He sent 3 of the crew with her, and 3 of the Indians he had on board, that they might open communications with her people. The sailors in the boat, who took her on shore, told the Admiral that she did not want to leave the ship, but would rather remain with the other women he had seized at the port of Mares, in the island of Juana or Cuba. The Indians who went to put the woman on shore said that the natives came in a canoe, which is their caravel, in which they navigate from one place to another; but when they came to the entrance of the harbour, and saw the ships, they turned back, left the canoe, and took the road to the village. The woman pointed out the position of the village. She had a piece of gold in her nose, which showed that three was gold in the island.

Thursday, 13th of December.
The three men who had been sent by the Admiral with the woman returned at 3 o'clock in the morning, not having gone with her to the village, because the distance appeared to be long, or because they were afraid. They said that next day many people would come to the ships, as they would have been reassured by the news brought them by the woman. The Admiral, with the desire of ascertaining whether there any profitable commodities in that land, being so beautiful and fertile, and of having some speech with the people, and being desirous of serving the Sovereigns, determined to send again to the village, trusting in the news brought by the woman that the Christians were good people. For this service he selected 9 men well armed, and suited for such an enterprise, with whom an Indian went from those who were on board. They reached the village, which is 4 1\2 leagues to the S.E., and found that it was situated in a very large and open valley. As soon as the inhabitants saw the Christians coming they all fled inland, leaving all their goods behind them. The village consisted of a thousand houses, with over three thousand inhabitants. The Indian whom the Christians had brought with them ran after the fugitives, saying that they should have no fear, for the Christians did not come from Cariba, but were from heaven, and that they gave many beautiful things to all the people they met. They were so impressed with what he said, that upwards of 2,000 came close up to the Christians, putting their hands on their heads, which was a sign of great reverence and friendship; and they were all trembling until they were reassured. The Christians related that, as soon as the natives had cast off their fear,

they all went to the houses, and each one brought what he had to eat, consisting of yams, which are roots like large radishes, which they sow and cultivate in all their lands, and is their staple food. They make bread of it, and roast it. The yam has the smell of a chestnut, and anyone would think he was eating chestnuts. They gave their guests bread and fish, and all they had. As the Indians who came in the ship had understood that the Admiral wanted to have some parrots, one of those who accompanied the Spaniards mentioned this, and the natives brought out parrots, and gave them as many as they wanted, without asking anything for them. The natives asked the Spaniards not to go that night, and that they would give them many other things that they had in the mountains. While all these people were with the Spaniards, a great multitude was seen to come, with the husband of the woman whom the Admiral had honored and sent away. They wore hair over their shoulders, and came to give thanks to the Christians for the honor the Admiral had done them, and for the gifts. The Christians reported to the Admiral that this was a handsomer and finer people than any that had hitherto been met with. But the Admiral says that he does not see how they can be a finer people than the others, giving to understand that all those he had found in the other islands were very well conditioned. As regards beauty, the Christians said there was no comparison, both men and women, and that their skins are whiter than the others. They saw two girls whose skins were as white as any that could be seen in Spain. They also said, with regard to the beauty of the country they saw, that the best land in Castile cold not be compared with it. The Admiral also, comparing the lands they had seen before with these, said that there was no comparison between them, nor did the plain of Cordova come near them, the difference being as great as between night and day. They said that all these lands were cultivated, and that a very wide and large river passed through the center of the valley, and could irrigate all the fields. All the trees were green and full of fruit, and the plants tall and covered with flowers. These roads were broad and good. The climate was like April in Castile; the nightingale and other birds sang as they do in Spain during that month, and it was the most pleasant place in the world. Some birds sing sweetly at night. The crickets and frogs are heard a good deal. The fish are like those of Spain. They saw much aloe and mastick, and cotton fields. Gold was not found, and it is not wonderful that it should not have been found in so short a time.

75--To America and Around the World

Here the Admiral calculated the number of hours in the day and night, and from sunrise to sunset. He found that 20 half-hour glasses passed, though he says that here there may be a mistake, either because they were not turned with equal quickness, or because some sand may not have passed. He also observed with a quadrant, and found that he was 34 degrees from the equinoctial line.

Friday, 14th of December.
The Admiral left the Puerto de la Concepcion with the land breeze, but soon afterwards it fell calm (and this is experienced every day by those who are on this coast). Later an east wind sprang up, so he steered N.N.E., and arrived at the island of Tortuga. He sighted a point which he named *Punta Pierna*, E.N.E. of the end of the island 12 miles; and from thence another point was seen and named *Punta Lanzada*, in the same N.E. direction 16 miles. Thus from the end of Tortuga to *Punta Aguda* the distance is 44 miles, which is 11 leagues E.N.E. Along this route there are several long stretches of beach. The island of Tortuga is very high, but not mountainous, and is very beautiful and populous, like Espanola, and the land is cultivated, so that it looked like the plain of Cordova. Seeing that the wind was foul, and that he could not steer for the island of Baneque, he determined to return to the Puerto de la Concepcion whence he had come; but he could not fetch a river which is two leagues to the east of that port.

Saturday, 15th of December.
Once more the Admiral left the Puerto de la Concepcion, but, on leaving the port, he was again net by a contrary east wind. He stood over to Tortuga, and then steered with the object of exploring the river he had been unable to reach yesterday; nor was he able to fetch the river this time, but he anchored half a league to leeward of it, where there was clean and good anchoring ground. As soon as the vessels were secured, he went with the boats to the river, entering an arm of the sea, which proved not to be the river. Returning, he found the mouth, there being only one, and the current very strong. He went in with the boats to find the villagers that had been seen they day before. He ordered a tow-rope to be got out and manned by the sailors, who hauled the boats up for a distance of 2 lombard shots. They could not get further owing to the strength of the current. He saw some houses, and the large valley where the villages were, and he

said that a more beautiful valley he had never seen, this river flowing through the center of it. He also saw people at the entrance, but they all took to flight. He further says that these people must be much hunted, for they live in such a state of fear. When the ships arrived at any port, they presently made smoke signals throughout the country; and this is done more in this island of Espanola and in Tortuga, which is also a large island, than in the others that were visited before. He called this valley *Valle del Paraiso*, and the river Quadalquivir at Cordova. The banks consist of shingle, suitable for walking.

Sunday, 16th December.

At midnight the Admiral made sail with the lang-breeze to get clear of that gulf. Passing along the coast of Espanola on a bowline, for the wind had veered to the east, he met a canoe in the middle of the gulf, with a single Indian in it. The Admiral was surprised how he could have kept afloat with such a gale blowing. Both the Indian and his canoe were taken on board, and he was given glass beads, bells, and brass trinkets, and taken in the ship, until she was off a village 17 miles from the former anchorage, where the Admiral came to again. The village appeared to have been lately built, for all the houses were new. The Indian then went on shore in his canoe, bringing the news that the Admiral and his companions were good people; although the intelligence had already been conveyed to the village from the place where the natives had their interview with the 6 Spaniards. Presently more than 500 natives with their king came to the shore opposite the ships, which were anchored very close to the land. Presently one by one, then many by many, came to the ship without bringing anything with them, except that some had a few grains of very fine gold in their ears and noses, which they readily gave away. The Admiral ordered them all to be well treated; and he says:

"...for they are the best people in the world, and the gentlest; and above all I entertain the hope in our Lord that your Highnesses will make them Christians, and that they will be all your subjects, for as yours I hold them."

He also saw that they all treated the king with respect, who was on the sea shore. The Admiral sent him a present, which he received in great state. He was a youth of about 21 years of age, and he had with him an aged tutor, and other councilors who advised and answered him, but he uttered very few words. One of the Indians who had come in the Admiral;s ship spoke to him, telling him how the Christians had come from heaven, and how they came in search of gold, and wished to find the island of Banueque. He said that it was well, and that there was much gold in the said island. He explained to the alguazil of the Admiral that they way they were going was the right way, and that in two days they would be there; adding, that if they wanted anything from the shore he would give it them with great pleasure. This king, and all the others, go naked as their mothers bore them, as do the women without any covering, and these were the most beautiful men and women that had yet been met with. They are fairly white, and if they were clothed and protected from the sun and air, they would be almost as fair as people in Spain. This land is cool, and the best that words can describe. It is very high, yet the top of the lightest mountain could be ploughed with bullocks; and all is diversified with plains and valleys. In all Castile there is no land that can be compared with this for beauty and fertility. All this island, as well as the island of Tortuga, is cultivated like the plain of Cordova. They raise on these lands crops of yams, which are small branches, at the foot of which grow roots like carrots, which serve as bread. They powder and knead them, and make them into bread; then they plant the same branch in another part, which again sends out 4 or 5 of the same roots, which are very nutritious, with the taste of chestnuts. Here they have the largest the Admiral had seen in any part of the world, for he says that they have the same plant in Guinea. At this place they were as thick as a man's leg. All the people were stout and lusty, not thin, like the natives that had been seen before, and of a very pleasant manner, without religious belief. The trees were so luxuriant that the leaves left off being green, and were dark with verdure. It was a wonderful thing to see those valleys, and rivers of sweet water, and the cultivated fields, and land fit for cattle, though they have none, for orchards, and for anything in the world that a man could seek for.

In the afternoon the king came on board the ship, where the Admiral received him in due form, and caused him to be told that the ships belonged to the Sovereigns of Castile, who were the greatest Princes in the world. But neither the Indians who were on board, who acted as interpreters, nor the king, believed a word of it. They maintained that the Spaniards came from heaven, and not in this world. They placed Spanish food before the king to eat, and he ate a mouthful, and gave the rest to his councilors and tutor, and to the rest who came with him.

"Your Highnesses many believe that these lands are so good and fertile, especially these of the island of Espanola, that there is no one who would know how to describe them, and no one who could believe if he had not seen them. And your Highnesses may believe that this island, and all the others, are as much yours as Castile. Here there is only wanting a settlement and the order to the people to do what is required. For I with the force I have under me, which is not large, could march over all these islands without opposition. I have seen only three sailors land, without wishing to do harm, and a multitude of Indians fled before them. They have no arms, and are without warlike instincts; they all go naked, and are so timid that a thousand would not stand before three of our men. So that they are good to be ordered about, to work and sow, and do all that may be necessary, and to build towns, and they should be taught to go about clothed and to adopt our customs."

Monday, 17th of December.
It blew very hard during the night from E.N.E., but there was not much at sea, as this part of the coast is enclosed and sheltered by the island of Tortuga. The sailors were sent away to fish with nets. They had much intercourse with the natives, who brought them certain arrows of the *Caribas* or *Canibales*. They are made of reeds, pointed with sharp bits of wood hardened by fire, and are very long. They pointed out two men who wanted certain pieces of flesh on their bodies, giving to understand that the Canibales had eaten them by mouthfuls. The Admiral did not believe it. Some Christians were again sent to the village, and, in exchange for glass beads, obtained some pieces of gold beaten out into fine leaf. They saw one man, whom the Admiral supposed to be Governor of that province, called by the *Cacique*, with a piece of gold leaf as large as a hand, and it appears that he wanted to barter with it. He went into his house, and the other remained in the open space outside. He cut the leaf into small pieces, and each time he came out he brought a piece and exchanged it. When he had no more left, he said by signs that he had sent for more, and that he would bring it another day. The Admiral says that all these things, and the manner of doing them, with their gentleness and the information they gave, showed these people to be more lively and intelligent than any that had hitherto been met with. In the afternoon a canoe arrived from the island of Tortuga with a crew of 40 men; and when they arrived on the beach, all the people of

the village sat down in sign of peace, and nearly all the crew came on shore. The Cacique rose by himself, and, with words that appeared to be of a menacing character, made them go back to the canoe and shove off. He took up stones from the beach and threw them into the water, all having obediently gone back into the canoe. He also took a stone and put it in the hands of my Alguazil, that he might throw it. He had been sent on shore with the Secretary to see if the canoe had brought anything of value. The Algauzil did not wish to throw the stone. The Cacique showed that he was well disposed to the Admiral. Presently the canoe departed, and afterwards they said to the Admiral that there was more gold in Tortuga than in Espanola, because it is nearer to Baneque. The Admiral did not think that there were gold mines either in Espanola or Tortuga, but that the gold was brought from Baneque in small quantities, there being nothing to give in return. That land is so rich that there is no necessity to work much to sustain life, nor to clothe themselves, as they go naked. He believed that they were very near the source, and that our Lord would point out where the gold has its origin. He had information that from here to Baneque was 4 day's journey, about 34 leagues, which might be traversed with a fair wind in a single day.

Tuesday, 18th of December.

The Admiral remained at the same anchorage, because there was no wind, and also because the Cacique had said that he had sent for gold. The Admiral did not expect much from what might be brought, but he wanted to understand better whence it came. Presently he ordered the ship and caravel to be adorned with arms and dressed with flags, in honor of the feast of Santa Maria de la O..., or commemoration of the Annunciation, which was on that day, and many rounds were fired from the lombards. The king of that island of Espanola had got up very early and left his house, which is about 5 leagues away, reaching the village at 3 in the morning. There were several men from the ship in the village, who had been sent by the Admiral to see if any gold had arrived. They said that the king came with 200 men; that he was carried in a litter by 4 men; and that he was a youth, as has already been said. Today, when the Admiral was dining under the poop, the king came on board with all his people. The Admiral says to the Sovereigns:

"Without doubt, his state, and the reverence with which he is treated by all his people, would appear good to your Highnesses, though they all go naked. When he came on board, he found that I was dining at a table under the poop, and, at a quick walk, he came to sit down by me, and did not wish that I should give place by coming to receive him or rising from the table, but that I should go on with my dinner. I thought that he would like to eat of our viands, and ordered them to be brought for him to eat. When he came under the poop, he made signs with his hand that all the rest should remain outside, and so they did, with the greatest possible promptitude and reverence. They all sat on the deck, except the men of mature age, whom I believe to be his councilors and tutor, who came and sat at his feet. Of the viands which I put before him, he took of each as much as would serve to taste it, sending the rest to his people, who all partook of the dishes. The same thing in drinking: he just touched with his lips, giving the rest to his followers. They were all of fine presence and very few words. What they did say, so far as I could make out, was very clear and intelligent. The two at his feet watched his mouth, speaking to him and for him, and with much reverence. After dinner, an attendant brought a girdle, made like those of Castile, but of different material, which he took and gave to me, with pieces of worked gold, very thin. I believe they get very little here, but they say that they are very near the place where it is found, and where there is plenty. I saw that he was pleased with some drapery I had over my bed, so I gave it to him, with some very good amber beads I wore on my neck, some colored shoes, and a bottle of orange-flower water. He was marvelously well content, and both he and his tutor and councilors were very sorry that they could not understand me, nor I them. However, I knew that they said, if I wanted anything, the whole island was at my disposal. I sent for some beads of mine, with which, as a charm, I had a gold *excelente*, on which your Highnesses were stamped. I showed it to him, and said, as I had done yesterday, that your Highnesses were stamped. I showed it to him, and said, as I had done yesterday, that your Highnesses ruled the best part of the world, and that there were no Princes so great. I also showed him the royal standards, and the others with a cross, of which he thought much. He said to his councilors what great lords your Highnesses must be to have sent me from so far, even from heaven to this country, without fear. Many other things passed between them which I did not understand, except that it was easy to see that they held everything to be very wonderful."

When it got late, and the king wanted to go, the Admiral sent him on shore in his boat very honorably, and saluted him with many guns. Having landed, he got into his litter, and departed with his 200 men, his son being carried behind on the shoulders of an Indian, a man highly respected. All the sailors and people from the ships were given to eat, and treated with much honor wherever they liked to stop. One sailor said that he had stopped in the road and seen all the things given by the Admiral. A man carried each one before the king, and these men appeared to be among those who were most respected. His son came a good distance behind the king, with a similar number of attendants, and the same with a brother of the king, except that the brother went on foot, supported under the arms by 2 honored attendants. This brother came to the ship after the king, and the Admiral presented him with some of the things used for barter. It was then that the Admiral learnt that a king was called *Cacique* in their language. This day little gold was got by barter, but the Admiral heard from an old man that there were many neighboring islands, at a distance of a 100 leagues or more, as he understood, in which much gold is found; and there is even one island that was all gold. In the others there was so much that it was said they gather it with sieves, and they fuse it and make bars, and work it in a thousand ways. They explained the work by signs. This old man pointed out to the Admiral the direction and position, and he determined to go there, saying that if the old man had not been a principal councillor of the king he would detain him, and make him go, too; or if he knew the language he would ask him, and he believed, as the old man was friendly with him and the other Christians, that he would go of his own accord. But as these people were now subjects of the King of Castile, and it would not be right to injure them, he decided upon leaving him. The Admiral set up a very large cross in the center of the square of that village, the Indians giving much help; they made prayers and worshipped it, and, from the feeling they show, the Admiral trusted in our Lord that all the people of those islands would become Christians.

Wednesday, 19th of December.

This night the Admiral got under weigh to leave the gulf formed between the islands of Tortuga and Espanola, but at dawn of day a breeze sprang up from the east, against which he was unable to get clear of the strait between the two islands during the whole day. At night he was unable to reach a port which was in sight. He made out

4 points of land, and a great bay with a river, and beyond he saw a large bay, where there was a village, with a valley behind it among high mountains covered with trees, which appeared to be pines. Over the Two Brothers there is a very high mountain-range running N.E. and S.W., and E.S.E. from the Cabo de Torres is a small island to which the Admiral gave the name of *Santo Tomas*, because tomorrow was his vigil. The whole circuit of this island alternates with capes and excellent harbors, so far as could be judged from the sea. Before coming to the island on the west side, there is a cape which runs far into the sea, in part high, the rest low; and for this reason the Admiral named it *Cabo alto y bajo*. From the road of Torres to E.S.E 60 miles, thee is a mountain higher than any that reaches the sea, and from a distance it looks like an island, owing to a depression on the land side. It was named *Monte Caribata*, because that province was called Caribata. It is very beautiful, and covered with green trees, without snow or clouds. The weather was then, as regards the air and temperature, like March in Castile, and as regards vegetation, like May. The nights lasted 14 hours.

Thursday, 20th of December.

At sunrise they entered a port between the island of Santo Tomas and the Cabo de Caribata, and anchored. This port is very beautiful, and would hold all the ships in Christendom. The entrance appears impossible from the sea to those who have never entered, owing to some reefs of rocks which run from the mountainous cape almost to the island. They are not placed in a row, but one here, another there, some towards the sea, others near the land. It is therefore necessary to keep a good look-out for the entrances, which are wide and with a depth of 7 fathoms, so that they can be used without fear. Inside the reefs there is a depth of 12 fathoms. A ship can lie with a cable made fast, against any wind that blows. At the entrance of this port there is a channel on the west side of a sandy islet with 7 fathoms, and many trees on its shore. But there are many sunken rocks in that direction, and a look-out should be kept up until the port is reached. Afterwards there is no need to fear the greatest storm in the world. From this port a very beautiful cultivated valley is in sight, descending from the S.E., surrounded by such lofty mountains that they appear to reach the sky, and covered with green trees. Without doubt there are mountains here which are higher than the island of Tenerife in the Canaries, which is held to be the highest yet known. On this side of the island of Santo Tomas, at a distance of a league, there is another islet, and beyond it another, forming wonderful harbors; though a good look-out must be kept for sunken rocks. The Admiral also saw villages, and smoke made by them.

Friday, 21st of December.

Today the Admiral went with the ship's boats to examine this port, which he found to be such that it could not be equalled by any he had yet seen; but, having praised the others so much, he knew not how to express himself, fearing that he will be looked upon as one who goes beyond the truth. He therefore contents himself with saying that he had old sailors with him who say the same. All the praises he has bestowed on the other ports are true, and that this is better than any of them is equally true. He further says:

"I have traversed the sea for 23 years, without leaving it for any time worth counting, and I saw all in the east and the west, going on the route of the north, which is England, and I have been to Guinea, but in all those parts there will not be found perfection of harbors... always found... better than another, that I, with good care, saw written; and I again affirm it was well written, that this one is better than all others, and will hold all the ships of the world, secured with the oldest cables. From the entrance to the end is a distance of 5 leagues."

The Admiral saw some very well cultivated lands, although they are all so, and he sent 2 of the boat's crew to the top of a hill to see if any village was near, for none could be seen from the sea. At about 10 o'clock that night, certain Indians came in a canoe to see the Admiral and the Christians, and they were given presents, with which they were much pleased. The two men returned, and reported that they had seen a very large village at a short distance from the sea. The Admiral ordered the boat to row towards the place where the village was until they came near the land, when he saw 2 Indians, who came to the shore apparently in a state of fear. So he ordered the boats to stop, and the Indians that were with the Admiral were told to assure the two natives that no harm whatever was intended to them. Then they came nearer the sea, and the Admiral nearer the land. As soon as the natives had got rid of their fear, so many came that they covered the ground, with women and children, giving a thousand thanks. They ran hither and thither to bring us bread made of yams, which they call *ajes*, which is very white and good, with water in calabashes, and in earthen jars made like those of Spain, and everything else they had and that they thought the Admiral could want, and all so willingly and cheerfully that it was wonderful.

"It cannot be said that, because what they gave was worth little, therefore they gave liberally, because those who had pieces of gold gave as freely as those who had a calabash of water; and it is easy to know when a thing is given with a hearty desire to give." These are the Admiral's words. "These people have no spears nor any other arms, nor have any of the inhabitants of the whole island, which I believe to be very large. They go naked as when their mothers bore them, both men and women. In Cuba and the other islands the women wear a small clout of cotton in front, as well as the men, as soon as they have passed the age of 12 years, but here neither old nor young do so. Also, the men in the other islands jealously hide their women from the Christians, but here they do not."

The women have very beautiful bodies, and they were the first to come and give thanks to heaven, and to bring what they had, especially things to eat, such as bread of ajes, nuts, and 4 or 5 kinds of fruits, some of which the Admiral ordered to be preserved, to be taken to the Sovereigns. He says that the women did not do less in other ports before they were hidden; and he always gave orders that none of his people should annoy them; that nothing should be taken against their wills, and that everything that was taken should be paid for. Finally, he says that no one could believe that there could be such good-hearted people, so free to give, anxious to let the Christians have all the wanted, and, when visitors arrived, running to bring everything to them.

afterwards the Admiral sent 6 Christians to the village to see what it was like, and the natives showed them all the honor they could devise, and gave them all they had; for no doubt was any longer entertained that the Admiral and all his people had come from heaven; and the same was believed by the Indians who were brought from the other islands, although they had now been told what they ought to think. When the 6 Christians had gone, some canoes came with people to ask the Admiral to come to their village when he left the place where he was. *Canoa* is a boat in which they navigate, some large and others small, Seeing that this village of the Chief was on the road, and that many people were waiting there for him, the Admiral went there; but, before he could depart, an enormous crowd came to the shore, men, women, and children, crying out to him not to go, but to stay with them. The messengers from the other Chief, who had come to invite him, were waiting with their canoes, that he might not go away, but come to see their Chief, and so he did. On arriving where the Chief was waiting for him with many things to eat, he ordered that all the people should sit down, and that the food should be taken to the boats, where the Admiral was, on the sea shore. When he saw that the Admiral had received what he sent, all or most of the Indians ran to the village, which was near, to bring more food, parrots, and other things they had, with such frankness of heart that it was marvelous. The Admiral gave them glass beads, brass trinkets, and bells: not because they asked for anything in return, but because it seemed right, and, above all, because he now looked upon them as future Christians, and subjects of the Sovereigns, as much as the people of Castile. He further says that they want nothing except to know the language and be under governance; for all they may be told to do will be done without any contradiction. The Admiral left this place to go to the ships, and the people, men, women, and children, cried out to him not to go, but remain with them. After the boats departed, several canoes full of people followed after them to the ship, who were received with much honor, and given to eat. There had also come before another Chief from the west, and many people even before another Chief from the west, and many people even came swimming, the ship being over a good half league from the shore. I sent certain persons to the Chief, who had gone back, to ask him about these islands. He received them very well, and took them to his village, to give them some large pieces of gold. They arrived at a large river, which the Indians crossed by swimming. The Christians were unable, so they turned back. In all this district there are very high mountains which seem to reach the sky, so that the mountain in the island of Tenerife appears as nothing in height and beauty, and they are all green with trees. Between them there are very delicious valleys, and at the end of this port, to the south, there is a valley so large that the end of it is not visible, though no mountains intervene, so that it seems to be 15 to 20 leagues long. A river flows through it, and it is all inhabited and cultivated, and as green as Castile in May or June; but the night contains 14 hours, the land being so far north. This port is very good for all the winds than can blow, being enclosed and deep, and the shores peopled by a good and gentle race without arms or evil designs. Any ship may lie within it without fear that other ships will enter at night to attack her, because, although the entrance is over 2 leagues wide, it is protected by reefs of rocks which are barely awash; and there is only a very narrow channel through the reef, which looks as if it had been artificially made, leaving an open door by which ships may enter. In the entrance there are 7 fathoms of depth up to the shore of a small flat island, which has a beach fringed with trees. The entrance is on the west side, and a ship can come without fear until she is close to the rock. On the N.W. side there are three islands, and a great river a league from the cape on one side of the port. It is the best harbor in the world, and the Admiral gave it the name of *Puerto de la mar de Santo Tomas*, because today it was the Saint's day. The Admiral called it a sea, owing to its size.

Saturday, 22nd of December.

At dawn the Admiral made sail to shape a course in search of the islands which the Indians had told him contained much gold, some of them having more gold than earth. But the weather was not favorable, so he anchored again, and sent away the boat to fish with a net. The Lord of that land, who had a place near there, sent a large canoe full of people, including one of his principal attendants, to invite the Admiral to come with the ships to his land, where he would give him all he wanted. The Chief sent, by this servant, a girdle which, instead of a bag, had attached to it a mask with two large ears made of beaten gold, the tongue, and the nose. These people are very open-hearted, and whatever they are asked for they give most willingly; while, when they themselves ask for anything, they do so as if receiving a great favor. So says the Admiral. They brought the canoe alongside the boat, and gave the girdle to a boy; then they came on board with their mission. It took a good part of the day before they could be understood. Not even the Indians who were on board understood them well, because they have some differences of words for the names of things. At last their invitation was understood by signs. The Admiral determined to start tomorrow, although he did not usually sail on a Sunday, owing to a devout feeling, and not on account of any superstition whatever. But in the hope that these people would become Christians through the willingness they show, and that they will be subjects of the Sovereigns of Castile, and because he now holds them to be so, and that they may serve with love, he wished and endeavoured to please them. Before leaving, today, the Admiral sent 6 men to a large village 3 leagues to the westward, because the Chief had come the day before and said that he had some pieces of gold. When the Christians arrived, the Secretary of the Admiral, who was one of them, took the Chief by the hand. The Admiral had sent him, to prevent the others from imposing upon the Indians. As the Indians are so simple, and the Spaniards so avaricious and grasping, it does not suffice that the Indians should give them all they want in exchange for a bead or a bit of glass, but the Spaniards would take everything without any return at all. The Admiral always prohibits this, although, with the exception of gold, the things given by the Indians are of little value. But the Admiral, seeing the simplicity of the Indians, and that they will give a piece of gold in exchange of 6 beads, gave the order that nothing should be received from them unless something had been given in exchange. Thus the Chief took the Secretary by the hand and led him to the house, followed by the whole village, which was very large. He made his guests eat, and the Indians brought them many cotton fabrics, and spun cotton in skeins. In the afternoon the Chief gave them 3 very fat geese and some small pieces of gold. A great number of people went back with them, carrying all the things they had got by barter, and they also carried the Spaniards themselves across streams and muddy places. The Admiral ordered some things to be given to the Chief, and both he and his people were very well satisfied, truly believing that the Christians had come from heaven, so that they considered themselves fortunate in beholding them. On this day more than 120 canoes came to the ships, all full of people, and all bringing something, especially their bread and fish, and fresh water in earthen jars. They also brought seeds of good kinds, and there was a grain which they put into a porringer of water and drank it. The Indians who were on board said that this was very wholesome.

Sunday, 23rd of December.

The Admiral could not go with the ships to that land whither he had been invited by the Chief, because there was no wind. But he sent, with the three messengers who were waiting for the boats, some people, including the Secretary. While they were gone, he sent two of the Indians he had on board with him to the villages which were near the anchorage. They returned to the ship with a chief, who brought the news that there was a great quantity of gold in that island of Espanola, and that people from other parts came to buy it. They said that here the Admiral would find as much as he wanted. Others came, who confirmed the statement that there was much gold in the island, and explained the way it was collected. The Admiral understood all this with much difficulty; nevertheless, he concluded that there was a very great quantity in those parts, and that, if he could find the place whence it was got, there would be abundance; and, if not, there would be nothing. He believed there must be a great deal, because, during the three days that he had been in that port, he had got several pieces of gold, and he could not believe that it was brought from another land.

"Our Lord, who holds all things in his hands, look upon me, and grant what shall be for his service."

These are the Admiral's words. He says that, according to his reckoning, a thousand people had visited the ship, all of them bringing something. Before they come alongside, at a distance of a crossbow-shot, they stand up in the canoe with what they bring in their hands, crying out, "Take it! Take it!" He also reckoned that 500 came to the ship swimming, because they had no canoes, the ship being near a league from the shore. Among the visitors, 5 chiefs had come, sons of chiefs, with all their families of wives and children, to see the Christians. The Admiral ordered something to be given to all, because such gifts were all well employed.

"May our Lord favor me by his clemency, that I may find this gold, I mean the mine of gold, which I hold to be here, many saying that they know it." These are his words.

The boats arrived at night, and said that there was a grand road as far as they went, and they found many canoes, with people who went to see the Admiral and the Christians, at the mountain of Caribatan. They held it for certain that, if the Christians festival was kept in that port, all the people of the island would come, which they calculated to be larger than England. All the people went with them to the village, which they said was the largest, and the best laid out with streets, of any they had seen. The Admiral says it is part of the Punta Santa, almost 3 leagues S.E. The canoes go very fast with paddles; so they went ahead to apprise the Cacique, as they call the chief. They also have another greater name *Nitayno*; but it was not clear whether they used it for lord, or governor, or judge. At last the Cacique came to them, and joined them in the square, which was clean-swept, as was all the village. The population numbered over 2,000 men. This king did great honor to the people from the ship, and every inhabitant brought them something to eat and drink. Afterwards the king gave each of the them cotton cloths such as women wear, with parrots for the Admiral, and some pieces of gold. The people also gave cloths and other things from their houses to the sailors; and as for the trifles they got in return, they seemed to look upon them as relics. When they wanted to return in the afternoon, he asked them to stay until the next day, and all the people did the same. When they saw that the Spaniards were determined to go, they accompanied them most of the way, carrying the gifts of the Cacique on their backs as far as the boats, which had been left at the mouth of the river.

Monday, 24th of December.
Before sunrise the Admiral got under weigh with the breeze. Among the numerous Indians who had come to the ship yesterday, and had made signs that there was gold in the island, naming the places whence it was collected, the Admiral noticed one who seemed more fully informed, or who spoke with more willingness, so he asked him to come with the Christians and show them the position of the gold mines. This Indian has a companion or relation with him, and many other places they mentioned where gold was found, they named *Cipango*, which they called *Civao*. Here they said that there was a great quantity of gold, and that the Cacique carried banners of beaten gold. But they added that it was very far off to the eastward.

Here the Admiral addresses the following words to the Sovereigns:

"Your Highnesses may believe that there is no better nor gentler people in the world. Your Highnesses ought to rejoice that they will soon become Christians, and that they will be taught the good customs of your kingdoms. A better race there cannot be, and both the people and lands are in such quantity that I know not how to write it. I have spoken in the superlative degree of the country and people of Juana, which they call Cuba, but there is as much difference between them and this island and people as between day and night. I believe that no one who should see them could say less than I have said, and I repeat that the things and the great villages of this island of Espanola, which they call Bohio, are wonderful. All here have a loving manner and gentle speech, unlike the others, who seem to be menacing when they speak. Both men and women are of good stature, and not black. It is true that they all paint, some with black, others with other colors, but most with red. I know that they are tanned by the sun, but this does not affect them much. Their houses and villages are pretty, each with a chief, who acts as their judge, and who is obeyed by them. All these lords use few words, and have excellent manners. Most of their orders are given by a sign with the hand, which is understood with surprising quickness." All these are the words of the Admiral.

He who would enter the sea of Santo Tome ought to stand for a good league across the mouth to a flat island in the middle, which was named *La Amiga*, pointing her head towards it. When the ship is within a stone's throw of it the course should be altered to make for the eastern shore, leaving the west side, and this shore, and not the other, should be kept on board, because a great reef runs out from the west, and even beyond that there are three sunken rocks. This reef comes within a lombard-shot of the Amiga island. Between them there are 7 fathoms at least, with a gravelly bottom. Within, a harbor will be found large enough for all the ships in the world, which would be there without need of cables. There is another reef, with sunken rocks, on the east side of the island of Amiga, which are extensive and run out to sea, reaching within two leagues of the cape. But it appeared that between them there was an entrance, within two lombard-shots of Amiga, on the west side of Monte Caribatan, where there was a good and very large port.

Tuesday, 25th of December. Christmas.

Navigating yesterday, with little wind, from Santo Tome to Punta Santa, and being a league from it, at about 11 o'clock at night the Admiral went down to get some sleep, for he had not had any rest for 2 days and night. As it was calm, the sailor who steered the ship thought he would go to sleep, leaving the tiller in charge of a boy. The Admiral had forbidden this throughout the voyage, whether it was blowing or whether it was calm. The boys were never to be entrusted with the helm. The Admiral had no anxiety respecting sand-banks and rocks, because when he sent the boats to that king on sunday, they had passed to the east of Punta Santa at least 3 leagues and a half, and the sailors had seen all the coast, and the rocks there are from Punta Santa, for a distance of 3 leagues to the E.S.E. They saw the course that should be taken, which had not been the case before, during this voyage. It pleased our Lord that, at 12 o'clock at night, when the Admiral had retired to rest, and when all had fallen asleep, seeing that it was a dead calm and the sea like glass, the tiller being in the hands of a boy, the current carried the ship on one of the sand banks. If it had not been night the bank could have been seen, and the surf on it could be heard for a good league. But the ship ran upon it so gently that it could scarcely be felt. The boy, who felt the helm and heard the rush of the sea, cried out. The Admiral at once came up, and so quickly that no one had felt that the ship was aground. Presently the master of the ship, whose watch it was, came on deck. The Admiral ordered him and others to launch the boat, which was on the poop, and lay out an anchor astern. The master, with several others, got into the boat, and the Admiral thought that they did so with the object of obeying his orders. But they did so in order to take refuge with the caravel, which was half a league to leeward. The caravel would not allow them to come on board, acting judiciously, and they therefore returned to the ship; but the caravel's boat arrived first. When the Admiral saw that his own people fled in this way, the water rising and the ship being across the sea, seeing no other course, he ordered the masts to be cut away and the ship to be lightened as much as possible, to see if she would come off. But, as the water continued to rise, nothing more could be done. Her side fell over across the sea, but it was nearly calm. Then the timbers opened, and the ship was lost. The Admiral went to the caravel to arrange about the reception of the ship's crew, and as a light breeze was blowing from the land, and continued during the greater part of the night, while it was unknown how far the bank extended, he hove her to until daylight. He then went back to the ship, inside the reef; first having sent a boat on shore with Diego de Arana of Cordova, Alguazil of the Fleet, and Pedro Gutierrez, Gentleman of the King's Bedchamber, to inform the king, who had invited the ships to come on the previous Saturday. His town was about a league and a half from the sand bank. They reported that he wept when he heard the news, and he sent all his people with large canoes to unload the ship. This was done, and they landed all there was between decks in a very short time. Such was the great promptitude and diligence shown by that king. He himself, with brothers and relations, were actively assisting as well in the ship as in the care of the property when it was landed, that all night be properly guarded. Now and then he sent one of his relations weeping to the Admiral, to console him, saying that he must not feel sorrow or annoyance, for he would supply all that was needed. The Admiral assured the Sovereigns that there could not have been such good watch kept in any part of Castile, for that there was not even a needle missing. He ordered that all the property should be placed by some houses which the king placed at his disposal, until they were emptied, when everything would be stowed and guarded in them. Armed men were place round the stores to watch all night.

"The king and all his people wept. They are a loving people, without covetousness, and fit for anything; and I assure your Highnesses, and fit for anything; and I assure you Highnesses that there is no better land nor people. They love their neighbors as themselves, and their speech is the sweetest and gentlest in the world, and always with a smile. Men and women go as naked as when their mothers bore them. Your Highnesses should believe that they have very good customs among themselves. The king ia a man of remarkable presence, and with a certain self-contained manner that is a pleasure to see. They have good memories, wish to see everything, and ask the use of what they see." All this is written by the Admiral.

Wednesday, 26th of December.
Today, at sunrise, the king of that land came to the caravel Nina, where the Admiral was, and said to him, almost weeping, that he need not be sorry, for that he would give him all he had; that he had placed 2 large houses at the disposal of the Christians who were on shore, and that he would give more if they were required, and as many canoes as could load from the ship and discharge on shore, with as many people as were wanted. This had all been done yesterday, without so much as a needle being missed.

"So honest are they," says the Admiral, "without any covetousness for the goods of others, and so above all was that virtuous king."

While the Admiral was talking to him, another canoe arrived from a different place, bringing some pieces of gold, which the people in the canoe wanted to exchange for a hawk's bell; for there was nothing they desired more than these bells. They had scarcely come alongside when they called and held up the gold, saying *Chuq chuq* for the bells, for they are quite mad about them. After the king had seen this, and when the canoes which came from other places had departed, he called the Admiral and asked him to give orders that one of the bells was to be kept for another day, when he would bring 4 pieces of gold the size of a man's hand. The Admiral rejoiced to hear this, and afterwards a sailor, who came from the shore, told him that it was wonderful what pieces of gold the men on shore were getting in exchange for next to nothing. For a needle they got a piece of gold worth 2 *castellano*, and that this was nothing to what it would be within a month. The King rejoiced much when he saw that the Admiral was pleased. He understood that his friend wanted much gold, and he said, by signs, that he knew where there was, in the vicinity, a very large quantity; so that he must be in good heart, for he should have as much as he wanted. He gave some account of it, especially saying that in Cipango, which they call Cibao, it is so abundant that it is of no value, and that they will bring it, although there is also much more in the island of Espanola, which they call Bohio, and in the province of Caritaba. The king dined on board the caravel with the Admiral and afterwards went on shore, where he received the Admiral with much honor. He gave him a collation consisting of 3 or 4 kinds of yams, with shellfish and game, and other viands they have, besides the bread they call *cazavi*. He then took the Admiral to see some groves of trees near the houses, and they were accompanied by at least a thousand people, all naked. The Lord had on a shirt and a pair of gloves, given to him by the Admiral, and he was more delighted with the gloves than with anything else. In his manner of eating, both as regards the high-bred air and the peculiar cleanliness he clearly showed his nobility. After he had eaten, he remained some time at table, and they brought him certain herbs, with which he rubbed his hands. The Admiral thought that this was done to make them soft, and they also gave him water for his hands. After the meal he took the Admiral to the beach. The Admiral then sent for a Turkish bow and a quiver of arrows, and took a shot at a man of his company, who had been warned. The chief, who knew nothing about arms, as they neither have them nor use them, thought this a wonderful thing. He, however, began to talk of those of Caniba, whom they call Caribes. They come to capture the natives, and have bows and arrows without iron, of which there is no memory in any of these lands, nor of steel, nor any other metal except gold and copper. Of copper the Admiral had only seen very little. The Admiral said, by signs, that the Sovereigns of Castile would order the Caribs to be destroyed, and that all should be taken with their heads tied together. He ordered a lombard and a hand gun to be fired off, and seeing the effect caused by its force and what the shots penetrated, the king was astonished. When his people heard the explosion they all fell on the ground. They brought the Admiral a large mask, which had pieces of gold for the eyes and ears and in other parts, and this they gave, with other trinkets of gold that the same king had put on the head and round the neck of the Admiral, and of other Christians, to whom they also gave many pieces. The Admiral received much pleasure and consolation from these things, which tempered the anxiety and sorrow he felt at the loss of the ship. He knew our Lord had caused the ship to stop here, that a settlement might be formed.

"From this," he says, "originated so many things that, in truth, the disaster was really a piece of good fortune. For it is certain that, if I had not lost the ship, I should have gone on without anchoring in this place, which is within a great bay, having two or three reefs of rock. I should not have left people in the country during this voyage, nor even, if I had desired to leave them, should I have been able to obtain so much information, nor such supplies and provisions for a fortress. And true it is that many people had asked me to give them leave to remain. Now I have given orders for a tower and a fort, both well built, and a large cellar, not because I believe that such defenses will be necessary. I believe that with the force I have with me I could subjugate the whole island, which I believe to be larger than Portugal, and the population double. But they are naked and without arms, and hopelessly timid. Still, it is advisable to build this tower, being so far from your Highnesses. The people may thus know the skill of the subjects of your Highnesses, and what they can do; and will obey them with love and fear. So they make preparations to build the fortress, with provisions of bread and wine for more than a year, with seeds for sowing, the ship's boat, a caulker and carpenter, a gunner and cooper. Many among these men have a great desire to serve your Highnesses and to please me, by finding out where the mine is whence the gold is brought. Thus everything is got in readiness to begin the work. Above all, it was so calm that there was scarcely wind nor wave when the ship ran aground."

This is what the Admiral says; and he adds more to show that it was great good luck, and the settled design of God, that the ship should be lost in order that people might be left behind. If it had not been for the treachery of the master and his boat's crew, who were all or mostly his countrymen, in neglecting to lay out the anchor so as to haul the ship off in obedience to the Admiral's orders, she would have been saved. In that case, the same knowledge of the land as has been gained in these days would not have been secured, for the Admiral always proceeded with the object of discovering, and never intended to stop more than a day at any one place, unless he was detained by the wind. Still, the ship was very heavy and unsuited for discovery. It was the people of Palos who obliged him to take such a ship, by not complying

"...with what they had promised to the King and Queen, namely, to supply suitable vessels for this expedition. This they did not do. Of all that there was on board the ship, not a needle, nor a board, nor a nail was lost, for she remained as whole as when she sailed, except that it was necessary to cut away and level down in order to get out the jars and merchandise, which were landed and carefully guarded."

He trusted in God that, when he returned from Spain, according to his intention, he would find a ton of gold collected by barter by those he was to leave behind, and that they would have found the mine, and spices in such quantities that the Sovereigns would, in three years, be able to undertake and fit out an expedition to go and conquer the Holy Sepulchre.

"Thus," he says, "I protest to your Highnesses that all the profits of this enterprise may be spent in the conquest of Jerusalem. Your Highnesses may laugh, and say that it is pleasing to you, and that, without this, you entertain that desire." These are the Admiral's words.

Thursday, 27th of December.

The king of that land came alongside the caravel at sunrise, and said that he had sent for gold, and that he would collect all he could before the Admiral departed; but he begged him not to go. The king and one of his brothers, with another very intimate relation, dined with the Admiral, and the two latter said they wished to go to Castile with him. At this time the news came that the caravel Pinta was in a river at the end of the island. Presently the Cacique sent a canoe there, and the Admiral sent a sailor in it. For it was wonderful how devoted the Cacique was to the Admiral. The necessity was now evident of hurrying on preparations for the return to Castile.

Friday, 28th of December.

The Admiral went on shore to give orders and hurry on the work of building the fort, and to settle what men should remain behind. The king, it would seem, had watched him getting into the boat, and quickly went into his house, dissimulating, sending one of his brothers to receive the Admiral, and conduct him to one of the houses that had been set aside for the Spaniards, which was the largest and best in the town. In it there was a couch made of palm matting, where they sat down. Afterwards the brother sent an attendant to say that the Admiral was there, as if the king did not know that he had come. The Admiral, however, believed that this was a feint in order to do him more honor. The attendant gave the message, and the Cacique came in great haste, and put a large soft piece of gold he had in his hand round the Admiral's neck. They remained together until the evening, arranging what had to be done.

Saturday, 29th of December.
A new youthful nephew of the king came to the caravel at sunrise, who showed a good understanding and disposition. As the Admiral was always working to find out the origin of the gold, he asked everyone, for he could now understand somewhat by signs. This youth told him that, at a distance of 4 days' journey, there was an island to the eastward called *Guarionex*, and others called *Macorix*, *Mayonic*, *Fuma*, *Cibao*, and *Coroay*, in which there was plenty of gold. The Admiral wrote these names down, and now understood what had been said by a brother of the king, who was annoyed with him, as the Admiral understood. At other times the Admiral had suspected that the king had worked against his knowing where the gold had its origin and was collected, that he might not go away to barter in another part of the island. For there are such a number of places in this same island that it is wonderful. After nightfall the king sent a large mask of gold, and asked for a washhand basin and jug. The Admiral thought he wanted them for patterns to copy from, and therefore sent them.

Sunday, 30th of December.
The Admiral went on shore to dinner, and came at a time when 5 kings had arrived, all with their crowns, who were subject to this king, named *Guacanagari*. They represented a very good state of affairs, and the Admiral says to the Sovereigns that it would have given them pleasure to see the manner of their arrival. On landing, the Admiral was received by the king, who led him by the arms to the same house where he was yesterday, where there were chairs, and a couch on which the Admiral sat. Presently the king took the crown off his head and put it on the Admiral's head, and the Admiral took from his neck a collar of beautiful beads of several different colors, which looked very well in all its parts, and put it on the king. He also took off a cloak of fine material, in which he had dressed himself that day, and dressed the king in it, and sent for some colored boots, which he put on his feet, and he put a large silver ring on his finger, because he had heard that he had admired greatly a silver ornament worn by one of the sailors. The king was highly delighted and well satisfied, and two of those kings who were with him came with him to where the Admiral was, and each gave him a large piece of gold. At this time an

Indian came and reported that it was 2 days since he left the caravel Pinta in a port to the eastward. The Admiral returned to the caravel, and Vicente Anes, the captain, said that he had seen the rhubarb plant, and that they had it on the island Amiga, which is at the entrance of the sea of Santo Tome, 6 leagues off, and that he had recognized the branches and roots. They say that rhubarb forms small branches above the ground, and fruit like green mulberries, almost dry, and the stalk, near the root, is as yellow and delicate as the best color for painting, and underground the root grows like a large pear.

Monday, 31st of December.

Today the Admiral was occupied in seeing that water and fuel were taken on board for the voyage to Spain, to give early notice to the Sovereigns, that they might despatch ships to complete the discoveries. For now the business appeared to be so great and important that the Admiral was astonished. He did not wish to go until he had examined all the land to the eastward, and explored the coast, so as to know the route to Castile, with a view to sending sheep and cattle. But as he had been left with only a single vessel, it did not appear prudent to encounter the dangers that are inevitable in making discoveries. He complained that all this inconvenience had been caused by the caravel Pinta having parted company.

Tuesday, 1st of January 1493.

At midnight the Admiral sent a boat to the island Amiga to bring the rhubarb. It returned at vespers with a bundle of it. They did not bring more because they had no spade to dig it up with; it was taken to be shown to the Sovereigns. The king of that land said that he had sent many canoes for gold. The canoe returned that had been sent for tidings of the Pinta, without having found her. The sailor who went in the canoe said that 20 leagues from there he had seen a king who wore 2 large plates of gold on his head, but when the Indians in the canoe spoke to him he took them off. He also saw much gold on other people. The Admiral considered that the King Guacanagari ought to have prohibited his people from selling gold to the Christians, in order that it might all pass through his hands. But the king knew the places, as before stated, where there was such a quantity that it was not valued. The spicery also is extensive, and is worth more than pepper or *manegueta*. He left instructions to those who wished to remain that they were to collect as much as they could.

Wednesday, 2nd of January.

In the morning the Admiral went on shore to take leave of the King Guacanagari, and to depart from him in the name of the Lord. He gave him one of his shirts. In order to show him the force of the lombards, and what effect they had, he ordered one to be loaded and fired into the side of the ship that was on shore, for this was opposite to the conversation respecting the Caribs, with whom Guacanagari was at war. The king saw whence the lombard-shot came, and how it passed through the side of the ship and went far away over the sea. The Admiral also ordered a skirmish of the crews of the ships, fully armed, saying to the Cacique that he need have no fear of the Caribs even if they should come. All this was done that the king might look upon the men who were left behind as friends, and that he might also have a proper fear of them. The king took the Admiral to dinner at the house where he was established, and the others who came with him. The Admiral strongly recommenced to his friendship Diego de Arana, Pedro Gutierrez, and Rodrigo Escovedo, whom he left jointly as his lieutenants over the people who remained behind, that all might be well regulated and governed for the service of their Highnesses. The Cacique showed much love for the Admiral, and great sorrow at his departure, especially when he saw him go on board. A relation of that king said to the Admiral that he had ordered a statue of pure gold to be made, as big as the Admiral, and that it would be brought within 10 days. The Admiral embarked with the intention of sailing presently, but there was no wind.

He left on that island of Espanola, which the Indians called Bohio, 39 men with the fortress, and he says that they were great friends of Guacanagari. The lieutenants placed over them were: Diego de Arana of Cordova, Pedro Gutierrez, Gentleman of the King's Bedchamber, and Rodrigo de Escovedo, a native of Segovia, nephew of Fray Rodrigo Perez, with all the powers he himself received from the Sovereigns. [Navarrete records 44 names left behind by Columbus]. He left behind all the merchandise which had been provided for bartering, which was much, that they might trade for gold. He also left bread for a year's supply, wine, and much artillery. He also left the ship's boat, that they, most of them being sailors, might go, when the time seemed convenient, to discover the gold mine, in order that the Admiral, on his return, might find much gold. They were also to find a good site for a town, for this was not altogether a desirable port;

especially if the gold the natives brought came from the east; also, the farther to the east the nearer to Spain. He also left seeds for sowing, and his officers, the Algauzil and Secretary, as well as a ship's carpenter, a caulker, a good gunner well acquainted with artillery, a cooper, a physician, and a tailor, all being seamen as well.

Thursday, 3rd of January.
The Admiral did not go today, because 3 of the Indians whom he had brought from the islands, and who had stayed behind, arrived, and said that the others with their women would be there at sunrise. The sea also was rather rough, so that they could not land from the boat. He determined to depart tomorrow, with the grace of God. The Admiral said that if he had the caravel Pinta with him he could make sure of shipping a ton of gold, because he could then follow the coasts of these islands, which he would not do alone, for fear some accident might impede his return to Castile, and prevent him from reporting all he had discovered to the Sovereigns. If it was certain that the caravel Pinta would arrive safely in Spain with Martin Alonso Pinzon, he would not hesitate to act as he desired; but as he had no certain tidings of him, and as he might return and tell lies to the Sovereigns, that he might not receive the punishment he deserved for having done so much harm in having parted company without permission, and impeded the good service that might have been done; the Admiral could only trust in our Lord that he would grant favorable weather, and remedy all things.

Friday, 4th of January.
At sunrise the Admiral weighed the anchor, with little wind, and turned her head N.W. to get clear of the reef, by another channel wider than the one by which he entered, which, with others, is very good for coming in front of the *Villa de la Navidad*, in all which the least depth is from 3 to 9 fathoms. These two channels run N.W. an S.E., and the reefs are long, extending from the Cabo Santo to the Cabo de Sierpe for more than 6 leagues, and then a good 3 leagues out to sea. At a league outside Cabo Santo there are not more than 8 fathoms of depth, and inside that cape, on the east side, there are many sunken rocks, and channels to enter between them. All this coast trends N.W. and S.E., and it is all beach, with the land very level for about a quarter of a league inland. After that distance there are very high mountains, and the whole is peopled with a very good race, as they showed themselves

to the Christians. Thus the Admiral navigated to the east, shaping a course for a very high mountain, which looked like an island, but is not one, being joined to the mainland by a very low neck. The mountain has the shape of a very beautiful tent. He gave it the name of *Monte Cristi*. It is due east of Cabo Santo, at a distance of 18 leagues. That day, owing to the light wind, they could not reach within 6 leagues of Monte Cristi. He discovered 4 very low and sandy islets, with a reef extending N.W. and S.E. Inside, there is a large gulf, which extends from this mountain to the S.E. at least 20 leagues, which must all be shallow, with many sand banks, and inside numerous rivers which are not navigable. At the same time the sailor who was sent in the canoe to get tidings of the Pinta reported that he saw a river into which ships might enter. The Admiral anchored at a distance of 6 leagues from Monte Cristi, in 19 fathoms, and so kept clear of many rocks and reefs. Here he remained for the night. The Admiral gives notice to those who would go to the Villa de la Navidad that, to make Monte Cristi, he should stand off the land 2 leagues, etc. (But as the coast is now known it is not given here.) The Admiral concluded that Cipango was in that island, and that it contained much gold, spices, mastick, and rhubarb.

Saturday, 5th of January.

At sunrise the Admiral made sail with the land breeze, and saw that to the S.S.E of Monte Cristi, between it and an island, there seemed to be a good port to anchor in that night. He shaped an E.S.E. course, afterwards S.S.E., for 6 leagues round the high land, and found a depth of 17 fathoms, with a very clean bottom, going on for 3 leagues with the same soundings. Afterwards it shallowed to 12 fathoms up to the *morro* of the mountain, and off the morro, at one league, the depth of 9 fathoms was found, the bottom clean, and all fine sand. The Admiral followed the same course until he came between the mountain and the island, where he found 3 1/2 fathoms at low water, a very good port, and here he anchored. He went in the boat to the islet, where he found remains of fire and footmarks, showing that fishermen had been there. Here they saw many stones painted in colors, or a quarry of such stones, very beautifully worked by nature, suited for the building of a church or other public work, like those he found on the island of San Salvador. On this islet he also found many plants of mastick. He says that this Monte Cristi is very fine and high, but accessible, and of a very beautiful shape, all the land round it being low, a very fine plain, from which the height rises, looking at a distance like an island disunited from other land. Beyond the mountain, to the east, he saw a cape at a distance of 24 miles, which he named *Cabo del Becerro*, whence to the mountain for 2 leagues there are reefs of rocks, though it appeared as if there were navigable channels between them. It would, however, be advisable to approach in daylight, and to send a boat ahead to sound. From the mountain eastward to Cabo del Becerro, for 4 leagues, there is a beach, and the land is low, but the rest is very high, with beautiful mountains and some cultivation. Inland, a chain of mountains runs N.E. and S.W., the most beautiful he had seen, appearing like the hills of Cordoba. Some other very lofty mountains appear in the distance towards the south and S.E., and very extensive green valleys with large rivers: all this in such quantity that he did not believe he had exaggerated a thousandth part. Afterwards he saw, to the eastward of the mountain, a land which appeared like that of Monte Cristi in size and beauty. Further to the east and N.E. there is land which is not so high, extending for some hundred miles or near it.

Sunday, 6th of January.
    That port is sheltered from all winds, except north and N.W., and these winds seldom blow in this region. Even when the wind is from those quarters, shelter may be found near the islet in 3 or 4 fathoms. At sunset the Admiral made sail to proceed along the coast, the course being east, except that it is necessary to look out for several reefs of stone and sand, within which there are good anchorages, with channels leading to them. After noon it blew fresh from the east. The Admiral ordered a sailor to go to the mast-head to look out for reefs, and he saw the caravel Pinta coming, with the wind aft, and she joined the Admiral. As there was no place to anchor, owing to the rocky bottom, the Admiral returned from 10 leagues to Monte Cristi, with the Pinta in company. Martin Alonso Pinzon came on board the caravel Nina, where the Admiral was, and excused himself by saying that he had parted company against his will, giving reasons for it. But the Admiral says that they were all false; and that on the night when Pinzon parted company he was influenced by pride and covetousness. He could not understand whence had come the insolence and disloyalty with which Pinzon had treated him during the voyage. The Admiral had taken no notice, because he did not wish to give place to the evil works of Satan, who desired to impede the voyage. It appeared that

one of the Indians, who had been put on board the caravel by the Admiral with others, had said that there was much gold in an island called Baneque, and, as Pinzon's vessel was light and swift, he determined to go there, parting company with the Admiral, who wished to remain and explore the coasts of Juana and Espanola, with an easterly course. When Martin Alonso arrived at the island of Baneque he found no gold. He then went to the coast of Espanola, on information from the Indians that there was a great quantity of gold and many mines in that island of Espanola, which the Indians call Bohio. He thus arrived near the Villa de Navidad, about 15 leagues from it, having then been absent more than 20 days, so that the news brought by the Indians was correct, on account of which the King Guacanagari sent a canoe, and the Admiral put a sailor on board; but the Pinta must have gone before the canoe arrived. The Admiral says that the Pinta obtained much gold by barter, receiving large pieces the size of 2 fingers in exchange for a needle. Martin Alonso took half, dividing the other half among the crew. The Admiral then says:

"Thus I am convinced that our Lord miraculously caused that vessel to remain here, this being the best place in the whole island to form a settlement, and the nearest to the gold mines."

He also says that he knew "of another great island, to the south of the island of Juana, in which there is more gold than in this island, so that they collect it in bits the size of beans, while in Espanola they find the pieces the size of grains of corn. They call that island *Yamaye*."

The Admiral also heard of an island further east, in which there were only women, having been told this by many people. He was also informed that Yamaye and the island of Espanola were 10 days' journey in a canoe from the mainland, which would be about 70 or 80 leagues, and that there the people wore clothes.

Monday, 7th of January.

This day the Admiral took the opportunity of caulking the caravel, and the sailors were sent to cut wood. They found mastick and aloes in abundance.

Tuesday, 8th of January.

As the wind was blowing fresh from the east and W.E., the Admiral did not get under weigh this morning. He ordered the caravel to be filled up with wood and water and with all other necessaries for the voyage. He wished to explore all the coast of Espanola in this direction. But those he appointed to the caravels as captains were brothers, namely, Martin Alonso Pinzon and Vicente Anes. They also had followers who were filled with pride and avarice, considering that all now belonged to them, and unmindful of the honor the Admiral had done them. They had not and did not obey his orders, but did and said many unworthy things against him; while Martin Alonso had deserted him from the 21st of November until the 6th of January without cause or reason, but from disaffection. All these things had been endured in silence by the Admiral in order to secure a good end to the voyage. He determined to return as quickly as possible, to get rid of such an evil company, with whom he thought it necessary to dissimulate, although they were a mutinous set, and though he also had with him many good men; for it was not a fitting time for dealing out punishment.

The Admiral got into the boat and went up the river which is near, towards the S.S.W. of Monte Cristi, a good league. This is where the sailors went to get fresh water for the ships. He found that the sand at the mouth of the river, which is very large and deep, was full of very fine gold, and in astonishing quantity. The Admiral thought that it was pulverized in the drift from the river, but in a short time he found many grains as large as horse-beans, while there was a great deal of the fine powder.

As the fresh water mixed with the salt when it entered the sea, he ordered the boat to go up for the distance of a stone's-throw. They filled the casks from the boat, and when they went back to the caravel they found small bits of gold sticking to the hoops of the casks and of the barrel. The Admiral gave the name of *Rio del Oro* to the river. Inside the bar it is very deep, though the mouth is shallow and very wide. The distance to the Villa de la Navidad is 17 leagues, and there are several large rivers on the intervening coast, especially 3 which probably contain much more gold than this one, because they are larger. This river is nearly the size of the Guadalquivir at Cordova, and from it to the gold mines the distance is not more than 20 leagues. The Admiral further says that he did not care to take the sand containing gold, because their Highnesses would have it all as their property at their town of Navidad; and because his first object was now to bring the news and to get rid of the evil company that was with him, whom he had always said were a mutinous set.

Wednesday, 9th of January.

The Admiral made sail at midnight, with the wind S.E., and shaped and E.N.E. course, arriving at a point named *Punta Roja*, which is 60 miles east of Monte Cristi, and anchored under its lee 3 hours before nightfall. He did not venture to go out at night, because there are many reefs, until they are known. Afterwards, if, as will probably be the case, channels are found between them, the anchorage, which is good and well sheltered, will be profitable. The country between Monte Cristi and this point where the Admirable anchored is very high land, with beautiful plains, the range running east and west, all green and cultivated, with numerous streams of water, so that it is wonderful to see such beauty. In all this country there are many turtles, and the sailors took several when they came on shore to lay their eggs at Monte Cristi, as large as a great wooden buckler.

On the previous day, when the Admiral went to the Rio del Oro, he saw 3 mermaids, which rose well out of the sea; but they are not so beautiful as they are painted, though to some extent they have the form of a human face. The Admiral says that he had seen some, at other times, in Guinea, on the coast of the Manequeta.

The Admiral says that this night, in the name of our Lord, he would set out on his homeward voyage without any further delay whatever, for he had found what he sought, and he did not wish to have further cause of offence with Martin Alonso until their Highnesses should know the news of the voyage and what had been done. Afterwards he says:

"I will not suffer the deeds of evil-disposed persons, with little worth, who, without respect for him to whom they owe their positions, presume to set up their own will with little ceremony."

Thursday, 10th of January.

He departed from the place where he had anchored, and at sunset he reached a river, to which he gave the name of *Rio de Gracia*, 3 leagues to the S.E. He came to at the mouth, where there is good anchorage on the east side. There is a bar with no more than 2 fathoms of water, and very narrow across the entrance. It is a good and well-sheltered port, except that there it is often misty, owing to which the caravel Pinta, under Martin Alonso, received a good deal of damage. He had been here bartering for 16 days, and got much gold, which was what Martin Alonso wanted. As soon as he heard from the Indians that the Admiral was on the coast of the same island of Espanola, and that he could not avoid him, Pinzon came to him. He

105--To America and Around the World

wanted all the people of the ship to swear that he had not been there more than 6 days. But his treachery was so public that it could not be concealed. He had made a law that half of all the gold that was collected was his. When he left this port he took 4 men and 2 girls by force. But the Admiral ordered that they should be clothed and put on shore to return to their homes.

"This", the Admiral says, "is a service of your Highnesses. For all the men and women are subjects of your Highnesses, as well in this island as in the others. Here, where your Highnesses already have a settlement, the people ought to be treated with honor and favor, seeing that this island has so much gold and such good spice-yielding lands."

Friday, 11th of January.
At midnight the Admiral left the Rio de Gracia with the land breeze, and steered eastward until he came to a cape named *Belprado*, at a distance of 4 leagues. To the S.E. is the mountain to which he gave the name of *Monte de Plata*, 8 leagues distant. Thence from the cape Belprado to E.S.E. is the point name *Angel*, 18 leagues distant; and rom this point to the Monte de Plata there is a gulf, with the most beautiful lands in the world, all high and fine lands which extend far inland. Beyond there is a range of high mountains running east and west, very grand and beautiful. At the foot of this mountain there is a very good port, with 14 fathoms in the entrance. The mountain is very high and beautiful, and all the country is well peopled. The Admiral believed there must be fine rivers and much gold. At a distance of 4 leagues E.S.E. of Cabo del Angel there is a cape named *Punta del Hierro*, and on the same course, 4 more leagues, a point is reached named *Punta Seca*. Thence, 6 leagues further on, is *Cabo Redondo*, and further on *Cabo Frances*, where a large bay is formed, but there did not appear to be anchorage in it. A league further on is *Cabo del Buen Tiempo*, and thence, a good league S.S.E., is *Cabo Tajado*. Thence, to the south, another cape was sighted at a distance of about 15 leagues. Today great progress was made, as wind and tide were favorable. The Admiral did not venture to anchor for fear of the rocks, so he was hove-to all night.

Saturday, 12 of January.
Towards dawn the Admiral filled and shaped a course to the east with a fresh wind, running 20 miles before daylight, and in 2 hours afterwards 24 miles. Thence he saw land to the south, and steered

towards it, distant 48 miles. During the night he must have run 28 miles N.N.E., to keep the vessels out of danger. When he saw the land, he named one cape that he saw *Cabo de Padre y Hijo*, because at the east point there are 2 rocks, one larger than the other. Afterwards, at 2 leagues to the eastward, he saw a very fine bay between 2 grand mountains. He saw that it was a very large port with a very good approach; but, as it was very early in the morning, and as the greater part of the time it was blowing from the east, and then they had a N.N.W. breeze, he did not wish to delay any more. He continued his course to the east as far as a very high and beautiful cape, all of scarped rock, to which he gave the name of *Cabo del Enamorado*, which was 32 miles to the east of the prot named *Puerto Sacro*. On rounding the cape, another finer and loftier point came in sight, like Cape St. Vincent in Portugal, 12 miles east of Cabo del Enamorado. As soon as he was abreast of the Cabo del Enamorado, the Admiral saw that there was a great bay between this and the next point, 3 leagues across, and in the middle of it a small island. The depth is great at the entrance close to the land. He anchored here 12 fathoms, and sent the boat on shore for water, and to see if intercourse could be opened with the natives, but they all fled. He also anchored to ascertain whether this was all one land with the island of Espanola, and to make sure that this was a gulf, and not a channel, forming another island. He remained astonished at the great size of Espanola.

Sunday, 13th of January.

The Admiral did not leave the port, because there was no land breeze with which to go out. He wished to shift to another better port, because this was rather exposed. He also wanted to wait in that haven, the conjunction of the sun and moon, which would take place on the 17th of this month, and their opposition with Jupiter and conjunction with Mercury, the sun being in opposition to Jupiter, which is the cause of high winds. He sent the boat on shore to a beautiful beach to obtain yams for food. They found some men with bows and arrows, with whom they stopped to speak, buying 2 bows and many arrows from them. They asked one of them to come on board the caravel and see the Admiral; who says that he was very wanting in reverence, more so than any native had had yet seen. His face was all stained with charcoal, but in all parts there is the custom of painting the body different colors. He wore his hair very long, brought together and fastened behind, and put into a small net of parrots' feathers. He was naked, like all the others. The Admiral asked about Caribs, and he pointed to the east, near at hand, which means that he saw the Admiral yesterday before he entered the bay. The Indian said there was much gold to the east, pointing to the poop of the caravel, which was a good size, meaning that there were pieces as large. He called gold *tuob*, and did not understand *caona*, as they call it in the first part of the island that was visited, nor *nozay*, the name in San Salvador and the other islands. Copper is called *tuob* in Espanola. He also spoke of the island of *Goanin*, where there was much *tuob*. The Admiral says that he had received notices of these islands from many persons; that in the other islands the natives were in great fear of the Caribs, called by some of them Caniba, but in Espanola Carib. He thought they must be an audacious race, for they go to all these islands and eat the people they can capture. He understood a few words, and the Indians who were on board comprehended more, there being a difference in the languages owing to the great distance between the various islands. The Admiral ordered that the Indian should be fed, and given pieces of green and red cloth, and glass beads, which they like very much, and then sent on shore. He was told to bring gold if he had any, and it was believed that he had, from some small things he brought with him. When the boat reached the shore there were 55 men behind the trees, naked, and with very long hair, as the women wear it in Castile. Behind the head they wore plumes of feathers of parrots and other birds, and each man carried a bow. The Indian landed, and signed to the others to put down their bows and arrows, and a piece of a staff, which is like..., very heavy, carried instead of a sword. As soon as they came to the boat the crew landed, and began to buy the bows and arrows and other arms, in accordance with an order of the Admiral. Having sold 2 bows, they did not want to give more, but began to attack the Spaniards, and to take hold of them. They were running back to pick up their bows and arrows where they had laid them aside, and took cords in their hands to bind the boat's crew. Seeing them rushing down, and being prepared--for the Admiral always warned them to be on their guard--the Spaniards attacked the Indians, and gave one a stab with a knife in the buttocks, wounding another in the breast with an arrow. Seeing that they could gain little, although the Christians were only 7 and they numbered over 50, they fled, so that none were left throwing bows and arrows away. The Christians would have killed many, if the pilot, who was in command, had not prevented them. The Spaniards presently returned to the caravel with the boat.

The Admiral regretted the affair for one reason , and was pleased for another. They would have fear of the Christians, and they were no doubt an ill-conditioned people, probably Caribs, who eat men. But the Admiral felt alarm lest they should do some harm to the 39 men left in the fortress and town of Navidad, in the event of their coming here in their boat. Even if they are not Caribs, they are a neighboring people, with similar habits, and fearless, unlike the other inhabitants of the island, who are timid, and without arms. The Admiral says all this, and adds that he would have liked to have captured some of them. He says that they lighted many smoke signals, as is the custom in this island of Espanola.

Monday, 14th of January.
This evening the Admiral wished to find the houses of the Indians and to capture some of them, believing them to be Caribs. For, owing to the strong east and northeast winds and the heavy sea, he had remained during the day. Many Indians were seen on shore. The Admiral therefore, ordered the boat to be sent on shore, with the crew well armed. Presently the Indians came to the stern of the boat, including the man who had been on board the day before, and had received presents from the Admiral. With him there came a king, who had given to the said Indian some beads in token of safety and peace for the boat's crew. This king, with 3 of his followers, went on board the boat and came to the caravel. The Admiral ordered them to be given biscuit and treacle to eat, and gave the chief a red cap, some beads, and a piece of red cloth. The others were also given pieces of cloth. The chief said that next day he would bring a mask made of gold, affirming that there was much here, and in Carib and Matinino. They afterwards went on shore well satisfied.

The Admiral here says that the caravels were making much water, which entered by the keel; and he complains of the caulkers at Palos, who caulked the vessels very badly, and ran away when they saw that the Admiral had detected the badness of their work, and intended to oblige them to repair the defect. But, notwithstanding that the caravels were making much water, he trusted in the favor and mercy of our Lord, for his high Majesty well knew how much controversy there was before the expedition could be despatched from Castile, that no one was in the Admiral's favor save Him alone who knew his heart, and after God came your Highnesses, while all others were against him without any reason. He further says:

109--To America and Around the World

"And this has been the cause that the royal crown of your Highnesses has not a hundred *cuentos*, of revenue more than after I entered your service, which is 7 years ago in this very month, the 20th of January. The increase will take place from now onwards. For the almighty God will remedy all things." These are his words.

Tuesday, 15th of January.

The Admiral now wished to depart, for there was nothing to be gained by further delay, after these occurrences and the tumult of the Indians. Today he had heard that all the gold was in the district of the town of Navidad, belonging to their Highnesses; and that in the island of Carib there was much copper, as well as in Matinino. The intercourse at Carib would, however, be difficult, because the natives are said to eat human flesh. Their island would be in sight from thence, and the Admiral determined to go there, as it was on the route, and thence to Matinino, which was said to be entirely people by women, without men. He would thus see both islands, and might take some of the natives. The Admiral sent the boat on shore, but the king of that district had not come, for his village was distant. He, however, sent his crown of gold, as he had promised; and many other natives came with cotton, and bread made from yams, all with their bows and arrows. After the bartering was finished, 4 youths came to the caravel. They appeared to the Admiral to give such a clear account of the islands to the eastward, on the same route as the Admiral would have to take, that he determined to take them to Castile with him. He says that they had no iron nor other metals; at least none was seen, but it was impossible to know much of the land in so short a time, owing to the difficulty with the language, which the Admiral could not understand except by guessing, nor could they know what was said to them, in such a few days. The bows of these people are as large as those of France or England. The arrows are similar to the darts of the natives who have been met with previously, which are made of young canes, which grow very straight, and a *vara* and a half or 2 varas in length. They point them with a piece of sharp wood, a *palmo* and a half long, and at the end some of them fix a fish's tooth, but most of them anoint it with an herb. They do not shoot as in other parts, but in a certain way which cannot do much harm. Here they have a great deal of fine and long cotton, and plenty of mastick. The bows appeared to be of yew, and there is gold and copper. There is also plenty of *aji*, which is their pepper, which is more valuable than pepper, and all the people eat nothing else, it being very wholesome. Fifty caravels might be annually loaded with it from Espanola. The Admiral says that he found a great deal of weed in this bay, the same as was met with at sea when he came on this discovery. He therefore supposed that there were islands to the eastward, in the direction of the position where he began to meet with it; for he considers it certain that this weed has its origin in shallow water near the land, and, if this is the case, these Indies must be very near the Canary Islands. For this reason he thought the distance must be less than 400 leagues.

Wednesday, 16th of January.
They got under weigh 3 hours before daylight, and left the gulf, which was named *Golfo de las Flechas*, with the land breeze. After-wards there was a west wind, which was fair to go to the island of Carib on a E.N.W. course. This was where the people live of whom all the natives of the other islands are so frightened, because they roam over the sea in canoes without number, and eat the men they can capture. The Admiral steered the course indicated by one of the four Indians he took yesterday in the Puerto de las flechas. After having sailed about 64 miles, the Indians made signs that the island was to the S.E. The Admiral ordered the sails to be trimmed for that course, but, after having proceeded on it for 2 leagues, the wind freshened from a quarter which was very favorable for the voyage to Spain. The Admiral had noticed that the crew were downhearted when he deviated from the direct route home, reflecting that both caravels were leaking badly, and that there was no help but in God. He therefore gave up the course leading to the islands, and shaped a direct course for Spain E.N.E. He sailed on this course, making 48 miles, which is 12 leagues, by sunset. The Indians said that by that route they would fall in with the island of Matinino, peopled entirely by women without men, and the Admiral wanted very much to take 5 or 6 of them to the Sovereigns. But he doubted whether the Indians understood the route well, and he could not afford to delay, by reason of the leaky condition of the caravels. He, however, believed the story, and that, at certain seasons, men came to them from the island of Carib, distant 10 or 12 leagues. If males were born, they were sent to the island of the men; and if females, they remained with their mothers. The Admiral says that these 2 islands cannot have been more than 15 or 20 leagues to the S.E. from where he altered course, the Indians not understanding how to point out the direction. After losing sight of the cape, which was named *San*

Theramo, which was left 16 leagues to the west, they went for 12 leagues E.N.E. The weather was very fine.

Thursday, 17 of January.

The wind went down at sunset yesterday, the caravels having sailed 14 glasses, each a little less than half-an-hour, at 4 miles an hour, making 28 miles. Afterwards the wind freshened, and they ran all that watch, which was 10 glasses. Then another 6 until sunrise at 8 miles an hour, thus making altogether 84 miles, equal to 21 leagues, to the E.N.E., and until sunset 44 miles, or 11 leagues, to the east. Here a booby came to the caravel, and afterwards another. The Admiral saw a great deal of gulf weed.

Friday, 18th of January.

During the night they steered E.S.E., with little wind, for 40 miles, equal to 10 leagues, and then 30 miles, or 7 1\2 leagues, until sunrise. All day they proceeded with little wind to E.N.E. and N.E. by E., more or less, her head being sometimes north and at others N.N.E., and, counting one with the other, they made 60 miles, or 15 leagues. There was little weed, but yesterday and today the sea appeared to be full of tunnies. The Admiral believed that they were on their way to the tunny-fisheries of the Duke, at Conil and Cadiz. He also thought they were near some islands, because a frigate-bird flew round the caravel, and afterwards went away to the S.S.E. He said that to the S.E. of the island of Espanola were the island of Carib, Martinino, and many others.

Saturday, 19th of January.

During the night they made good 56 miles N.N.E., and 64 N.E. by N. After sunrise they steered N.E. with the wind fresh from S.W., and afterwards W.S.W. 85 miles, equal to 21 leagues. The sea was again full of small tunnies. There were boobies, frigate-birds, and terns.

Sunday, 20th of January.

It was calm during the night, with occasional slants of wind, and they only made 20 miles to the N.E. After sunrise they went 11 miles S.E., and then 36 miles N.N.E., equal to 9 leagues. They saw an immense quantity of small tunnies, the air very soft and pleasant, like Seville in April or May, and the sea, for which God be given many thanks, always very smooth. Frigate-birds, sandpipers, and other birds were seen.

Monday, 21st of January.

Yesterday, before sunset, they steered N.E. b. E., with the wind east, at the rate of 8 miles an hour until midnight, equal to 56 miles. Afterwards they steered N.N.E. 8 miles an hour, so, that they made 104 miles, or 26 leagues, during the night N.E. by N. After sunrise they steered N.N.E. with the same wind, which at times veered to N.E., and they made good 88 miles in the 11 hours of daylight, or 21 leagues; except one that was lost by delay caused by closing with the Pinta to communicate. The air was colder, and it seemed to get colder as they went further north, and also that the nights grew longer owing to the narrowing of the sphere. Many boatswain-birds and terns were seen as well as other birds, but not so many fish, perhaps owing to the water being colder. Much weed was seen.

Tuesday, 22nd of January.

Yesterday, after sunset, they steered N.N.E. with an east wind. They made 8 miles an hour during 5 glasses, and 3 before the watch began, making 8 glasses, equal to 72 miles, or 18 leagues. Afterwards they went N.E. by N. for 6 glasses, which would be another 18 miles. Then, during 4 glasses of the second watch N.E. at 6 miles an hour, or 3 leagues. From that time to sunset, for 7 glasses, E.N.E. at 6 leagues an hour, equal to 7 leagues. Then E.N.E. until 11 o'clock, 32 miles. Then the wind fell, and they made no more during that day. The Indians swam about. They saw boatswain-birds and much weed.

Wednesday, 23rd of January.

Tonight the wind was very changeable, but, making the allowances applied by good sailors, they made 84 miles, or 21 leagues, N.E. by N. Many times the caravel Nina had to wait for the Pinta, because she sailed badly when on a bowline, the mizen being of little use owing to the weakness of the mast. If her captain, Martin Alonso Pinzon, had taken the precaution to provide her with a good mast in the Indies, where there are so many and such excellent spars, instead of deserting his commander from motives of avarice, he would have done better. They saw many boatswain-birds and much weed. The heavens have been clouded over during these last days, but there has been no rain. The sea has been as smooth as a river, for which many thanks be given to God. After sunrise they went free, and made 30 miles, or 7 1\2 leagues N.E. During the rest of the day E.N.E. another 30 miles.

Thursday, 24th of January.
They made 44 miles, or 11 leagues, during the night, allowing for many changes in the wind, which was generally N.E. After sunrise until sunset E.N.E. 14 leagues.

Friday, 25th of January.
They steered during part of the night E.N.E for 13 glasses, making 9 1\2 leagues. Then N.N.E. 6 miles. The wind fell, and during they day they only made 28 miles E.N.E., or 7 leagues. The sailors killed a tunny and a very large shark, which was very welcome, as they now had nothing but bread and wine, and some yams from the Indies.

Saturday, 26th of January.
The night they made 56 miles, or 14 leagues, E.S.E. After sunrise they steered E.S.E., and sometimes S.E. making 40 miles up to 11 o'clock. Afterwards they went on another tack, and then on a bowline, 24 miles, or 6 leagues, to the north, until night.

Sunday, 27th of January.
Yesterday, after sunset, they steered N.E. and N.E. by N. at the rate of 5 miles an hour, which in 13 hours would be 65 miles, or 16 1\2 leagues. After sunrise they steered N.E. 24 miles, or 6 leagues, until noon, and from that time until sunset 3 leagues E.N.E.

Monday, 28th of January.
All night they steered E.N.E. 36 miles, or 9 leagues. After sunrise until sunset E.N.E. 20 miles, or 5 leagues. The weather was temperate and pleasant. They saw boatswain-birds, sandpipers, and much weed.

Tuesday, 29th of January.
They steered E.N.E. 39 miles, or 9 1\2 leagues, and during the whole day 8 leagues. The air was very pleasant, like April in Castile, the sea smooth, and fish they call *dorados* came on board.

Wednesday, 30th of January.

All this night they made 6 leagues E.N.E., and in the day S.E. by S. 13 1\2 leagues. Boatswain-birds, much weed, and many tunnies.

Thursday, 31st of January.
This night they steered N.E. by N. 30 miles, and afterwards N.E. 35 miles, or 16 leagues. From sunrise to night E.N.E. 13 1\2 leagues. They saw boatswain-birds and terns.

Friday, 1st of February.
They made 16 1\2 leagues E.N.E. during the night, and went on the same course during the day 19 1\2 leagues. The sea very smooth, thank be to God.

Saturday, 2nd of February.
They made 40 miles, or 10 leagues, E.N.E. this night. In the daytime, with the same wind aft, they went 7 miles an hour, so that in 11 hours they had gone 77 miles, or 9 1\4 leagues. The sea was very smooth, thanks be to God, and the air very soft. They saw the sea so covered with weed that, if they had not known about it before, they would have been fearful of sunken rocks. They saw terns.

Sunday, 3rd of February.
This night, the wind being aft and the sea very smooth, thanks be to God, they made 29 leagues. The North Star appeared very high, as it does off Cape St. Vincent. The Admiral was unable to take the altitude, either with the astrolabe or with the quadrant, because the rolling caused by the waves prevented it. That day he steered his course E.N.E., going 10 miles an hour, so that in 11 hours he made 27 leagues.

Monday, 4th of February.
During the night the course was N.E. by E., going 12 miles an hour part of the time, and the rest 10 miles. Thus they made 130 miles, or 32 leagues and a half. The sky was very threatening and rainy, and it was rather cold, by which they knew that they had not yet reached the Azores. After sunrise the course was altered to east. During the whole day they made 77 miles, or 19 1\4 leagues.

Tuesday, 5th of February.

This night they steered east, and made 55 miles, or 13 1\2 leagues. In the day they were going 10 miles an hour, and in 11 hours made 110 miles, or 27 1\2 leagues. They saw sandpipers, and some small sticks, a sign that they were near land.

Wednesday, 6th of February.

They steered east during the night, going at the rate of 11 miles an hour, so that in the 13 hours of the night they made 143 miles, or 35 1\4 leagues. They saw many birds. In the day they went 14 miles an hour, and made 154 miles, or 38 1\2 leagues; so that, including night and day, they made 74 leagues, more or less. Vicente Anes said that they had left the island of Flores to the north and Madeira to the east. Roldan said that the island of Fayal, or San Gregorio, was to the N.N.E. and Puerto Santo to east. There was much weed.

Thursday, 7th of February.

This night they steered east, going 10 miles an hour, so that in 13 hours they made 130 miles, or 32 1\2 leagues. In the daytime the rate was 8 miles an hour, in 11 hours 88 miles, or 22 leagues. This morning the Admiral found himself 65 leagues south of the island of Flores, and the pilot Pedro Alonso, being further north, according to his reckoning, passed between Terceira and Santa Maria to the east, passing to windward of the island of Madeira, 12 leagues further north. The sailors saw a new kind of weed, of which there is plenty in the islands of the Azores.

Friday, 8th of February.

They went 3 miles an hour to the eastward for some time during the night, and afterwards E.S.E, going 12 miles an hour. From sunrise to noon they made 27 miles, and the same distance from noon till sunset, equal to 13 leagues S.S.E.

Saturday, 9th of February.

For part of this night they went 3 leagues S.S.E., and afterwards S. by E., then N.E. 5 leagues until 10 o'clock in the forenoon, then 9 leagues east until dark.

Sunday, 10th of February.

From sunset they steered east all night, making 130 miles, or 32 1\12 leagues. During the day, they went at the rate of 9 miles an hour, making 99 miles, or 24 1\2 leagues, in 11 hours.

In the caravel of the Admiral, Vicente Yanez and 2 pilots, Sancho Ruiz and Pedro Alonso Nino, and Roldan, made charts and plotted the route. They all made the position a good deal beyond the islands of the Azores to the east, and, navigating to the north, none of them touched Santa Maria, which is the last of the Azores. They made the position 5 leagues beyond it, and were in the vicinity of the islands of Madeira and Puerto Santo. But the Admiral was very different from them in his reckoning, finding the position very much in rear of theirs. This night he found the island of Flores to the north, and to the east he made the direction to be towards Nafe in Africa, passing to leeward of the island of Madeira to the north... leagues. So that the pilots were nearer to Castile than the Admiral by 150 leagues. The Admiral says that, with the grace of God, when they reach the land they will find out whose reckoning was most correct. He also says that he went 263 leagues from the island of Hierro to the place where he first saw the gulf weed.

Monday, 11th of February.

This night they went 12 miles an hour on their course, and during the day they ran 16 1\2 leagues. They saw many birds, from which they judged that land was near.

Tuesday, 12th of February.

They went 6 miles an hour on an east course during the night, altogether 73 miles, or 18 1\4 leagues. At this time they began to encounter bad weather with a heavy sea; and, if the caravel had not been very well managed, she must have been lost. During the day they made 11 or 12 leagues with much difficulty.

Wednesday, 13th of February.

From sunset until daylight there was great trouble with the wind, and the high and tempestuous sea. There was lightning 3 times to the N.N.E.--a sign of a great storm coming either from that quarter or its opposite. They were lying-to most of the night, afterwards showing a little sail, and made 52 miles, which is 13 leagues. In the day the wind moderated a little, but it soon increased again. The sea was terrific, the waves crossing each other, and straining the vessels. They made 55 miles more, equal to 13 1\2 leagues.

Thursday, 14th of February.
This night the wind increased, and the waves were terrible, rising against each other, and so shaking and straining the vessel that she could make no headway, and was in danger of being stove in. They carried the mainsail very closely reefed, so as just to give her steerage-way, and proceeded thus for 3 hours, making 20 miles. Meanwhile, the wind and sea increased, and, seeing the great danger, the Admiral began to run before it, there being nothing else to be done. The caravel Pinta began to run before the wind at the same time, and Martin Alonso ran her out of sight, although the Admiral kept showing lanterns all night, and the other answered. It would seem that she could do no more, owing to the force of the tempest, and she was taken far from the route of the Admiral. He steered that night E.N.E., and made 54 miles, equal to 13 leagues. At sunrise the wind blew still harder, and the cross sea was terrific. They continued to show the closely-reefed mainsail, to enable her to rise from between the waves, or she would otherwise have been swamped. An E.N.E. course was steered, and afterwards N.E. by E. for 6 hours, making 7 1\2 leagues. The Admiral ordered that a pilgrimage should be made to Our Lady of Guadaloupe, carrying a candle of 6 lbs. of weight in wax, and that all the crew should take an oath that the pilgrimage should be made by the man on whom the lot fell. As many beans were got as there were persons on board, and on one a cross was cut with a knife. They were then put into a cap and shaken up. The first who put in his hand was the Admiral, and he drew out the bean with a cross, so the lot fell on him; and he was bound to go on the pilgrimage and fulfil the vow. Another lot was drawn, to go on pilgrimage to Our Lady of Loreto, which is in the march of Ancona, in the Papal territory, a house where Our Lady works many and great miracles. The lot fell on a sailor of the port of Santa Maria, named Pedro de Villa, and the Admiral promised to pay his traveling expenses. Another pilgrimage was agreed upon to watch for one night in Santa Clara at Moguer, and have a Mass said, for which they again used the beans, including the one with a cross. The lot again fell on the Admiral. After this the Admiral and all the crew made a vow that, on arriving at the first land, they would all go in procession, in their shirts, to say their prayers in a church dedicated to Our Lady.

Besides these general vows made in common, each sailor made a special vow; for no one expected to escape, holding themselves for lost, owing to the fearful weather from which they were suffering. The want of ballast increased the danger of the ship, which had become light, owing to the consumption of the provisions and water. On account of the favorable weather enjoyed among the islands, the Admiral had omitted to make provision for this need, thinking that ballast might be taken on board at the island inhabited by women, which he had intended to visit. The only thing to do so was to fill the barrels that contained wine or fresh water with water from the sea, and this supplied a remedy.

Here the Admiral writes of the causes which made him fear that he would perish, and of others that gave him hope that God would work his salvation, in order that such news as he was bringing to the Sovereigns might not be lost. It seemed to him that the strong desire he felt to bring such great news, and to show that all he had said and offered to discover had turned out true, suggested the fear that he would not be able to do so, and that each stinging insect would be able to thwart and impede the work. He attributed this fear to his little faith, and to his want of confidence in Divine Providence. He was comforted, on the other hand, by the mercies of God in having vouchsafed him such a victory, in the discoveries he had made, and in that God had complied with all his desires in Castile, after much adversity and many misfortunes. As he had before put all his trust in God, who had heard him and granted all he sought, he ought now to believe that God would permit the completion of what had been begun, and ordain that he should be saved. Especially as he had freed him on the voyage out, when he had still greater reason to fear, from the trouble caused by the sailors and people of his company, who all with one voice declared their intention to return, and protested that they would rise against him. But the eternal God gave him force and valor to withstand them all, and in many other marvelous ways had God shown his will in this voyage besides those known to their Highnesses. Thus he ought not to fear the present tempest, though his weakness and anxiety prevent him from giving tranquillity to his mind. He says further that it gave him great sorrow to think of the two sons he had left at their studies in Cordova, who would be left orphans, without father or mother, in a *strange* land; while the Sovereigns would not know of the services he had performed in this voyage, nor would they receive the prosperous news which would move them to help the orphans. To remedy this, and that their Highnesses might know how our Lord had granted a victory in all that could be desired respecting the Indies, and that they might understand that there were no storms in those parts, which may be known by the herbs and trees which grow even within the sea; also that the Sovereigns might still have information, even if he perished in the storm, he took a parchment and wrote on it as good an account as he could of all he had discovered, entreating anyone who might pick it up to deliver it to the Sovereigns. He rolled this parchment up in waxed cloth, fastened it very securely, ordered a large wooden barrel to be brought, and put it inside, so that no one else knew what it was. They thought that it was some act of devotion, and so he ordered the barrel to be thrown into the sea. Afterwards, in the showers and squalls, the wind veered to the west, and they went before it, only with the foresail, in a very confused sea, for 5 hours. They made 2 1\2 leagues N.E. They had taken in the reefed mainsail, for fear some wave of the sea should carry all away.

Friday, 15th of February.
Last night, after sunset, the sky began to clear towards the west, showing that the wind was inclined to come from that quarter. The Admiral added the bonnet to the mainsail. The sea was still very high, although it had gone down slightly. They steered E.N.E., and went 4 miles an hour, which made 13 leagues during the 11 hours of the night. After sunrise they sighted land. It appeared from the bows to bear E.N.E. Some said it was the island of Madeira, others that it was the rock of Cintra, in Portugal, near Lisbon. Presently the wind headed to E.N.E., and a heavy sea came from the west, the caravel being 5 leagues from the land. The Admiral found by his reckoning that he was close to the Azores, and believed that this was one of them. The pilots and sailors thought it was the land of Castile.

Sunday, 16th of February.
All that night the Admiral was standing off and on to keep clear of the land, which they now knew to be an island, sometimes standing N.E., at others N.N.E., until sunrise, when they tacked to the south to reach the island, which was now concealed by a great mist. Another island was in sight from the poop, at a distance of 8 leagues. Afterwards, from sunrise until dark, they were tacking to reach the land against a strong wind and head-sea. At the time of repeating the *Salve*, which is just before dark, some of the men saw a light to leeward, and

it seemed that it must be on the island they first saw yesterday. All night they were beating to windward, and going as near as they could, so as to see some way to the island at sunrise. That night the Admiral got a little rest, for he had not slept nor been able to sleep since Wednesday, and his legs were very sore from long exposure to the wet and cold. At sunrise he steered S.S.W., and reached the island at night, but could not make out what island it was, owing to the thick weather.

Monday, 18th of February.

Yesterday, after sunset, the Admiral was sailing round the island, to see where he could anchor and open communications. He let go one anchor, which he presently lost, and then stood off and on all night. After sunrise he again reached the north side of the island, where he anchored, and sent the boat on shore. They had speech with the people, and found that it was the island of Santa Maria, one of the Azores. They pointed out the port to which the caravel should go. They said that they had never seen such stormy weather as there had been for the last 15 days, and they wondered how the caravel could have escaped. They gave many thanks to God, and showed great joy at the news that the Admiral had discovered the Indies. The Admiral says that his navigation had been very certain, and that he had laid the discoveries down on the chart. Many thanks were due to our Lord, although there had been some delay. But he was sure that he was in the region of the Azores, and that this was one of them. He pretended to have gone over more ground, to mislead the pilots and mariners who pricked off the charts to the Indies, as, in fact, he did. For none of the others kept an accurate reckoning, so that no one but himself could be sure of the route to the Indies.

Tuesday, 19th of February.

After sunset 3 natives of the island came to the beach and hailed. The Admiral sent the boat, which returned with fowls and fresh bread. It was carnival time, and they brought other things which were sent by the captain of the island, named Juan de Castaneda, saying that he knew the Admiral very well, and that he did not come to see him because it was night, but that at dawn he would come with more refreshments, bringing with him 3 men of the boat's crew, whom he did not send back owing to the great pleasure he derived from hearing their account of the voyage. The Admiral ordered much respect to be shown to the messengers, and that they should be given beds to sleep in that night, because it was late, and the town was far off. As on the previous Thursday, when they were in the midst of the storm, they had made a vow to go in procession to a church of Our Lady as soon as they came to land, the Admiral arranged that half the crew should go to comply with their obligation to a small chapel, like a hermitage, near the shore; and that he would himself go afterwards with the rest. Believing that it was a peaceful land, and confiding in the offers of the captain of the island, and in the peace that existed between Spain and Portugal, he asked the 3 men to go to the town and arrange for a priest to come and say Mass. The half of the crew then went in their shirts, in compliance with their vow. While they were at their prayers, all the people of the town, horse and foot, with the captain at their head, came and took them all prisoners. The Admiral, suspecting nothing, was waiting for the boat to take him and the rest to accomplish the vow. At 11 o'clock, seeing that they did not come back, he feared that they had been detained, or that the boat had been swamped, all the island being surrounded by high rocks. He could not see what had taken place, because the hermitage was round a point. He got up the anchor and made sail until he was in full view of the hermitage, and he saw many of the horsemen dismount and get into the boat with arms. They came to the caravel to seize the Admiral. The Captain stood up in the boat, and asked for an assurance of safety from the Admiral, who replied that he granted it; but, what outrage was this, that he saw none of his people in the boat? The Admiral added that they might come on board, and that he would do all that might be proper. The Admiral tried, with fair words, to get hold of this captain, that he might recover his own people, not considering that he broke faith by giving him security, because he had offered peace and security, and had then broken his word. The captain, as he came with an evil intention, would not come on board. Seeing that he did not come alongside, the Admiral asked that he might be told the reason for the detention of his men, an act which would displease the King of Portugal, because the Portuguese received much honor in the territories of the King of Castile, and were as safe as if they were in Lisbon. He further said that the Sovereigns had given him letters of recommendation to all the Lords and Princes of the world, which he would show the captain if he would come on board; that he was the Admiral of the Ocean Sea, and Viceroy of the Indies, which belonged to their Highnesses, and that he would show the commissions signed with their signatures, and attested by their seals, which he held up from a distance. He added that his Sovereigns were in friendship and amity with the King of Portugal, and had ordered that all honor should be shown to ships that came from Portugal. Further, that if the captain did not surrender his people, he would still go on to Castile, as he had quite sufficient to navigate as far as Seville, in which case the captain and his followers would be severely punished for their offence. Then the captain and those with him replied that they did not know the King and Queen of Castile there, nor their letters, nor were they afraid of them, and they would give the Admiral to understand that this was Portugal, almost menacing him. On hearing this the Admiral was much moved, thinking that some cause of disagreement might have arisen between the two kingdoms during his absence, yet he could not endure that they should not be answered reasonably. Afterwards he turned to the captain, and said that he should go to the port with the caravel, and that all that had been done would be reported to the King his Lord. The Admiral made those who were in the caravel bear witness to what he said, calling to the captain and all the others, and promising that he would not leave the caravel until a hundred Portuguese had been taken to Castile, and all that island had been laid waste. He then returned to anchor in the port where he was first, the wind being very unfavorable for doing anything else.

Wednesday, 20th of February.

The Admiral ordered the ship to be repaired, and the casks to be filled alongside for ballast. This was a very bad port, and he feared he might have to cut the cables. This was so, and he made sail for the island of San Miguel; but there is no good port in any of the Azores for the weather they then experienced, and there was no other remedy but to go to sea.

Thursday, 21st of February.

Yesterday the Admiral left that island of Santa Maria for that of San Miguel, to see if a port could be found to shelter his vessel from the bad weather. There was much wind and a high sea, and he was sailing until night without being able to see either one land or the other, owing to the thick weather caused by wind and sea. The Admiral says he was in much anxiety, because he only had 3 sailors who knew their business, the rest knowing nothing of seamanship. He was lying-to all that night, in great danger and trouble. Our Lord showed him mercy in that the waves came in one direction, for if there had been a cross sea they would have suffered much more. After sunrise the island of San Miguel was not in sight, so the Admiral determined to return to Santa Maria, to see if he could recover his people and boat, and the anchors and cable he had left there.

The Admiral says that he was astonished at the bad weather he encountered in the region of these islands. In the Indies he had navigated throughout the winter without the necessity for anchoring, and always had fine weather, never having seen the sea for a single hour in such a state that it could not be navigated easily. But among these islands he had suffered from such terrible storms. The same had happened in going out as far as the Canary Islands, but as soon as they were passed there was always fine weather, both in sea and air. In concluding these remarks, he observes that the sacred theologians and wise men said well when they placed the terrestrial paradise in the Far East, because it is a most temperate region. Hence these lands that he had now discovered must, he says, be in the extreme East.

Friday, 22nd of February.

Yesterday the Admiral came-to off Santa Maria, in the place or port where he had first anchored. Presently a man came down to some rocks at the edge of the beach, hailing that they were not to remain there. Soon afterwards the boat came with 5 sailors, 2 priests, and a scrivener. They asked for safety, and when it was granted by the Admiral, they came on board, and, as it was night they slept on board, the Admiral showing them all the civility he could. In the morning they asked to be shown the authority of the Sovereigns of Castile, by which the voyage had been made. The Admiral felt that they did this to give some color of right to what they had done, and to show that they had right on their side. As they were unable to secure the person of the Admiral, whom they intended to get into their power when they came with the boat armed, they now feared that their game might not turn out so well, thinking, with some fear, of what the Admiral had threatened, and which he proposed to put into execution. In order to get his people released, the Admiral displayed the general letter of the Sovereigns to all Princes and Lords, and other documents, and having given them of what he had, the Portuguese went on shore contended, and presently released all the crew and the boat. The Admiral heard from them that if he had been captured also, they never would have been released, for the captain said that those were the orders of the King his Lord.

Saturday, 23rd of February.

Yesterday the weather began to improve, and the Admiral got under weigh to seek a better anchorage, where he could take in wood and stones for ballast; but he did not find one until late.

Sunday, 24th of February.

He anchored yesterday in the afternoon, to take in wood and stones, but the sea was so rough that they could not land from the boat, and during the first watch it came on to blow from the west and S.W. He ordered sail to be made, owing to the great danger there is off these islands in being at anchor with a southerly gale, and as the wind was S.W. it would go round to south. As it was a good wind for Castile, he gave up his intentions of taking in wood and stones, and shaped an easterly course until sunset, going 7 miles an hour for 6 hours and a half, equal to 45 1\2 miles. After sunset he made 6 miles an hour, or 66 miles in 11 hours, altogether 111 miles, equal to 28 leagues.

Monday, 25th of February.

Yesterday, after sunset, the caravel went at the rate of 5 miles an hour on an easterly course, and in the 11 hours of the night she made 65 miles, equal to 16 1\4 leagues. From sunrise to sunset they made another 16 1\2 leagues with a smooth sea, thanks be to God. A very large bird, like an eagle, came to the caravel.

Tuesday, 26th of February.

Yesterday night the caravel steered her course in a smooth sea, thanks be to God. Most of the time she was going 8 miles an hour, and made a 100 miles, equal to 25 leagues. After sunrise there was little wind and some rain-showers. They made about 8 leagues E.N.E.

Wednesday, 27th of February.

During the night and day she was off her course, owing to contrary winds and a heavy sea. She was found to be 125 leagues from Cape St. Vincent, and 80 from the island of Madeira, 106 from Santa Maria. It was very troublesome to have such bad weather just when they were at the very door of their home.

Thursday, 28th of February.

The same weather during the night, with the wind from south and S.E., sometimes shifting to N.E. and E.N.E, and it was the same all day.

Friday, 1st of March.

Tonight the course was E.N.E., and they made 12 leagues. During the day, 23 1\2 leagues on the same course.

Saturday, 2nd of March.

The course was E.N.E., and distance made good 28 leagues during the night, and 20 in the day.

Sunday, 3rd of March.

After sunset the course was east; but a squall came down, split all the sails, and the vessel was in great danger; but God was pleased to deliver them. They drew lots for sending a pilgrim in a shirt to Santa Maria de la Cinta at Huelva, and the lot fell on the Admiral. The whole crew also made a vow to fast on bread and water during the first Saturday after their arrival in port. They had made 60 miles before the sails were split. Afterwards they ran under bare poles, owing to the force of the gale and the heavy sea. They saw signs of the neighborhood of land, finding themselves near Lisbon.

Monday, 4th of March.

During the night they were exposed to a terrible storm, expecting to be overwhelmed by the cross-seas, while the wind seemed to raise the caravel into the air, and there was rain and lightning in several directions. The Admiral prayed to our Lord to preserve them, and in the first watch it pleased our Lord to show land, which was reported by the sailors. As it was advisable not to reach before it was known whether there was any port to which he could run for shelter, the Admiral set the mainsails, as there was no other course but to proceed, though in great danger. Thus God preserved them until daylight, though all the time they were infinite fear and trouble. When it was light, the Admiral knew the land, which was the rock of Cintra, near the river of Lisbon, and he resolved to run in because there was nothing else to be done. So terrible was the storm, that in the village of Cascaes, at the mouth of the river, the people were praying for the little vessel all that morning. After they were inside, the people came off, looking upon their escape as a miracle. At the third hour they passed Rastelo, within the river of Lisbon, where they were told that such a winter, with so many storms, had never before been known, and that 25 ships had been lost in Flanders, while others had been wind-bound in the river for 4 months. Presently the Admiral wrote to the King of Portugal, who was then at a distance of nine leagues, to state that the Sovereigns of Castile had ordered him to enter the ports for payment, and requesting that the King would give permission for the caravel to come to Lisbon, because some ruffians, hearing that he had much gold on board, might attempt robbery in an unfrequented port, knowing that they did not come from Guinea, but from the Indies.

Tuesday, 5th of March.

Today the great ship of the King of Portugal was also at anchor off Rastelo, with the best provision of artillery and arms that the Admiral had ever seen. The master of her, named Bartolome Diaz, of Lisbon, came in an armed boat to the caravel, and ordered the Admiral to get into the boat, to go and give an account of himself to the agents of the king and to the captain of that ship. The Admiral replied that he was the Admiral of the Sovereigns of Castile, and that he would not give an account to any such persons, nor would he leave the ship by force, as he had not the power to resist. The master replied that he must then send the master of the caravel. The Admiral answered that neither the master nor any other person should go except by force, for if he allowed anyone to go, it would be as if he went himself; and that such was the custom of the Admirals of the Sovereigns of Castile, rather to die than to submit, or to let any of their people submit. The master then moderated his tone, and told the Admiral that if that was his determination he might do as he pleased. He, however, requested that he might be shown the letters of the Kings of Castile, if they were on board. The Admiral readily showed them, and the master returned to the ship and reported what had happened to the captain, named Alvaro Dama. That officer, making great festival with trumpets and drums, came to the caravel to visit with the Admiral, and offered to do all that he might require.

Wednesday, 6th of March.

As soon as it was known that the Admiral came from the Indies, it was wonderful how many people came from Lisbon to see him and the Indians, giving thanks to our Lord, and saying that the heavenly

Majesty had given all this to the Sovereigns of Castile as a reward for their faith and their great desire to serve God.

Thursday, 7th of March.
Today an immense number of people came to the caravel, including many knights, and amongst them the agents of the king, and all gave infinite thanks to our Lord for so wide an increase of Christianity granted by our Lord to the Sovereigns of Castile; and they said that they received it because their Highnesses had worked and labored for the increase of the religion of Christ.

Friday, 8th of March.
Today the Admiral received a letter from the King of Portugal, brought by Don Martin de Norona, asking him to visit him where he was, as the weather was not suitable for the departure of the caravel. He complied, to prevent suspicion, although he did not wish to go, and went to pass the night at Sacanben. The King had given orders to his officers that all that the Admiral, his crew, and the caravel were in need of should be given without payment, and that all the Admiral wanted should be complied with.

Saturday, 9th of March.
Today the Admiral left Sacanben, to go where the King was residing, which was at Valparaiso, 9 leagues from Lisbon. Owing to the rain, he did not arrive until night. The King caused him to be received very honorably by the principal officers of his household; and the King himself receive the Admiral with great favor, making him sit down, and talking very pleasantly. He offered to give orders that everything should be done for the service of the Sovereigns of Castile, and said that the successful termination of the voyage had given him great pleasure. He said further that he understood that, in the capitulation between the Sovereigns and himself, that conquest belonged to him. The Admiral replied that he had not seen the capitulation, nor knew more than that the Sovereigns had ordered him not to go either to Lamina or to any other port of Guinea, and that this had been ordered to be proclaimed in all the ports of Andalusia before he sailed. The King graciously replied that he held it for certain that there would be no necessity for any arbitrators. The Admiral was assigned as a guest to the Prior of Crato, who was the principal person present, and from whom he received many favors and civilities.

Sunday, 10th of March.

Today, after Mass, the King repeated that if the Admiral wanted anything he should have it. He conversed much with the Admiral respecting his voyage, always ordering him to sit down, and treating him with great favor.

Monday, 11th of March.

Today the Admiral took leave of the King, who entrusted him with some messages to the Sovereigns, and always treating him with much friendliness. He departed after dinner, Don Martin de Norona being sent with him, and all the knights set out with him, and went with him some distance, to do him honor. Afterwards he came to a monastery of San Antonio, near a place calle Villafrance, where the Queen was residing. The Admiral went to do her reverence and to his her hand, because she had sent to say that he was not to go without seeing her. The Duke and the Marquis were with her, and the Admiral was received with much honor. He departed at night, and went to sleep at Llandra.

Tuesday, 12th of March.

Today, as he was leaving Llandra to return to the caravel, an esquire of the King arrived, with an offer that if he desired to go to Castile by land, that he should be supplied with lodgings, and beasts, and all that was necessary. When the Admiral took leave of him, he ordered a mule to be supplied to him, and another for his pilot, who was with him, and he says that the pilot received a present of 20 *espadines*. He said this that the Sovereigns might know all that was done. He arrived on board the caravel that night.

Wednesday, 13th of March.

Today, at 8 o'clock, with the flood tide, and the wind N.N.W., the Admiral got under weigh and made sail for Seville.

Thursday, 14th of March.

Yesterday, after sunset, a southerly course was steered, and before sunrise they were off Cape St. Vincent, which is in Portugal. Afterwards he shaped a course to the east for Saltes, and went on all day with little wind, "until now that the ship is off Furon."

129--To America and Around the World

Friday, 15th of March.

Yesterday, after sunset, she went on her course with little wind, and at sunrise she was off Saltes. At noon, with the tide rising, they crossed the bar of Saltes, and reached the port which they had left on the 3rd of August of the year before. The Admiral says that so ends this journal, unless it becomes necessary to go to Barcelona by sea, having received news that their Highnesses are in that city, to give an account of all his voyage which our Lord had permitted him to make, and saw fit to set forth in him. For, assuredly, he held with a firm and strong knowledge that his high Majesty made all things good, and that all is good except sin. Nor can he value or think of anything being done without His consent.

"I know respecting this voyage", says the Admiral, "that he has miraculously shown his will, as may be seen from this journal, setting forth the numerous miracles that have been displayed in the voyage, and in me who was so long at the court of your Highnesses, working in opposition to and against the opinions of so many chief persons of your household, who were all against me, looking upon this enterprise as folly. But I hope, in our Lord, that it will be a great benefit to Christianity, for so it has ever appeared."

These are the final words of the Admiral Don Cristobal Colon respecting his first voyage to the Indies and their discovery.

Landing of Columbus
(John Vanderlyn)

A Frontespiece of Marco Polo, Il Milione
(Nürmberg, 1477)

Ferdinand Magellan

Antonio Pigafetta
From the Museo Civico,
Vicenza, Italy

VOYAGE
AROUND THE
THE WORLD

by
Antonio Pigafetta
A Gentleman from Vicenza
Knight of Rhodes

Translated by
John Pinkerton

Book I

Departure from Seville,
and thence to leaving the Strait of Magellan

The captain-general Fernandez Magellan had resolved on undertaking a long voyage over the ocean, where the winds blow with violence, and storms are very frequent. He had also determined on taking a course as yet unexplored by any navigator; but this bold attempt he was cautious of disclosing, lest any one should strive to dissuade him from it by magnifying the risk he would have to encounter, and thus dishearten his crew. To the perils naturally incident on a similar voyage was joined the unfavorable circumstance of the four other vessels he commanded besides his own being under the direction of captains who were inimical to him, merely on account of his being a Portuguese, they themselves being Spaniards.

Before his departure he made some regulations, as well respecting signals as the discipline of the squadron. That the ships might constantly be kept together, he established the following rules for the pilots and masters: his vessel was constantly to lead the van; and, in order that the other vessels should not lose sight of it during the night, he had a torch of wood called *farol* burning on the poop. If besides the farol he lighted a lanthorn, or a rope made of rushes, the other vessels were to do the same, that he might be certain of their following him. When he showed two lights without the farol, the vessels were to alter their course, either to make slower progress, or on account of adverse winds. When three fires were lighted, it was the signal for lowering the bonnet, a sail affixed beneath the mainsail in fine weather to accelerate the speed of the ship. The bonnet is lowered when a storm is threatened, in order that it may not be in the way of the mariners on raising the mainsail. If four were shown, it was a signal to take in all the sails; but if they were previously reefed, these fires were a direction for setting them. A greater number of lights, or the firing of a few lombards, denoted the approach to land or shallows, and, consequently, that much caution was to be used in steering. He had also another signal for casting anchor.

The night was divided into three watches, the first at the beginning of night; the second, called medora, taking place at midnight; and the thirds towards the morning. The crew in consequence were formed into three divisions: the first watch was under the orders of the captain; the pilot commanded the second, and the master the third. The commander in chief enforced the most rigid discipline, the better to secure success to the voyage.

Monday morning the 10th August 1519, the squadron having every thing requisite on board, and a complement of 237 men, its departure was announced by a discharge of artillery, and the foresail was set. We dropped down the river Betis to the bridge of Guadalquivir, passing near Juan d'Alfaraz, formerly a thickly-peopled city belonging to the Moors, where there was a bridge, of which no vestige now remains but two piers, which are yet standing in the river below the surface, and which must be guarded against; indeed, in order to run no hazard, this part should not be navigated without pilots on board, and but at high water.

Continuing to descend the Betis we passed by Coria, and several other villages to San Lucar, a castle belonging to the Duke of Medina Sidonia. Here is the port which opens on the ocean, 10 leagues distant from Cape St. Vincent, in 37 degrees of latitude north. From Seville to this port the distance is 17 to 20 leagues.

Some days after the commander in chief, and the captains of the other vessels, arrived in boats at San Lucar from Seville; and the stock of provisions was completed. Every morning we landed to hear mass in the church of N.D. de Barrameda; and before we sailed the commodore obliged every man to go to confession; he also strictly forbade any woman being taken on board.

The 20th September we sailed from San Lucar, steering towards the south-west, and on the 26th reached one of the Canary islands called Teneriffe, situated in 28 degrees of latitude north. We stopped here for three days, at a spot where we could take in wood and water:

afterwards we entered a port of the same island called Monte Rosso, where we passed two days.

A singular phenomenon was related to us respecting this island; viz, that it never rains here, and that it has neither spring nor river, but that it produces a large tree, the leaves of which continually distil excellent water; this is collected in a pit at the foot of the tree, and hither the inhabitants go for what water they want, and all the animals tame and wild to quench their thirst. This tree is perpetually encircled by a thick mist which doubtless supplies its leaves with water.

On Monday 3rd October we made sail directly towards the south. We passed between Cape Verd and its islands in latitude 14 degrees 30 minutes north. After coasting along the shores of Guinea for several days we arrived in latitude 8 degrees north, where is a mountain called Sierra Leona. We here experienced contrary winds, or dead calms with rain, which continued to the equinoctial line; the duration of the rainy weather was 60 days, a circumstance that controverts the hypothesis of the ancients.

In latitude 14 degrees north we experienced very impetuous squalls, which, joined to the currents, prevented our advancing. On the approach of these squalls we had the precaution of taking in our sails, and laid to until the wind abated.

In clear and calm weather, large fish called tiburoni (sharks) swam about our vessel. These fish have several rows of frightful teeth; and if unhappily they chance to meet with a man in the sea they instantly devour him. We caught several with iron hooks; the large ones are by no means good to eat, and the smaller are but of little esteem.

In stormy weather we frequently saw what is called the corpo santo, or St. Elme. On one very dark night it appeared to us like a brilliant flambeau on the summit of a large tree, and thus remained for the space of two hours, which was a matter of great consolation to us during the tempest. At the instant of its disappearing, it diffused such a resplendent blaze of light as almost blinded us. We gave ourselves up for lost; but the wind ceased momentarily.

We saw birds of many kinds. Some appeared to us to have no rump; others make no nests for want of feet; but the female lays and hatches her eggs on the back of the male in the midst of the sea. There are others called cagassela, or caca uccello (stercorarius), which live on the excrements of other birds; and I have myself oftentimes seen one of these birds pursuing another without interruption until it voided its excrement, upon which it seized with avidity. I likewise saw many flying-fish, and other fish in such amazing shoals, they resembled a bank in the sea.

After we had passed the equinoctial line, we lost sight of the polar star. We then steered S.S.W., making for the Terra di Verzino (Brazil), in latitude 23 degrees 30 minutes south. This land is a continuation of that on which Cape Augustin is situated in latitude 8 degrees 30 minutes south.

Here we laid in a good stock of fowls, potatoes, a kind of fruit which resembles the cone of a pine-tree (pineapple), but which is very sweet, and of an exquisite flavor, sweet reeds, the flesh of the anta, which resembles that of a cow, etc. We made excellent bargains here: for a hook or a knife we purchased five or six fowls; a comb brought us two geese; and a small looking-glass, or a pair of scissors, as much fish as would serve ten people; the inhabitants, for a little bell or a ribbon, gave a basked of potatoes, which is the name the give to roots somewhat resembling our turnips, and which are nearly like chestnuts in taste. Our playing-cards were an equally advantageous object of barter; for a king of spades I obtained half a dozen fowls, and the hawker even deemed his bargain an excellent one.

We entered this port on St. Lucy's day the 13th of December. The sun at noon was vertical, and we suffered much more from the heat than on passing the line.

The land of Brazil, which abounds in all kinds of productions, is as extensive as Spain, France, and Italy united: it belongs to Portugal.

The Brazilians are not Christians; still they are not idolaters, for they worship nothing; natural instinct is the only law they acknowledge. They are very long lived, for they generally reach 105, and sometimes 140. They go entirely naked, the women as well as the men. Their houses are long cabins, termed by them boi, and they lie on nets of cotton, called hamaks, fastened by the two extremities to two strong posts. Their hearths are on the ground. One of these bois sometimes contains 100 men, with their wives and children; there is consequently always much noise in them. Their boats, which they call canoes, are formed of the trunk of a tree, hollowed by means of a sharp stone; for stone is their substitute for iron, of which they are destitute. These trees are so large that a single canoe is capable of containing 30 or even 40 persons, who paddle with oars similar to bakers' shovels. On seeing them so black, naked, dirty, and bald, one might mistake them easily for Charon's ferrymen.

The men and women are well made, and formed as we are. They sometimes eat human flesh; but only that of their enemies. It is neither from want or inclination they follow this practice, but owing to a custom the origin of which they thus relate. An old woman had but one son, who was killed by the enemy. Shortly after the murderer of her son was taken prisoner, and brought before her: full of revenge the mother flew upon him like a beast of prey, and tore away part of his shoulder with her teeth. This man had the good fortune not only to escape from the woman, but to rejoin his own people, to whom he exhibited the print of teeth on his shoulder, and whom he made believe (what perhaps he himself fancied to be the case) that the enemy were disposed to devour him alive. That they might not be inferior in cruelty to the others, these resolved on really devouring the enemies they might take in battle, and those again retaliated. Still they do not devour their prisoners at the instant, nor while alive; they cut them in pieces and divide the parts among the conquerors. Each individual carries away with him his allotment, dries it in smoke; and every 8 days cooks a small portion. This fact I learn from John Carvajo, our pilot, who passed four years in the Brazils.

The Brazilians paint their bodies, and especially their faces, in a strange manner, and in different figures, the men as well as the women. They have short and woolly hair on the head, but none on any other part of the body, for they root it out. They have a vest made of the interwoven feathers of the parrot, and so arranged that the large quills of the pinions and tail form a circle round their loins, which gives them a whimsical and ridiculous appearance. Almost all the men have the lower lip pierced with three holes through which they run cylindrical stone, very narrow and about two inches long. Women and children do not wear this incommodious ornament. Add to this, the front of their bodies is perfectly uncovered. Their color is more an olive than a black. Their King is called a Cacique.

The country produces an immense number of parrots, so many indeed that a small mirror will purchase 8 or 10. They have likewise very handsome monkeys of a yellow color, and resembling small lions.

The inhabitants eat white bread made into a round shape, but which we did not fancy. It is made with the pith, or rather the epidermis of a certain tree, which has much resemblance to curdled milk. They likewise have hogs, which seemed to us to have their navel on the back; and large birds, the beak of which resembles a spoon, but which are without tongues.

Occasionally, for a thatcher or cutlass, the offered us one or more of their young daughters, but never their wives; nor indeed would these consent to have connection with any but their husbands; for notwithstanding the freedom allowed to unmarried girls, when married so great is their modesty that they never submit to the embraces even of those to whom they are espoused but under the veil of night. They are subject to the most laborious toil, and often are they seen descending from the mountains, with baskets on their head, very heavy laden; never however do they go alone, their husbands, who are highly jealous, constantly accompanying them, the bow in one hand and arrows in the other. The bow is made of Brazil wood, or the black palm. If the women chance to have young children they hang them in a net of cotton, which is suspended from the neck. I could relate much more respecting their manners, but to avoid prolixity I pass over the rest.

These people are exceeding credulous and well inclined, whence their conversion to Christianity would be no difficult task. As chance would have, we excited respect and veneration. A great drought had long prevailed in the country, and as rain fell on our arrival, they attributed it to our coming. When we landed to say mass they listened with silence and an air of inquiry; and seeing us unship our boats which hung from the sides, or which followed the ships, they imagined them to be the children of the vessels, and these the mothers who gave them sustenance.

The captain-general and myself were one day present at a singular incident. The young girls frequently came on board to barter their favors with the crew; one of the most handsome among them on this occasion made a visit with this intention to our vessel; but perceiving a nail about as long as my finger, and thinking herself unobserved, she seized it, and chose a singular place for its concealment. Was it truly for the purpose of concealment; or was it for decoration sake? This we could never learn.

We stayed 13 days at this port; after which, resuming our course, we coasted along this country as far as 34 degrees 40 minutes south where we found a large river of fresh water. Here it is that cannibals reside, or anthropophagy. One of them of gigantic size, and whose voice was loud as the bellowing of a bull, approached our vessel for the purpose of enheartening his comrades, who, apprehensive of injury from us, were withdrawing from the coast, and retiring with their effects to the interior. That we might not lose the opportunity afforded of seeing them at hand, and conversing with them, we landed about 100 men, and pursued them with an intention of catching one or another of the party: but they made such huge strides that even though we ran and jumped we were unable to cover any thing like a similar space.

This river contains 7 small islands: in the largest called Sta. Maria, precious stones are found. It was formerly imagined that this was not a river, but a channel which communicated with the South Sea; but it was shortly found to be truly a river, which at its mouth is 17 leagues across. Here John de Solis, while on a voyage of discovery like us, was with 60 of his crew devoured by cannibals, in whom they placed too great confidence.

Coasting constantly along this land towards the antarctic pole, we stopped at two islands, which we found peopled by geese and sea-wolves alone. The former are so numerous and so little wild that we caught a sufficient store for the five ships in the space of a single hour. They are black, and seem to be covered alike over every part of the body, with short feathers, without having wings with which to fly; in fact they cannot fly, and live entirely on fish: they are so fat that we were obliged to singe them, as we could not pluck their feathers. Their beak is curved like a horn.

The sea-wolves are of different color, and nearly of the size of a calf, with a head much like the head of that animal. Their ears are round and short, and their teeth very long. They have no legs; and their paws, which adhere to the body, somewhat resemble our hands, having also small nails. They are, however, web-footed like a duck. Were these animals capable of running they would be much to be dreaded for they seem very ferocious. They swim with great swiftness, and subsist on fish.

We experienced a dreadful storm between these islands, during which the lights of St. Elme, St. Nicholas, and St. Clare were often-times perceived at the tops of the masts; instantly as they disappeared the fury of the tempest abated.

On leaving these islands to continue our course, we ascended as high as 49 degrees 30 minutes south where we discovered an excellent port; and as winter approached (the month was May), we thought best to take shelter here during the bad weather.

Two months elapsed without our perceiving any inhabitant of the country. One day when the least we expected any thing of the kind, a man of gigantic figure presented himself before us. He capered almost naked on the sands, and was singing and dancing, at the same time casting dust on his head. The captain sent one of our seamen on shore, with orders to make similar gestures as a token of friendship and peace, which were well understood, and the giant suffered himself to be quietly led to a small island where the captain had landed. I likewise went on shore there with many others. He testified great surprise of seeing us; and, holding up his finger, undoubtedly signified to us that he thought us descended from heaven.

This man was of such immense stature that our heads scarcely reached to his waist. He was of handsome appearance, his face broad and painted red, except a rim of yellow round his eyes, and two spots in shape of a heart on his cheeks. His hair, which was thin, appeared whitened with some kind of powder. His coat, or rather his cloak, was made of furs, well sewed together, taken from an animal which, as we had afterwards an opportunity of seeing, abounds in this country. This animal has the head and ears of a mule, the body of a camel, the legs of a stag, and the tail of a horse; and like this last animal, it neighs. This man likewise wore a sort of shoe, made of the same skin. He held in his left hand a short and massive bow, the string of which, somewhat thicker than that of a lute, was made of the intestines of the same animal; in the other hand he held arrows, made of short reeds, with feathers at one end, similar to ours, and at the other, instead of iron, a white and black flint stone. With the same stone they likewise form instruments to work wood with.

The captain-general gave him victuals and drink, and among other trifles presented him with a large steel mirror. The giant, who had not the least conception of this trinket, and who saw his likeness, now, perhaps, for the first time, started back in so much fright, as to knock down four of our men who happened to stand behind him. We gave him some little bells, a small looking-glass, a comb, and some glass beads; after which he was set on shore, accompanied by four men well armed.

His comrade, who had objected to coming on board the ship, seeing him return, ran to advise his comrades, who perceiving that our armed men advanced towards them ranged themselves in file without arms, and almost naked: they immediately began dancing and singing, in the course of which they raised the fore-finger to heaven, to make us comprehend that it was thence they reckoned us to have descended. They at the same time showed us a white powder, in clay pans, and presented it to us, having nothing else to offer us to eat; our people invited them by signs to come on board our ship, and proffered to carry on board with them whatever they might with. They accepted the initiation; but the men, who merely carried a bow and arrow, loaded every thing on the women, as if they had been so many beasts of burden.

The women are not of equal size with the men, but in recompense they are much more lusty. Their breasts, which hang down, are more than a foot in length; they paint, and dress in the same manner as their husbands, but they have a thin skin of some animal, with which they cover their nudity. They were, in our contemplation, far from handsome, nevertheless their husbands seemed very jealous.

The women led four of the animals, of which I have previously spoken, in a string, but they were young ones. They make use of these young to catch the old ones: they fasten them to a tree, the old ones come to play with them, when from their concealment the men kill them with their arrows. The inhabitants of the country, both men and women, being invited by our people to repair to the vicinage of the ships, divided themselves into two parties, one on each side the port, and diverted us with an exhibition of the mode of hunting before recited.

Six days afterwards, while out people were employed in selling wood for the ships, they saw another giant, dressed like those we had parte with, and like them armed with a bow and arrow. On approaching our people he touched his head and body, afterwards raising his hands to heaven, gestures which the men imitated. The captain-general, informed of this circumstance, sent the skiff on shore, to conduct him to the islet, in the port, on which a house had been erected, to serve as a forge, and a magazine for different articles of merchandise.

This man was of higher stature, and better made than the others; he was moreover of gentler manners; he danced and sprang so high, and with such might, that his feet sunk several inches deep into the sand; he remained with us some days; we taught him to pronounce the name of Jesus, to say the Lord's Prayer, etc. which he did with equal ease with ourselves, but in a much stronger tone of voice. Finally, we baptized him by the name of John; the captain-general made him a present of a shirt, a vest, cloth drawers, a cap, a looking-glass, comb, some little bells, and other trifling things: he returned towards his own people, apparently well contented. The next day he brought us one of the large animals, of which we have made mention, and received other presents to induce him to repeat his gift; but from that day we saw nothing of him, and suspected his companions had killed him on account of his attachment to us. At the end of a fortnight four other of these men repaired to us; they were without arms, but we afterwards found they had concealed them behind some bushes, where they pointed out to us by tow of the party, whom we detained. They were all of them painted, but in a different manner to those we had seen before.

The captain wished to keep the two youngest, who, as well, were of handsomest form, to carry them with us on our voyage, and even take them to Spain; but, aware of the difficulty of securing them by forcible means, he made use of the following artifice. He presented them a number of knives, mirrors, glass-beads, etc. so that both their hands were full; he afterwards offered them two of those iron rings used for chaining felons, and when he saw their anxiety to be possessed of them (for they are passionately fond of iron), and moreover, that they could not hold them in their hands, he proposed to fasten them to their legs, that they might more easily carry them home, to which they consented; upon this our people put on the irons and fastened the rings, by which means they were securely chained. As soon as they became aware of the treachery used towards them they were violently enraged, and puffed and roared aloud, invoking Setebos, their chief demon, to come to their assistance.

Not content with having these men, the captain was anxious of securing their wives also, in order to transport a race of giants to Europe: with this view he ordered the two others to be arrested, to oblige them to conduct our people to the spot where they were; nine of our strongest men were scarcely able to cast them to the ground, and bind them, and still even one of them succeeded in freeing himself, while the other exerted himself so much that he received a slight wound in the head from one of the men; but they were in the end obliged to show our people the way to the abode of the wives of our two prisoners. These women, on learning what had happened to their husbands, made such loud outcries as to be heard at a great distance. Johan Carvajo, the pilot, who was at the head of our people, as night was drawing on, did not choose to bring away at that time the women to whose house he had been conducted, but remained there till morning, keeping a good guard. In the mean time came there two other men, who without expressing any dissatisfaction or surprise, continued all night in the hut; but soon as dawn began to break, upon saying a few words, in an instant every one took to flight, man, woman, and child; the children even scampering away with greater speed than the rest. They abandoned their hut to us, and all that it contained; in the mean time one of the men drove off, to a distance, the little animals which they used in hunting; while another, concealed behind the bush, wounded one of our men in the thigh, who died immediately. Though our people fired on the runaways, they were unable to hit any, on account of their not escaping in a straight line, but leaping from one side to another, and getting on as swiftly as horses at full gallop. Our people burned the hut of these savages, and buried their dead companions.

Savage as they are, these Indians are yet not without their medicaments. When they have a pain in the stomach, for example, in lieu of an operative medicine, they thrust an arrow pretty deeply down the throat, to excite a vomit, and throw up a matter of a greenish color, mixed with blood. The green is occasioned by a sort of thistle, on which the fee. If they have the headache, they make a gash in their forehead, and do the same with the other parts of their body, where they experience pain, in order to draw from the affected part a considerable quantity of blood. Their theory, as explained to us by one of those we had taken, is on a par with their practice: pain, they say, proceeds from the reluctance of the blood to abide any longer in the part where it is felt; by releasing it, consequently, the pain is removed.

Their hair is cut circularly like that of monks, but is longer, and supported round the head by a cotton string, in which they place their arrows when they go hunting. When the weather is very cold, they tie their private parts closely to the body. It appears that their religion is limited to adoring the devil: they pretend that when one of them is on the point of death, 10 or 12 demons appear dancing and singing around him. One of these, who makes a greater noise than the rest, is termed Setebos, the inferior imps are called Cheleule; they are painted like the people of the country. Our giant pretends to have once seen a devil, with horns, and hair of such length as to cover his feet; he cast out flames, added hie, from his mouth and his posteriors.

These people, as I have already noticed, clothe themselves in the skin of an animal, and with the same kind of skin do they cover their huts, which they transport whither suits them best, having no fixed place of abode, but wandering about from spot to spot like gypsies. They generally live upon raw meat, and a sweet root called capac; they are great feeders: the two we took daily consumed a basket full of bread each, and drank half a pail of water at a draught, they eat mice raw, and without even slaying them. Our captain gave these people the name of *Patagonians*. We spent 5 months in this port, to which we gave the denomination of *St. Julian*, and met with no accidents on shore, during the whole of our stay, save what I have noticed.

Scarcely had we anchored in this port before the four captains of the other vessels plotted to murder the captain-general. These were Juan of Carthagena, vehador of the squadron; Lewis de Mendoza, the treasurer, Antonio Cocca, the paymaster, and Gaspar de Casada. The plot was discovered, the first was slayed alive, and the second was stabbed to the heart; Gaspar de Casada was forgiven, but a few days after he meditated treason anew. The captain-general then, who dared not take his life, as he was created a captain by the Emperor himself, drove him from the squadron, and left him in the country of the Patagonians, together with a priest, his accomplice.

Another mishap befell part of the squadron while we remained at this station. The ship St. Jago, which had been detached to survey the coast, was cast upon rocks; nevertheless, as if by a miracle, the whole of the crew were saved; two seamen came over-land to the port where we were to acquaint us of this disaster, and the captain-general sent men to the spot immediately, with some sacks of biscuit. The crew stopped two months near the place where the vessel was stranded, to collect the wreck and merchandise, which the sea successively cast off shore; and during all this time means of subsistence was transported them over land, although 100 miles distant from the port of St. Julian, and by a very bad and fatiguing road, through thickets and briars, among which the bearers of provision were obliged to pass the whole night, without any other beverage than what they obtained from the ice they found, and which they were able with difficulty to break.

As for us, we fared tolerably in this port, though certain shell-fish, of great length, some of which contained pearls, but of very small size, were not edible. We found ostriches here, foxes, rabbits much smaller than ours, and sparrows. The trees yield frankincense.

We planted a cross on the summit of a neighboring mountain, which we termed *Monte Christo*, and took possession of the country in the name of the King of Spain.

We at length left this port (21st August) and keeping along the coast, in latitude 50 degrees 40 minutes south, discovered a river of fresh water, into which we entered. The whole squadron nearly experienced shipwreck here, owing to the furious winds with which it was assailed, and which occasioned a very rough sea; but God and the Corpora Sancta (that is to say, the lights which shone on the summits of the masts) brought us succor, and saved us from harm. We spent two months here, to stock our vessels with wood and water; we laid in provision, also, of a species of fish nearly two feet in length, and covered with scales; it was tolerable eating, but we were unable to take a sufficient number of them. Before we quitted this spot, our captain ordered all of us to make confession, and, good Christians, to receive the communion.

Continuing our course towards the south, on the 21st October, in latitude 52 degrees, we discovered a strait, which we denominated the strait of *Elen Thousand Virgins*, in honor of the day. This strait, as will appear in the sequel, is 440 miles, or 110 maritime leagues in length; it is a league in breadth, sometimes more, sometimes less, and terminates in another sea, which we denominated the *Pacific Ocean*. This strait is inclosed between lofty mountains, covered with snow, and it is likewise very deep, so that we were unable to anchor, except quite close to shore, where was from 25 to 35 fathoms water.

The whole of the crew were so firmly persuaded that this strait had no western outlet, that we should not, but for the deep science of the captain-general, have ventured on its exploration. This man, as skilful as he was intrepid, knew that he would have to pass by a strait very little known, but which he had seen laid down on a chart of Martin de Boheme, a most excellent cosmographer, in the treasury of the King of Portugal.

As soon as we entered on this water, imagined to be only a bay, the captain sent forward two vessels, the Sto. Antonio, and La Concepcion, to examine where it terminated, or whither it led; while we in the Trinidad and the Vittoria awaited them in the mouth of it.

At night came on a terrible hurricane, which lasted six and thirty hours, and forced us to quit our anchors, and leave our vessels to the mercy of the winds and waves in the gulf. The two other vessels, equally buffeted, were unable to double a cape, in order to rejoin us; so that by abandoning themselves to the gale, which drove them constantly towards what they conceived to be the bottom of a bay, they were apprehensive momentarily of being driven on shore. But at the instant they gave themselves up for lost, they saw a small opening, which they took for an inlet of the bay, into this they entered, and perceiving that this channel was not closed, they threaded it, and found themselves in another, through which they pursued their course to another strait, leading into a third bay still larger than the preceding. Then, in lieu of following up their exploration, they deemed it most prudent to return, and render account of what they had observed to the captain-general.

Two days passed without the two vessels returning, sent to examine the bottom of the bay, so that we reckoned they had been swallowed up during the tempest; and seeing smoke on shore, we conjectured that those who had had the good fortune to escape, had kindled those fires to inform us of their existence and distress. But while in this painful incertitude as to their fate, we saw them advancing towards us under full sail, and their flags flying; and when sufficiently near, heard the report of their bombards, and their loud exclamations of joy. We repeated the salutation; and when we learnt from them that they had seen the prolongation of the bay, or, better speaking, the strait, we made towards them, to continue our voyage in this course, if possible.

When we had entered into the third bay, which I have before notice, we saw two openings, or channels, the one running to the south-east, the other to the south-west. The captain-general sent the two vessels, the Sant Antonio and La Conception to the south-east, to examine whether or no this channel terminated in an open sea. The first set sail immediately, under press of canvas, not choosing to wait for the second, which the pilot wished to leave behind, as he had intention to avail himself of the darkness of the night to retrace his course, and return to Spain by the same way we came.

The pilot was Emanuel Gomez, who hated Magellan, for the sole reason that, when he came to Spain to lay his project before the Emperor of proceeding to the Moluccas by a western passage, Gomez himself had requested, and was on the point of obtaining, some caravellas for an expedition of which he would have had the command. This expedition had for its object to make new discoveries; but the arrival of Magellan prevented his request from being complied with, and he could only obtain the subaltern situation of pilot; what, however, no less served to increase his irritation, was the reflection of his serving under a Portuguese. In the course of the night he conspired with the other Spaniards on board the ship. They put in irons, and even wounded the Captain, Alvaro de Mefchita, the cousin-german of the captain-general, and carried him thus to Spain. They reckoned likewise on transporting thither one of the two giants we had taken, and who was on board their ship; but we learnt, on our return, that he died on approaching the equinoctial line, unable to bear the heat of the tropical regions.

The vessel, the Conception, which could not keep up with the Sant Antonio, continued to cruise in the channel to await its return, but in vain.

We, with the two other vessels, entered the remaining channel, on the south-west; and, continuing our course, came to a river which we called *Sardine* river, on account of the vast number of the fish of this denomination we found in it. We anchored here to wait for the two other ships, and remained in the river four days; but in the interim we dispatched a boat, well manned, to reconnoitre the cape of this channel, which promised to terminate in another sea. On the third day the sailors sent on this expedition returned, and announced their having seen the cape where the strait ended, and with it a great sea, that is to say, ocean. We wept for joy: this cape was denominated *Il Capo Defeado* (Wished for Cape) for in truth we had long wished to see it.

We returned to join the two other vessels of the squadron, and found the Conception alone. On enquiring of the pilot, Johan Serano, what had become of the other vessel, we learnt that he conceived it to be lost, as he had not once seen it since he entered the channel. The captain-general then ordered it to be sought for every where, but especially in the channel into which it had penetrated. He sent back the Vittoria to the mouth of the strait, with directions, if they should not find it, to hoist a standard on some eminent spot at the foot of which, in a small pot, should be placed a letter, pointing out the course the captain-general would take, in order to enable the missing ship to follow the squadron. This mode of communication, in case of a division, was concerned at the instant of our departure. Two other signals were hoisted in the same manner on eminent sites in the first bay, and on a small island of the third bay, on which we saw a number of sea-wolves and birds. The captain-general, with the Conception, awaited the return of the Victory, near the river of Sardines, and erected a cross on a small island, at the foot of two mountains, covered with snow, where the river had its source.

Had we not discovered this strait, leading from one sea to the other, it was the intention of the captain-general to continue his course towards the south, as high as 75 degrees, where in summer there is no night, or very little, as in winter there is scarcely any day. While we were in the straits, in the month of October, there were but three hours night.

The shore in this strait, which, on the left, turns to the south-east, is low. We called it the *Strait of the Patagonians*. At every half league it contains a safe port, with excellent water, cedar-wood, sardines, and a great abundance of shell-fish. There were here also some vegetable, part of them of bitter taste, but others fit to eat, especially a species of sweet celery, which grows on the margin of springs, and which, for want of other, served us for food. In short, I do not think the world contains a better strait than this.

At the very instant of our launching into the ocean we witnessed a singular chase of fish pursued by others. There are three species, that is to say, dorados, albicores and bonitos, which pursue the fish called colondrins, a kind of flying-fish. These, when followed close, issue from the water, extend their fins, of sufficient length to serve them as wings, and fly the distance of a cross-bow's shot; after this they return into the water. In the mean time their enemies, directed by the shadow of them, continue the pursuit, and instantly as they re-enter the water, make them their prey. These flying-fish are upwards of a foot in length, and are excellent eating.

During the voyage I talked with the Patagonian giant on board our ship, and by means of a species of pantomime, enquired of him the Patagonian name of a number of objects, and was thus enable to form a small vocabulary. He had accustomed himself so perfectly to this practice, that no sooner did he see me take my pen in hand, than he came immediately to tell the name of the different things before him, and what was passing. Among other things he showed us the manner of kindling fire in this country; that is to say, by rubbing one piece of pointed wood against another, until fire catches to a kind of pith of a tree, placed between the two pieces of wood. One day when I showed him and kissed the cross, he gave me to understand by his gestures that Setebos would enter into my body, and caused me to burst. When at death's door, on his last illness, he called for the cross, which he kissed; he also begged to be baptized, which was done; he receiving the name of Paul.

Book II

Departure from the Strait, and thence to the Death of Captain Magellan, and our leaving Zubu.

On Wednesday, 28th November, we left the strait, and entered the ocean to which we afterwards gave the denomination of *Pacific*, and in which we sailed the space of three months and 20 days, without tasting any fresh provisions. The biscuit we were eating no longer deserved the name of bread; it was nothing but dust, and worms which had consumed the substance; and what is more, it smelled intolerably, being impregnated with the urine of mice. The water we were obliged to drink was equally putrid and offensive. We were even so far reduced, that we might not die of hunger, to each pieces of the leather with which the main-yard was covered to prevent it from wearing the rope. These pieces of leather, constantly exposed to the water, sun, and wind, were so hard that they required being soaked four or five days in the sea in order to render them supple; after this we broiled them to eat. Frequently indeed we were obliged to subsist on saw-dust, and even mice, a food so disgusting, were sought after with such avidity that they sold for half a ducat a piece.

Nor was this all, our greatest misfortune was being attacked by a malady in which the gums swelled so as to hide the teeth, as well in the upper as the lower jaw, whence those affected thus were incapable of chewing their food. Nineteen of our number died of this complaint,

154--To America and Around the World

among whom was the Patagonian giant, and a Brazilian, whom we had brought with us from his own country. Besides those who died, we had from 25 to 30 sailors ill, who suffered dreadful pains in their arms, legs, and other parts of the body; but these all of them recovered. As for myself, I cannot be too grateful to God for the continued health I enjoyed; though surrounded with sick I experienced not the slightest illness.

In the course of these three months and 20 days we traveled nearly 4000 leagues in the Ocean denominated by the Pacific, on account of our not having experienced throughout the whole of this period any the least tempestuous weather. We did not either in this whole length of time discover any land, except two desert islands; on these we saw nothing but birds and trees, for which reason we named them *Las Islas Desdichados* (the Unfortunate Islands). We found no bottom among their shores, and saw no fish but sharks. The two islands are 200 leagues apart. The first lies in latitude 15 degrees south, the second in latitude 9 degrees. From the run of our ship, as estimated by the log, we traveled a space of from 60 to 70 leagues a day; and if God and his Holy Mother had not granted us a fortunate voyage, we should all have periled of hunger in so vast a sea. I do not think that any one for the future will venture upon a similar voyage.

If, on leaving the straits, we had continued a western course under the same parallel, we should have made the tour of the world; and without seeing any land should have returned by Wishead-for-Cape (Il Capo Deseado), to the cape of the Eleven Thousand Virgins, both of which are in latitude 52 degrees south.

The antarctic has not the same stars as the arctic pole, but here are seen two clusters of small nebulous stars, which look like small clouds, and are but little distant the one from the other. In midst of these clusters of small stars two are distinguished very large and very brilliant, but of which the motion is scarcely apparent: these indicate the antarctic pole. Though the needle declined somewhat from the north pole, it yet oscillated towards it, but not with equal force as in the northern hemisphere. When out at sea, the captain-general directed the course the pilots should steer, and enquired how they pointed. They unanimously replied they bore in that direction he ordered them: he then informed them that their course was wrong, and directed them to correct the needle, because, being in the southern, it had not an equal power to designate the true north as in the northern hemisphere. When in midst of the ocean we discovered, in the west, five stars of great brilliance, in form of a cross.

We steered north-west by west till we reached the equinoctial line in one 120 degrees longitude, west of the line of demarcation. This line is 30 degrees west of the meridian, and 3 degrees west of Cape Vert.

In our course we coasted along two very lofty islands, one of which in latitude 20 degrees south, the other in 15 degrees south. The first is called *Cipangu*, the second *Sumbdit Pradit*.

After we had crossed the line we steered west-by-north. We then ran 200 leagues towards the west; when, changing our course again, we ran west-by-south until in the latitude of 13 degrees north; we trusted by this course to reach Cape Gatticara which cosmographers have placed in this latitude, but they are mistaken, this cape lying 12 degrees more towards the north. They must, however, be excused the error in their plan, as they have not like us had the advantage of visiting these parts.

When we had run 70 leagues in this direction and were in latitude 12 degrees north, longitude 140 degrees, on Wednesday the 6th of March, we discovered in the north-west a small island, and afterwards tow others in the south-west. The first was more lofty and larger than the other two. The captain-general meant to stop at the largest to victual and refresh; but this was rendered impossible, as the islanders came on board our ships, and stole, first one thing and then another, without our being able to prevent them. They invited us to take in our sails and come on shore, and even had the address to steal the skiff which hung astern of our vessel. Exasperated at length, our captain landed with 40 men, burnt 40 or 50 of their houses, and several of their boats, and killed 7 of the people. By acting thus he recovered his skiff; but he did not deem it prudent to stop any longer after such acts of hostility. We therefore continued our course in the same direction as before.

On our entering the boats to land and punish the islanders, our sick people besought us, if any of them should chance to be killed, to bring them their intestines, persuaded that they would soon effect their cure.

When our people wounded any of the islanders with their arrows, (of which weapon they had no conception), and chanced to pierce with them through, the unfortunate sufferers endeavoured to draw out these arrows from their bodies, now by one end, now by the other; after which they looked at them with astonishment, and sometimes died of their wounds, a circumstance that did not fail to excite our pity. Still, when they saw us about to depart, they followed us with more than a 100 canoes, and showed us fish as if disposed to sell it; but when near us they pelted us with stones, and took to flight. We sailed through the midst of them under full sail, but they avoided our vessels with much dexterity. We likewise saw in their boats, crying and tearing their hair, some women, whose husbands probably had been killed.

These people are ignorant of any law, and are guided merely by their inclinations. They have no king, nor any chief; adore no Being or image, and go naked. Some among them have a long beard, and black hair, tied over the forehead and hanging down to the girdle. They likewise wear small hats made of palm. They are of good size and well built. Their complexion is an olive brown, but we were told they are born fair, and become dark as they increase in years. They possess the art of staining their teeth red and black, which with them is a mark of beauty. The women are pretty, of handsome shape, and less dark than the men. Their hair is very black, sleek, and hangs to the ground. They go naked like the men, except their privites, which they cover with a very narrow strip of cloth, or rather of the inner bark of the palm-tree. Their whole employment is in their houses, in making mats and baskets of the leaves of the palm-tree, and in other similar works. Both men and women anoint their hair, and the whole of the body, with the oil of the cocoa-nut and seseli.

These people live on birds, flying-fish, potatoes, a sort of figs half a foot long, sugar-canes and other similar productions. Their houses are of wood covered with planks, over which leaves of their fig-trees four feet in length are spread. They have tolerably decent rooms, with rafters and window frames; and their beds are pretty soft, being made of very fine matting of the palm-tree laid upon straw. Their only arms are a lance tipped with pointed fish-bone. The inhabitants of these islands are poor, but very dexterous, and above all at thieving; for this reason we gave the name *De los Ladrones* to the islands.

Their chief amusement consists in sailing about with their wives in canoes similar to the gondolas of Fusine near Venice, but they are still more narrow; all of them are painted, either black, white, or red. The sail is made of the leaves of the palm-tree, sewed together, and has the shape of a latine sail. It is always placed on one side; and on the opposite side, to form an equipoise to the sail, they fasten a large wooden log, pointed at one end, with poles laid across and fixed in it, which keeps the boat steady and admits of their sailing without apprehension; their rudder resembles a baker's shove, that is to say, it consists of a pole fastened into a plank. They make no difference between head and stern, as they have a rudder at each end. They are excellent swimmers, and have as little fear of the sea as dolphins. They were so much astonished at the sight of us, that we had reason to believe they had never seen any other than the inhabitants of their own island.

The 16th of March, at sunrise, we found ourselves near an elevated land, 300 leagues from the island De los Ladrones. We soon discovered it to be an island. It is called *Zamal.* Behind this island is another not inhabited, and we afterwards learnt that its name is *Humunu.* Here the captain-general resolved on landing the next day to take in water in greater security, and take some rest after so long and tedious a voyage. Here likewise he caused two tents to be erected for the sick, and ordered a sow to be killed.

On Monday the 18th, in the afternoon, we saw a bark with nine men making towards us. The captain-general hereupon issued orders that none should make the least motion, or utter a single word without his leave. When they had landed, the chief of the party addressed our commander, and testified by signs the pleasure he experienced on seeing us. Four of the best dressed remained with us; the residue went to fetch their companions, who were fishing, and returned with them.

The captain, seeing them so peaceable, placed food before them, and at the same time offered them some red caps, small looking-glasses, combs, bells, moccasins, ivory trinkets, and other similar articles. The islanders, delighted with the kindness of the captain, presented him fish, a vase full of palm-wine, which they call uraca, bananas more than a span long, with others of a smaller size and superior flavor, and two cocoa-nuts. They signified at the same time by their gestures, that they had nothing else to offer us at that time, but that in four days they would return, and bring us rice, which they call umai, cocoa-nuts, and other provision.

Cocoa-nuts are the fruit of a species of palm-tree, which furnishes them with their substitute for bread, with wine, oil, and vinegar. In order to obtain wine they make an incision at the top of the palm-tree, penetrating to the pith of the tree, from which drops a liquor resembling white must, but which is rather tart. This liquor is caught in the hollow of a reed the thickness of a man's leg, which is suspended to the tree, and which is carefully emptied twice a day, at morning and night. The fruit of this palm-tree is of the size of a man's head, and sometimes larger. Its outward rind is green, and two fingers thick: it is composed of filaments of which they made cordage for their boats. Beneath the outward rind is a shell much harder and thicker than that of the walnut. This shell they burn, and reserve for making into a powder which they use. Within, the shell is lined with a white kernel about as thick as a finger, which is eaten in lieu of bread with meat and fish. In the center of the nut encircled by the kernel, a sweet and limpid liquor is found, of a corroborative nature. After pouring this liquor into a glass, if it be suffered to stand, it assumes the consistence of an apple. To obtain an oil, the kernel and the liquor are left to ferment; they are afterwards boiled, and yield an oil as thick as butter. To obtain vinegar, the liquor itself is exposed to the sun, and the acid which results from it resembles that vinegar we make from white wine. We likewise made a beverage which resembled goat's milk, by rasping the nut, mixing with the liquor, and straining the liquor through a cloth. The cocoa-trees resemble those palm-trees which produce dates, but their trunks, without being very smooth, have not so large a number of knots. A family of ten persons might be supported from two cocoa-trees, by alternately tapping each every week, and letting the other rest, that a perpetual drainage of liquor may not kill the tree. We were told that a cocoa-tree lives a century.

The islanders became very familiar with us, by which means we were enabled to learn from them the names of many things, especially surrounding objects. From them also we learnt that their island, which is not very large, is called *Zuluan*. They were polite and well behaved. Out of friendship towards our captain they took him in their canoes to the warehouses where they kept their merchandise, cloves, for example, cinnamon, pepper, nutmeg, mace, gold, etc. etc.; and by signs informed us that the countries towards which we directed our course produced these articles in abundance. The captain-general in return invited them on board his vessel, where he spread before them whatever by its novelty was likely to fix their attention. At the instant they were about to depart he caused a bombard to be fired, which strangely frightened them, so much indeed that they were on the point of throwing themselves into the sea in order to get away; but, with little difficulty, we succeeded in persuading them that they had no cause for apprehension, and they left us at length tranquillized, and with courtesy assured us, as they had promised before, that they would return immediately. The desert island on which we had landed was called *Humuna* by the islanders; but we have it the name of *Acquada degli Buoni Signali* (the Watering-place of Good Promise), on account of our finding here two fountains of excellent water, and the first indices of gold in this country. Here also white coral is found; and there are some trees, the fruit of which, smaller than our almonds, resemble the kernel of the pine cone. Many kinds of palm are likewise seen, some of which yield fruit good to eat, while others produce none.

Perceiving around us a number of islands on the fifth Sunday of Lent, which also is the feast of St. Lazarus, we called the archipelago by the name of that saint. It lies in 10 degrees of north latitude, and 151 degrees of longitude from the line of demarkation.

On Friday, the 22nd of the month, the islanders kept their word, and came with two canoes full of cocoa-nuts, oranges, a pitcher-full of palm-wine, and a cock, in order to show us that they had poultry. We bought the whole of what they brought us. Their chief was an old man; his face was painted and he wore pendants in his ears. The people in his suite wore bracelets of gold on their arms, and handkerchiefs round their heads.

We laid eight days off this island, and the captain every day went on shore to visit the sick, taking with him the wine of the cocoa-tree, which was highly serviceable to them.

The inhabitants of the islands contiguous to that at which we were, had such large holes in their ears, and the ends of them were drawn down so much, that one might thrust an arm through the orifice.

These people are Caffres, that is to say Gentiles. They go naked, merely wearing a piece of the bark of a tree to hide their privites, which some of their chiefs cover with a girdle of cotton cloth, embroidered with silk at the two extremities. They are of an olive color, and generally pretty plump. They tattoo themselves, and grease the body all over with the oil of the cocoa-tree and gengeli, in order, they say, to preserve themselves from the sun and wind. They have black hair, of such length it reaches to their waist. Their arms are cutlasses, bucklers, clubs, and lances, adorned with gold. The fishing instruments they use are darts, harpoons, and nets made nearly in the same manner as ours. Their boats likewise resemble those in use with us.

On Holy Monday, 25th March, I was in the most imminent danger. We were about to set sail, and I was intent on fishing: being about to place myself for greater convenience on a yard wetted by rain, my foot slipped, and I fell into the sea without being perceived. Fortunately a rope, belonging to one of the sails, which was hanging in the water, presented itself within my grasp; I seized it and hollored with all my might, till I was heard, and the skiff was sent round to relieve me from peril. My salvation was certainly not to be attributed to my individual merit, but to the merciful protection of the Holy Virgin.

We left the island the same day, and steered west-south-west between four islands called *Cenato, Huinangan, Ibusson,* and *Abarien.*

On Thursday, 28th March, having distinguished fire during the night on an island near us, we steered for it in the morning, and when but little distant saw a small bark, called a boloto, with eight men in it, making for our vessel. The captain had a slave on board, a native of Sumatra, anciently called Tapobrana: we endeavoured to converse with the inhabitants by his means, and found they comprehended his language. They came to within a short distance of us, but would not come on board, and seemed even to be fearful of approaching us too closely. The captain, seeing their mistrust, threw into the sea a red cap and some other trifles, attached to a plank. They took it, and seemed greatly pleased, but immediately after departed: we afterwards learnt that they hastened to make their King acquainted with our arrival.

Two hours after we saw two balanghais proceeding towards us (for thus do they call their large boats), which were full of people. The King was in the largest, under a sort of canopy formed of matting. When the King came near enough to our vessel the slave of the captain spoke to him, and was understood, for the monarchs of these islands speak several languages. He ordered some of the men who accompanied him to go on board the ship, but himself remained in his balanghay; and as soon as his people returned he took his departure.

The captain gave a very kind reception to those who came on board, and made them presents. The King, informed of this, was desirous before he departed of presenting the captain in return with an ingot of gold and a basked full of ginger; but he refused the present, expressing thanks for his civility. Towards the evening the squadron anchored near the King's house.

The next day the captain sent the slave on shore, who served him as an interpreter, to tell the King if he would furnish us with provisions we would pay him liberally; assuring him at the same time that we had not come with any hostile intention against him, but as friends. Upon this the King himself came on board in our boat, with six or eight of his chief subjects. He embraced our captain, and presented him with three vases of porcelain full of rice, and covered with leaves, two pretty large dorados, and some other articles. The captain in turn offered him a robe a la Turque, made of red and yellow cloth, and a fine red cap. He also made several presents to the people who accompanied him: to some he gave mirrors, and to others knives. At length he caused breakfast to be served up, and directed the slave who acted as interpreter to tell the King he wished to live with him on brotherly terms, which seemed to afford him great pleasure.

He afterwards spread out cloths of different colors before the King, linens, coral, and other merchandise. He likewise showed him all our fire-arms, and the great guns; and even caused several to be fired, the report of which created great consternation in the inhabitants. He caused one of us to be completely clothed in armor, and directed three men to cut at him with swords, and strive to stab him, in order to show the King that nothing could affect a man armed after this fashion; this occasioned him great surprise, and turning towards the interpreter he observed that a man so guarded would be able to fight with a hundred:

"Yes," replied the interpreter, in the name of the captain, "and each of the three vessels has 200 men armed in the same manner."

He was afterwards allowed to examine separately each distinct piece of armor, and all our arms; and the men went through the different exercises with them before him.

After this the captain conducted him to the hind-castle, or poop, and causing the chart and a compass to be brought forward, he explained to him, through the interpreter, by what means he had discovered the strait which led to the sea in which we were, and how many moons he had passed at sea without sight of land.

The King, astonished at all he had seen and heard, took leave of the captain, beseeching him in return to send two of his people to view the curiosities of his country. For this purpose the captain deputed me and another to accompany him on shore.

As soon as we landed the King raised his hands up to heaven, and afterwards turned towards us; we, as well as all who accompanied us, then did the same. The King then took me by the hand, and one of his chief people did the same with my comrades, in which manner we repaired to a sort of shed formed of reeds, under which was a balanghay about 50 feet long resembling a galley. We seated ourselves on the poop, and endeavoured by gestures to render ourselves understood, as we had no interpreter with us. Those in the suite of the King encircled him round, standing, and armed with spears and bucklers.

They now served up a dish of port, with a large pitcher of wine. At every mouthful of meat we took a spoonful of wine; and when we did not wholly empty the spoon, which seldom was the case, the residue was poured into another pitcher. The spoon from which the King drank was always covered, and no one but himself was suffered to touch it. Previous to drinking, the King constantly raised his hands to heaven before he took the spoon, afterwards turning them towards us; and on taking it with the right hand, extended his left closed towards me, in such a manner that, on his first using this ceremony, I thought he was about to give me a blow with his fist; in this attitude he remained the whole time he was drinking; perceiving that all the others imitated him in this I did the same. In this manner we finished our repast, and I was unable to dispense with eating meat notwithstanding it happened to be on a Good Friday.

Before supper I presented several articles to the King, which I had brought with me for the purpose; and at the same time enquired of him the name of several things in his language, which he was surprised to see me write down.

For supper two large dishes of porcelain were set before us, one containing rice, the other pork in the liquor in which it was boiled. At supper the same ceremony was observed as at the collation. After supper we repaired to the King's palace, which resembled in form a hay-stack. It was covered with the leaves of the bananier, and was supported at some height in the air by four large posts. So that we were obliged to use a ladder on ascending to it.

When we had entered the palace the King caused us to be seated on mats of reeds, with our legs across like tailors. Half an hour afterwards a dish of broiled fish was brought in cut in slices, some ginger fresh gathered, and wine. The King's eldest son now coming in, he was directed to seat himself beside us. Two other dishes were then served up, one of boiled fish swimming in its liquor, the other of rice, that we might eat with the heir apparent. My companion drank to excess, and was intoxicated.

Their candles are made of a kind of gum, which they call anime, and which is enveloped in the leaves of the palm or fig-tree.

The King, after signifying he was about to retire, to rest, went away and left us with his son, with whom we slept on a matting of reeds, our heads being supported on pillows of leaves.

The next day the King came to see me in the morning, and taking me by the hand led me to the spot where we supped the preceding evening, that we might breakfast there together; but as our boat had come for us, I excused myself, and departed with my companion. The King was extremely good humored; he kissed our hands, and we kissed his in turn.

His brother, who was King of another island, accompanied us, together with three other persons. The captain-general retained him to dinner, and made him a present of several trifles.

The King who accompanied us informed us that gold was found in his island in lumps as large as a walnut, and even as an egg, mingled with earth; that they used a sieve for sifting it; and that all his vessels, and even many of the ornaments of his house, were of this metal. He was handsomely dressed in the fashion of his country, and was the finest man we saw among these people. His black hair fell down over his shoulders: his head was covered with a silken veil, and in his ears were two gold rings. From the waist to the knees he wore a tunic of cotton cloth embroidered with silk; at his side was a species of sword or dagger with a long golden hilt, and a wooden scabbard of exquisite workmanship. On each of his teeth were three golden dots, so placed one would have thought his teeth had been fastened with this metal. He was perfumed with storax and gum benjamin. His skin was painted, but its ground color was an olive. He resides generally in an island, in which are the two countries of Butuan and Calagan; but when the two Kings wish to hold a conference they repair to the island Massana, at which we then were. The first King is denominated Rajah Colambu, the other Rajah Siagu.

On Easter day, which fell on the last day in March, the captain-general early in the morning sent our almoner on shore with some sailors to make preparations for saying mass; and at the same time he sent a message by the interpreter to the King, to inform him that we should land on his island, not to dine with him, but to perform a religious ceremony: the King approved our intention, and at the time of signifying his pleasure sent us two hogs just killed.

We landed, 50 in number, not completely armed, but at the same time armed and dressed in the best manner possible: at the instant our boats touched the shore six guns were fired as a salute.

We jumped on shore, where the two Kings, who had come down to meet us at the water-side embraced our captain, and placed him between them. We proceeded thus in an orderly manner to the spot where mass was to be said, which was but a short distance from the sea.

Before mass was said the captain sprinkled the two Kings with sweet scented water. At the period of the oblation they kissed the cross as we did, but made no offering. On the elevation of the host they adored the eucharist with joined hands, imitating us in all we did. At this instant, upon signal given, a general discharge of artillery was fired from the ships. After mass some of us received the communion; which effected, the captain exhibited a dance with swords, with which the two Kings seemed much delighted.

After this he caused a large cross to be brought, garnished with nails and a crown of thorns, before which we prostrated ourselves; and in this action were again imitated by the islanders. The captain then told the two Kings, by means of the interpreter, that this cross was the standard confided to him by the Emperor his master, to plant wherever he landed; and that in consequence he should erect it on the island, to which this symbol would moreover be auspicious; as all European ships which in future should visit it would know, on seeing the cross, that we had been received as friends, and would refrain from any violence to the persons or property of their subjects; and should any be taken prisoners, they would only have to make the sign of it to regain their liberty. He added that this cross should be placed on the most lofty spot in the neighborhood, so that every one might see it, and that every morning it was to be worshipped. To this he added further, that by following such advice neither storms or thunder would hereafter do them injury. The Kings, who gave implicit faith to all the captain said, thanked him, and assured him by means of the interpreter that they were perfectly satisfied, and would with pleasure do as he desired.

He enquired what their religion, and whether they were Moors (Mohometans) or Gentiles (Pagans)? They replied that they adored no terrestrial object, but, raising their hands towards heaven, on Supreme Being only, whom they called Abba; which afforded much pleasure to our captain. The Rajah Colambu then, raising his hands to heaven, expressed his desire of showing him some marks of his friendship. The interpreter having inquired of him wherefore provisions were so scarce, he answered that it was owing to that island not being the place of their residence, but only a spot to which he casually resorted for hunting, or to hold intercourse with his brother; and that he generally dwelt on another island where his family then was.

The captain told the King that if he had any enemies he would willingly combine with him to combat them with all his vessels and warriors. The King answered that he was indeed at war with the inhabitants of two islands; but that the present was not a fit time to attack them, and returned him thanks. In the afternoon we determined on erecting the cross on the summit of a mountain, and the festival terminated with a discharge of musketry, our men being formed into battalions; after this the King and the captain embraced, and we returned to our ships.

Dinner ended, we all landed, dressed merely in our jackets; and, accompanied by the two Kings we ascended the highest mountain in the neighborhood and there planted the cross. In the interim the captain expatiated on the advantages which would accrue from it to the inhabitants. We all adored the cross, and the Kings did the same. As we came down the mountain we traversed some fields in culture, and proceeded to the spot where the balanghay was, to which the Kings ordered refreshments to be brought.

The captain-general had previously inquired which was the best ports in the neighborhood for obtaining provisions and for traffic, and learned there were three; to wit, Ceylon, Zubu, and Calagan; but that the best of these was Zubu; and as he resolved on failing thither, they offered him pilots for the purpose. The ceremony of adoring the cross being ended, the captain fixed upon the next day for our departure, and offered to leave an hostage with the kings to answer for the safe return of the pilots, which they accepted.

In the morning, when on the point of heaving anchor, King Colambu caused to be intimated to us that he would willingly himself serve as a pilot, but that he was obliged to defer his departure for some days in order to gather the harvest of rice and other produce of the earth: he at the same time entreated the captain to lend him part of the crew in order to hasten the conclusion of the harvest. The captain accordingly sent him some men; but the Kings had eaten and drunk so much the day before, that whether their health suffered in consequence, whether they had not yet recovered from inebriety, they were unable to give any directions, and our men were consequently idle. The two succeeding days they worked very hard, and completed what they had to do.

We passed 7 days on this island; in the course of which we had full opportunity of noticing the manners and customs of the people. The men go naked, merely covering their privities with a piece of cloth, and their bodies are painted. The women wear a petticoat made of the rind of a tree which descends from their waist downwards. Their hair is black, and sometime so long as to reach to the ground. Their ears are bored, and adorned with rings and pendants of gold. They are great drinkers; and are constantly chewing a fruit called areca, which resembles a pear: they cut it in quarters, and fold it in the leaves of the same tree called betre, which resemble those of the mulberry, and mix with it a portion of lime: after well chewing it, they spit out the masticated fruit, etc. and their mouth is deeply reddened with the juice. There are none of these islanders but chew this fruit of the betre, which, as they pretend, serves to enliven them; I am even assured that were they to abstain from this practice they would die. The animals of this island are dogs, cats, hogs, goats, and fowls; and of edible vegetables are found rice, millet, panicle, maize, cocoa-nuts, oranges, lemons, bananas, and ginger. Wax also is found on the island.

Gold abounds, as is evident from two facts to which I was witness. A man brought us a large bowl of rice and figs for which in exchange he demanded a knife. The captain in lieu of a knife, offered him some pieces of money, and among others a doubloon; but he refused the money and preferred the knife. Another offered a large ingot of massive gold for six strings of glass beads; but the captain forbade the bargain, lest the islanders should thence comprehend that we placed a higher value on gold than on glass and other merchandise.

The island Massana lies in latitude 9 degrees 40 minutes north, and in longitude 162 degrees west of the line of demarcation. It is 25 leagues distant from the island Humunu.

We sailed from this island on the 5th April 1521, and steered south east, threading between five islands called Ceylon, Bohol, Canigan, Baybay, and Gatigan. In this last we saw bats as large as eagles. One of them we killed and ate, and found it much resembled a fowl in taste. Here also are pigeons, doves, parrots, and other birds, black and as large as fowls, which lay eggs equal in size to those of the duck, and an excellent food. We were told that the female lays her eggs in the sand, and that they are hatched by the heat of the sun. From Massana to Gatigan the distance is 20 leagues.

On leaving Gatigan we steered westward, and, as the King of Massana was unable to keep pace with us in his pirogue, we waited for him near three islands called Polo, Ticobon, and Pozon: when he had overtaken us we caused him, with some of his attendants, to come on board our vessel, which greatly pleased him; finally we arrived at the island Zubu. From Gatigan to Zubu, the distance is 15 leagues.

On Sunday, 7th April, we entered the port of Zubu. We passed by several village, in which we saw houses built upon trees. When near the town the captain ordered all our colors to be hoisted, and all our sails to be taken in; and a general salute was fired, which caused great alarm among the islanders.

The captain then sent one of his pupils, with the interpreter, as ambassador to the King of Zubu. On arriving at the town they found the King surrounded by an immense concourse of people alarmed at the noise occasioned by the discharge of our bombards. The interpreter began with removing the apprehension of the monarch, informing him that this was a custom with us, and meant as a mark of respect towards him, and as a token of friendship and peace. Upon this assurance the fears of all were dissipated.

The King enquired by his minister what brought us to his island, and what we wanted. The interpreter answered that his master who commanded the squadron was a captain in the service of the greatest monarch upon the earth, and that the object of his voyage was to proceed to Malucho; but that the King of Massana, at whose island we had touched, having spoken very highly of him, he had come hither to pay him his respects, and at the same time to take in provisions and give merchandise in exchange.

The King replied he was welcome, but at the same time he advised him that all vessels which might enter his port in view of trading were subject previously to pay duties: in proof of the truth of which he added, that four days had not yet elapsed since his having received port dues for a junk from Ciam, which had come thither to take in slaves and gold; he moreover sent for a Moorish merchant, who came from Ciam with the same view, to bear witness to what he stated.

The interpreter answered, that his master being the captain of so great a king could not consent to pay duty to any monarch upon earth; that if the King of Zubu wished for peace, he brought peace with him; but if he wished to be hostile, he was prepared for war. The merchant from Ciam then approaching the King, said to him in his own language, "Cata rajah chita"; that is to say, "Take care, Sire, of that. These people", added he, for he thought us Portuguese, "are those who conquered Calicut, Malacca, and Upper India." The interpreter, who comprehended what the Moor said, then remarked that his monarch was one vastly more powerful than the King of Portugal, to whom the Ciamese alluded, as well by seas as by land; that it was the King of Spain, the Emperor of the whole Christian world; and that if he had preferred to have him for an enemy rather than a friend he would have sent a sufficient number of men and vessels entirely to destroy his island. The Moor confirmed what the interpreter said. The King then, finding himself embarrassed, said he would advise with his ministers, and return and answer the next day. In the mean time he ordered a breakfast, consisting of several dishes, to be set before the deputy of the captain-general and the interpreter, all the dishes of meat served up in porcelain.

After breakfast our deputies returned, and reported what had taken place. The King of Massana, who next to that of Zubu was the most powerful monarch of these islands, went on shore to announce to the King the friendly intentions of our captain-general with respect to him.

The next day the secretary of our ship and the interpreter went to Zubu. The King advanced to meet them, accompanied by his chiefs, and after causing them to be seated before him, told them that, convinced from what he had heard, he not only desisted from exacting any dues, but was ready himself to become tributary to the Emperor. They then answered that they exacted no other concession on his part than that of an exclusive commerce with the island. To this the King agreed, and charged them to assure the captain that if he truly wished to be esteemed his friend he had only to draw some little blood from his right arm and sent it him, and he would do the same, which on either side would be a compact of true and substantial friendship. The interpreter answered for this being effected. The King then added, that all friendly captains who visited his port made presents to him, and received others in return; and that he left to the captain the choice of being the first to make or receive them. On this observation the captain remarked, that as he seemed to lay such stress on this usage, he had only to set the example, which he consented to do.

Tuesday, in the morning, the King of Massana came on board our vessel, in company with the Moorish merchant, and after saluting the captain on the part of the King of Zubu, told him he was authorized to communicate that the King was busied in collecting all the provisions he could to make a present of them to hi, and that in the afternoon he would send his nephew with some of his ministers to confirm a treaty of peace. The captain thanked the deputation, and at the same time exhibited to them a man armed cap-a-pie, observing, in case of a necessity to fight, we should all of us be armed in the same manner. The Moor was terribly frightened at sight of a man armed in this manner; but the captain tranquillized him with the assurance that our arms were as advantageous to our friends as fatal to our enemies; and that we were able as readily to disperse all the enemies of our sovereign and our faith as to wipe the sweat form our brows. The captain made use of this lofty and threatening tone purposely that the Moor might make report of it to the King.

As promised, the presumptive heir to the throne came on board us in the afternoon with the King of Massana, the Moor, the governor or minister, the provost-major, and eight chiefs of the island, to establish a treaty of peace. The captain received them with great state: he was seated in a chair covered with red velvet, and other chairs covered in the same manner were assigned to the King of Massana and the Prince; the chiefs were seated on chairs covered with leather, and the rest of the party on mats.

The captain inquired by means of the interpreter, if it was usual with them to form treaties in public, and if the Prince and the King of Massana were duly authorized to conclude a treaty with him. The answer was, that they were duly authorized, and that the conditions might be publicly discussed. The captain then made them sensible of all the advantages to be derived from this alliance, called on the God of Heaven to witness it, and added many other things which inspired them with love and veneration for our religion. He enquired if the King had any male children, and learnt that he had none but females, the eldest of whom was the wife of his nephew, who then was his ambassador, and who, in virtue of this marriage, was regarded as the hereditary prince. On speaking to them of the course of succession, we learnt that when parents attain a certain age they are no longer held in esteem, and that their authority then devolves to their sons. Our captain was much displeased at hearing of this usage, which he strongly condemned, seeing the Almighty who created heaven and earth, as he observed, has strictly commanded children to honor their parents, and threatened with eternal fire those who should transgress this commandment; and to make them the better apprehend the force of this divine precept, he told them that we were all alike subject to the same divine laws, as we were all alike descended from Adam and Eve. He added other observations from holy writ, which afforded much pleasure to these islanders, and inspired them with desire of being instructed in our religion; so much so indeed that they besought the captain to leave with them at their departure, one or two men capable of teaching them, who would not fail of being held in great honor. But the captain informed them that the most essential thing was that they should be baptized, which could be effected before he should quit the country; that he could not on this occasion leave any of his people behind him; but that he would return on a future day, and bring with him priests and monks to instruct them in all things belonging to our religion.

At this they expressed their satisfaction, and added that they themselves would be glad to receive baptism; but that beforehand they wished to consult their monarch on this subject. The captain then admonished them by no means to be baptized through any dread with which we might have inspired them, nor through any expectation of temporal advantage; for it was not his intention to molest any one on account of his preferring the religion of his fathers: he did not, however, disguise that those who should become Christians would be more beloved and better dealt with. Every one upon this exclaimed that it was neither out of dread of nor complaisance towards us, that they sought to embrace our religion, but from a spontaneous emotion, and of their own will

The captain then promised them, in consonance to orders he had received from his sovereign, to leave with them arms and a complete set of armor; but he told them at the same time that it was requisite their wives should likewise be baptized, as otherwise they must be divorced from and hold no communication with them if they would escape sin. Learning that they pretended to be tormented by frequent apparitions of the devil, he assured them that if they became Christians the devil would not afterwards dare to appear before them, but at the hour of death. These islanders, much affected and firmly persuaded of the truth of all they heard, answered, that they placed full reliance in him: on this the captain, weeping for joy, embraced them all.

He then took hold of the hand of the Prince and that of the King of Massana, and said that by the trust he had in God, by his allegiance to his sovereign the Emperor, and by the dress he wore, he now established and vowed perpetual peace between the King of Spain and King of Zubu. The two ambassadors made similar profession.

After this ceremony breakfast was served up. The Indians then presented to the captain, on the part of the King of Zubu, large baskets full of rice, hogs, goats, and fowls, making excuses at the same time for the unsuitableness of the present to the dignity of so great personage.

The captain-general in return presented to the Prince a very fine piece of white woolen cloth, a red cap, some strings of glass beads, and a glass goblet gilt, glass being in high request among these people. He made no present to the King of Massana, as he had just previously given him a Cambayan vest and several other things. He made presents at the same time to all the suite of the embassy.

After the islanders had left us, the captain sent me on shore, in company with another person, to carry the present designed for the King, which consisted of a vest of yellow and violet colored silk, made after the Turkish fashion, a red cap, and some strings of crystal beads in a silver dish; with two gilt glasses, which we carried in our hands.

On reaching the town we found the King in his palace surrounded by a large concourse of people. He was seated on the ground on a mat of palm. He was naked, a girdle excepted which he wore about his loins, and which served to hide his sexual parts; around his head he wore a veil embroidered with the needle, on his neck a collar of great value, and in his ears two gold rings of great size set with precious stones. He was small in stature, plump, and painted with different figures burnt into the skin. Before him on another mat, in two vases of porcelain, were some turtle eggs, of which he was eating, and near them four pitchers of palm wine covered with odoriferous herbs. In each of these pitchers was a hollow reed, by means of which he drank.

After salutation on our part, the interpreter informed the King that the captain returned thanks for the present made him, and on his part had sent him certain articles, not as a compensation, but as testimonials of the sincere friendship he had lately contracted. After this preface we clothed him in the vest we brought, put the cap on his head, and proffered the other presents. Before I gave him the glass goblets, I kissed and raised them above my head: the King on receiving them did the same. He then made us partake of his eggs, and drink of his wine through the reeds he used himself. While we were regaling, those who had come from the ship related to him what the captain had said respecting peace, and the manner in which he had exhorted them to embrace Christianity.

The King wished us to stay and sup with him, but we excused ourselves and took our leave. The Prince, his son-in-law, conducted us to his own house, where we found four girls playing music after their manner: one was beating a drum similar to our own, but placed on the ground; another had two kettle drums beside her, and in each hand a small drum stick, the end of it armed with cloth made of the palm, with which she struck first one and then the other; the third was beating in the same manner a large kettle-drum; and the fourth held in her hands two small cymbals, which she alternately struck one against the other and which rendered an extremely pleasing sound. They all of them kept such excellent time, that we conceived them to posses great knowledge of music. The kettle-drums, which are of metal or bronze, are made in the country of the Sign Magno, and serve the people of that country in lieu of bells; they are called _agon_. These islanders likewise play on a kind of violin, the strings of which are of copper.

These girls were very pretty, and almost as fair as Europeans; and although they were adult, they nevertheless were naked: part of them however had a piece of cloth, made of the inner bark of a tree, fastened round their waists, which descended as low as the knees; but nothing veiled from the eye any part of the body of the residue. The hole in their ears was very large, and was furnished with a wooden ring to keep it extended and preserve it of a round figure. Their hair was black and long, and their head was encircled by a small veil. They never wear shoes nor any covering whatever for the legs and feet. We partook of a collation with the Prince, and afterwards returned to our ships.

One of our people dying in course of the night, I returned to the King on Wednesday morning, 10th April, accompanied by the interpreter, to beg permission of him to inter the corpse, and to request he would point out to us some spot for the purpose. The King, who was encircled by a number of people, replied, that as the captain was at liberty to dispose of himself and all his subjects, he might with full propriety do what he pleased with their lands. I added that, before we could bury the defunct, it would be necessary we should consecrate the ground, and erect a cross there. The King not only gave his approbation to this measure, but stated that, as well as we did, he would adore the cross.

We consecrated, as well as we were able, the whole ground in the town set apart for sepulture of the dead, according to the rites of the church, that we might inspire the Indians with a good opinion of us, and here we interred the dead body. The same evening we again buried another.

173--To America and Around the World

Having this day landed a quantity of our merchandise, we placed them in a house assigned for the purpose by the King, which he took under his protection, as well as four men which the captain left in it for the purpose of trading by wholesale. These people, who are great lovers of justice, have their weights and measures. Their scales are made of a beam of wood supported in the middle by a cord. At one end is the scale to receive the things to be weighed, on the other a leaden weight equivalent to that of the scale, to which the different weights are suspended. They have likewise their measures of length and capacity.

The inhabitants of these islands are addicted to pleasure and idleness. We have already remarked the manner in which the girls play on the gongs: they have also a species of bag-pipe which much resembles ours, and which they call *subin*.

Their houses are constructed with beams, planks, and reeds, and are like ours divided into apartments. They are raised on posts; so that beneath them there is an empty space, which serves as a farm and poultry-yard, in which they keep their hogs, goats, and fowls.

We were told that in these seas are birds of a black color, resembling our crows, which, when the whale appears on the surface of the water, watch the moment it opens its mouth to fly into it, and thence proceed directly to pluck out its heart, which they carry away with them to some other spot to feed upon. The only proof they have however of this fact is their having seen this black bird feeding on the heart of the whale, and their finding the whale dead and without a heart. They add that this bird is called *lagan*; that it has a dentated beak, and a black skin; but that its flesh is white and fit to eat.

On Friday we opened our warehouse, and exhibited our different merchandise, which excited much admiration among the islanders. For brass, iron, and other weighty articles, they gave us gold in exchange: our trinkets, and articles of a lighter kind, were bartered for rice, hogs, goats, and other edibles. For 14 pounds of iron we received 10 pieces of gold, of the value of a ducat and a half. The captain-general forbade too great an anxiety for receiving gold; without which order every sailor would have parted with all he had to obtain this metal, which would have ruined our commerce forever.

The King having promised our captain to embrace the Christian faith, Sunday the 14th of April was fixed upon for the ceremony. With this intent a scaffold was raised, in the place we had already consecrated, which was covered with tapestry and branches of palm. About

40 of us landed, exclusive of two men armed cap-a-pie, who preceded the royal standard. At the instant of our landing the vessels fired a general salute, which did not fail of alarming the islanders. The captain and the King embraced. We ascended the scaffold, on which were placed two chairs for them, covered with green and blue velvet. The chiefs of the island were seated on cushions, and the rest of the assemblage on mats.

The captain then told the King that among the other advantages that would accrue to him from embracing the Christian faith would be that of his being strengthened, so as with greater facility to overcome his enemies. The King answered, that without this consideration he felt himself disposed to become a Christian; but that he certainly should be much pleased at being enabled to enforce respect from different chiefs of the island who refused him homage, saying they were men as well as himself, and would not obey his mandates. The captain having summoned them before him, gave them, through the interpreter, to understand that, if they failed in obeying the King as their liege lord, he would cause them all to be put to death, and give their possessions to the King. Upon this the intimidated chiefs universally promised to acknowledge the King's authority.

The captain furthermore promised the King that, after he should have returned to Spain, he would come back to his country with forces far more considerable, and that he would render him the most powerful monarch in all these islands; a recompense which he considered due to him for being the first who had embraced the Christian faith. The King, raising his hands to heaven, returned him thanks, and earnestly entreated him to leave some of his people behind him, to instruct him in the mysteries of the Christian religion; which the captain promised he would do, but on condition that two of the sons of the chief men in the island should be allowed to accompany him to Spain, where they should be taught the Spanish language, in order that on their return they might give account of all they might see and hear.

After erecting a large cross in the middle of the place, a proclamation was issued ordering that all who were inclined to become Christians should destroy their idols and substitute the cross in their stead. The captain then taking the King by the hand, conducted him to the platform, where he was dressed entirely in white, and was baptized, together with the King of Massana, the Prince his nephew, the Moorish merchant, and others, in number 500. The King, who was called Rajah Humabon, received the name of Charles, after the

Emperor: the others received other names. Mass was afterwards celebrated, after which the captain invited the King to dinner; but his Majesty excused himself, accompanying us however to the boats which took us back to the squadron, on which another general salute was fired.

Soon as we had dined we went on shore in great numbers, with our almoner, to baptize the queen and other women. We ascended the platform with them. I showed the Queen a small image of the Virgin with the infant Jesus, with which she was much affected and delighted. She begged it of me to replace her idols, and with great willingness I acceded to her request. The Queen received the name of Jane, from the mother of the Emperor; the Prince's spouse that of Catherine, and the Queen of Massana that of Isabella. On that day we baptized altogether more than 800 persons, men, women, and children.

The Queen, a young and handsome woman, was completely dressed in black and white cloth; on her head she wore a very large hat in the shape of an umbrella, formed of the leaves of the palm-tree, and surmounted by a triple crown formed of similar leaves and resembling the papal tiara. This hat she constantly wears, never going abroad without it. Her mouth and nails were of a very lively red.

Towards evening the King and Queen came to the sea-shore where we were, and listened with satisfaction to the innocent noise of our guns, a noise which before had occasioned them so much alarm.

At this time all the inhabitants of Zubu and the neighboring islands were baptized, those of one village in one of the islands alone excepted, who refused obedience to the injunctions of the King or our captain-general: after burning the village, a cross was erected on the spot, because it was a village of idolaters; if the inhabitants had been Moors, i.e. Mahometans, a pillar of stone would have been raised to mark the hardness of their hearts.

The captain-general landed every day to hear mass, on which occasion many new Christians also attended, for whom he made a kind of catechism in which many points of our religion were explained.

One day the Queen also came in state to hear mass. She was preceded by three young girls, with each one of her hats in their hands: she was dressed in black and white, and with her head and shoulders covered by a large veil of silk striped with gold. Many women accompanied her, each wearing a small veil surmounted by a hat; they were otherwise naked, save a small girdle of palm cloth about their middle: their hair hung loose. The Queen, after bowing to the altar, seated herself on a cushion of embroidered silk; and the captain sprinkled her and her attendants with rose water, a scent in which the women of this country much delight.

That the King might obtain more respect and be better obeyed, our captain-general caused him to attend mass one day dressed in silk, and ordered his two brothers to be conducted to the ceremony, one of whom was called Bondora, and was the father of the hereditary prince, the other Cadaro; with these also were brought thither several chiefs, whose names were Simicut, Sibuaia, Sisacai, Magalibe, etc. From these severally he exacted on the altar an oath to obey the King; after which all of them kissed his hand.

The captain next caused the King of Zubu to swear that he would continue submissive and faithful to the King of Spain. After his having taken this oath, the captain-general drew his sword before the King of Spain. After his having taken this oath, the captain-general drew his word before the image of Our Lady, and told the King that after a similar engagement, a man ought rather to die than sail in observance of it; and that for his part he was ready to undergo a thousand deaths rather than falsify an oath thus sworn by the image of Our Lady, by the life of the Emperor his master, and by his own habit. He then made him a present of a velvet chair, recommending him to cause it to be carried before him by one of his chiefs wherever he went, and instructing him how this was to be effected.

The King promised the captain to do exactly as he was desired; and to give him a fresh mark of his personal attachment to him, he caused some jewels to be worked, which he designed as a present for him: these consisted of two gold pendants for the ears, of pretty large size, two bracelets of gold for the arms, and two others for the small of the leg, all of them ornamented with precious stones. These rings are the chief ornaments of the Kings of these islands, who constantly go naked and without any shoes or stockings, their only vestment being a bit of cloth which hangs down from the waist to the knees.

The captain, who had directed the King and the other newly made Christians to burn their idols, which they had promised to do, seeing they not only continued to preserve them but made sacrifices to them of meat according to custom, complained loudly of and highly blamed this breach of promise. They did not deny the fact; but sought to excuse themselves by saying, it was not on their own account they made these sacrifices; but for a sick person to whom they hoped the idols would restore health. This sick man was the brother of the

Prince, who was looked upon as the wisest and most valiant personage in the island; and his illness had attained such a height that four days had already elapsed since he had lost his speech.

The captain hearing this, animated with holy zeal, said, if they had truly faith in Jesus Christ, they must immediately burn all their idols and cause the sick man to be baptized, who would then recover. He moreover added that he was so perfectly convinced of what he said, that he would consent to lose his head if what he promised did not immediately take place. The King consented to all he required. We then made a procession with all imaginable pomp from the place where we were to the house of the sick man, whom we found in reality in a very sad condition, such indeed that he could neither speak nor move. We baptized him, together with two of his wives and his ten daughters. The captain then asked him how he found himself, and he answered, of a sudden recovering his speech, that, thanks to the Lord, he found himself very well. We were all of us ocular witness of this miracle. The captain then, with greater fervor than the rest of us, returned praise to God. He administered a restorative cordial to the sick man, and repeated the same every day until he was perfectly recovered. He at the same time sent him a mattress, blankets, a coverlid of yellow linen, and a pillow.

On the fifth day the sick man was perfectly recovered and quitted his couch. His first care was to cause an idol which was held in great veneration, and which was secreted with greatest care by some old women in his hose, to be burned in presence of the King and all the people. He likewise caused several temples to be demolished which were built on the margin of the sea, and where the people assembled to eat the meat offerings presented to the idols. All the inhabitants approved of these doings, and determined on utterly destroying every idol, those even which ornamented the King's house, crying at the same time, "Viva la Castilla," in honor of the King of Spain.

The idols of these countries are of wood hollowed behind; their arms and legs are extended and their feet turned up; they have a disproportionately large face with four very large teeth in front similar to those of the wild boar. Generally speaking they are painted.

Now I am speaking of their idols, I shall relate to your lordship some of their superstitious, one of which is blessing the hog. The ceremony begins with beating large gongs. Three large dishes are afterwards brought, two of which contain broiled fish, and cakes or rice and millet folded in leaves; on the third are Cambayan cloths and two fillets of cloth made from the palm tree. Two old women then advance, each of which holds in her hand a large trumpet of bamboo. They place themselves upon the cloth, salute the sun, and clothe themselves in the other cloths which were in the dish. The first of these old women covers her head with a handkerchief tied round her forehead in such manner as to present two horn; and taking another handkerchief in her hand she dances, and at the same time sounds the trumpet, invoking the sun at intervals. The other old woman takes one of the fillets of palm tree cloth, and in a like manner dances and sounds the trumpet, and turning towards the sun addresses some words to that luminary. The fist then snatches up the other fillet of palm tree cloth, throws away the handkerchief she held in her hand, and both together the two sound the trumpets and dance round the hog, which is tied and lies on the ground. In the mean time the first old woman addresses the sun in a low tone of choice, and is answered by the other. After this a cup of wine is presented to the first which she takes, but without stopping her dancing or her addresses to the sun, and brings the cup to her mouth four or five times pretending to drink, but the liquor she pours over the heart of the hog. She then return the cup and receives a lance which she brandishes, still continuing to dance and speak, and directs it repeatedly to the heart of the hog, which in the end she pierces with a sudden and forcible blow. As soon as the lance is withdrawn from the wound it is closed and dressed with salutary herbs. During the whole of this ceremony a flambeau is kept burning, which the old woman, who pierced the hog through the heart, seizes and extinguishes by thrusting it into the mouth of the animal. The other old woman dips the end of her trumpet in the blood of the hog, and with the blood on it stains the forehead of all persons present, beginning with her husband; but she did not come towards us. This being finished, the two old women undress themselves, eat what had been brought in the two first plates, and then invite the women, but not the men, to partake with them. The hog is then seared. Never is this animal eaten before it has undergone a similar purification, and none but old women officiate on the occasion.

At the death of one of their chiefs the ceremonies practiced are, likewise, very singular, as I have myself witnessed. The most distinguished women in the country repaired to the house of the defunct, in the middle of which the corpse was placed in a case, round which a barrier of cords was made. To these cords branches of trees were fastened; and between these branches hangings of cotton were suspended so as to form alcoves. Beneath these alcoves the women alluded to seated themselves, covered with a white cloth. Each woman was attended by a servant who cooled her with a fan of palm. The other women with mournful countenances were seated round the chamber. One among them had a knife with which she gradually cut off the hair of the dead. Another, who had been the principal wife of the deceased, (for though a man many have as many wives as he pleases, there is but one mistress), stretched herself in such a manner on the corpse that her mouth, hands, and feet were opposed to those of the dead. While the one was cutting off his hair, the other was crying; and she began to sing as soon as the work was completed. All round the chamber vases of porcelain were placed containing fire, into which at intervals myrrh, storax, and gum benjamin were cast, which diffused a most pleasing fragrance. These ceremonies continue five or six days, during which the corpse remains in the house; I believe the precaution is used of embalming it with camphor to prevent putrefaction. At length the body is fastened down with wooden pins and interred in the cemetery, which is an enclosure covered with canopies.

We were assured that every night a black bird, the size of a crow, came at midnight and perched on the houses, and by its screams frightened the dogs, who never ceased barking till break of day. We never were able to learn the cause of this singular phenomenon of which we were all of us witness.

I shall mention another of their strange customs. I have already said that these Indians go naked, or with only a piece of cloth of the palm to cover their privities. All the men, young as well as old, have a sort of fibula consisting of a bar of gold or tin of the size of a goose quill, which traverses the prepuce from one side to the other over the glans, leaving an opening in the middle for the passage of the urine; this bar, at the two ends, is fastened by means of heads similar to those of our large nails; these even are oftentimes jagged with points so as to represent a star.

They informed me that this extraordinary ornament is never removed, not even in the act of coition; that it was their wives who invented and insisted on this usage; and that it was they themselves who prepared their children for its affixture from their early infancy; what, however, is certain, notwithstanding this strange invention, all the women gave us a preference to their husbands.

Provisions abound in this island. Besides the animals I have already mentioned, there are dogs and cats which, like the others, are both of them eaten. There also grow rice, millet, panicle, and maize, oranges, lemons, sugar canes, cocoa nuts, pompions, garlic and ginger; honey also abounds, with various other productions; palm wine is made; and a great quantity of gold is collected.

When any of us went on shore, whether it happened by day or by night, the Indians constantly invited us to eat and drink. They never thoroughly dress their meat, and salt it very much, which excites them to drink, and at their meals they drink often, by means of hollow reeds, from the vases which contain their wine. The commonly remain 5 or 6 hours at table.

In this island are many villages, the chiefs of each of which are one or several in number, and persons much respected. The following are the names of the villages and their respective chiefs: *Cingapola*, its chiefs Cilaton, Cighibucan, Cimanenga, Cimaticat, and Cicanbul; *Mandani*, its chief Aponoan; *Lalan*, its chief Teten; *Lalutan*, its chief Japaa; and *Lubucin*, the chief of which is Cilumai. All these villages were subjects to us, and paid us a kind of tribute.

Contiguous to the island Zubu is another called *Matan*, which has a port of the same name, in which our vessels laid at anchor. The chief village of this island is likewise called Tatan, over which Zula and Cilapulapu presided as chiefs. In this island the village of Bulaia was situate, which we burnt.

On Friday 26th April, Zula, one of these chiefs, sent one of his sons with two goats to the captain-general, and observed, that if he did not send him the whole of what he had promised, the blame was not to be imputed to himself, but to the other chief Cilapulapu, who would not acknowledge the authority of the King of Spain: he further stated, that if the captain-general would only send to his assistance the following night a boat with some armed men, he would engage to beat and entirely subjugate his rival.

On receiving this message the captain-general determined on going himself with these boats. We entreated him not to hazard his person on this adventure, but he answered, that as a good pastor he ought not to be away from his flock.

At midnight we left the ship 60 in number, armed with helmets and cuirasses. The Christian King, the Prince his nephew, and several Chiefs of Zubu, with a number of armed men, followed us in 20 or 30 balanghays. We reached Matan three hours before day. The captain would not then begin the attack; but he sent the Moor on shore to inform Cipapulapu and his people, that if he would acknowledge the sovereignty of the King of Spain, obey the Christian King of Zubu, and pay the tribute he demanded, they should be looked upon as friends, otherwise they should experience the strength of our lancers. The islanders, nothing intimidated, replied, they had lances as well as we, although they were only sticks of bamboo pointed at the end, and staves hardened in the fire. They merely requested that they might not be attacked in the night, as they expected reinforcements, and should then be better able to cope with us: this they said designedly to induce us to attack them immediately, in hope that thus we should fall in the dikes they had dug between the sea and their houses.

We accordingly waited day-light, when we jumped into the water up to our thighs, the boats not being able to approach near enough to land, on account of the rocks and shallows. The number which landed was 49 only, as 11 were left in charge of the boats. We were obliged to wade some distance through the water before we reached the shore.

We found the islanders, 1500 in number, formed into three battalions, who immediately on our landing fell upon us, making horrible shouts; two of these battalions attacked us in flank, and the third in front. Our captain divided his company into two platoons. The musketeers and cross-bowmen fired from a distance the space of half an hour without making the least impression on the enemy; for though the balls and arrows penetrated their bucklers made of thin wood, and even wounded them at times in their arms, this did not make them halt, as the wounds failed of occasioning them instant death as they expected, on the contrary, it only made them more bold and furious. Moreover, trusting to the superiority of their numbers, they showered on us such clouds of bamboo lances, staves hardened in the fires, stones, and even dirt, that it was with difficulty we defended ourselves. Some even threw spears headed with iron at our captain-general, who, to intimidate and cause them to disperse, ordered away a party of our men to set fire to their houses, which they immediately effected. The sight of the flames served only to increase their exasperation: some of them even ran to the village which was set on fire, and in which 20 or 30 houses were consumed, and killed two of our men on the spot. They seemed momentarily to increase in number and impetuosity. A poisoned arrow struck the captain in the leg, who on this ordered a retreat in slow and regular order; but the majority of our men took to flight precipitously, so that only seven or eight remained about the captain.

The Indians perceiving their blows were ineffectual when aimed at our body or head, on account of our amour, and noticing at the same time that our legs were uncovered, directed against these their arrows, javelins, and stones, and these in such abundance, that we could not guard against them. The bombards we had in our boats were of no utility, as the levelness of the strand would not admit of the boats being brought sufficiently close in shore. We retreated gradually, still continuing to fight, and were now at a bow's-shot from the islanders, and in the water up to our knees, when they renewed their attack with fury, throwing at us the same lance five or six times over as they picked it up on advancing. As they knew our captain, they chiefly aimed at him, so that his helmet was twice struck from his head; still he did not give himself up to despair, and we continued in a very small number fighting by his side. This combat, so unequal, lasted more than an hour. An islander at length succeeded in thrusting the end of his lance through the bars of his helmet, and wounding the captain in the forehead, who irritated on the occasion, immediately ran the assailant through the body with his lance, the lance remaining in the wound. He now attempted to draw his sword, but was unable, owing to his right arm being grievously wounded. The Indians, who perceived this, pressed in crowds upon him; and one of them having given him a violent cut with a sword on the left leg, he fell on his face: on this they immediately fell upon him. Thus perished our guide, our light, and our support. On falling, and seeing himself surrounded by the enemy, he turned towards us several times, as if to know whether we had been able to save ourselves. As there was not one of those who remained with him but was wounded, and as we were consequently in no condition either to afford him succor or revenge his death, we instantly made for our boats, which were on the point of putting off. To our captain indeed did we owe our deliverance, as the instant he fell, all the islanders rushed towards the spot where he laid.

The Christian King had it in his power to render us assistance, and this he would no doubt have done; but the captain general, far from foreseeing what was about to happen when he landed with his people, had ordered him not to leave his balanghay, but merely to remain a spectator of our manner of fighting. His Majesty bitterly bewailed his fate on seeing him fall.

But the glory of Magellan will survive him. He was adorned with every virtue; in midst of the greatest adversity he constantly possessed an immoveable firmness. At sea he subjected himself to the same privations as his men. Better skilled than any one in the knowledge of nautical charts, he was a perfect master or navigation, as he proved in making the tour of the world, an attempt on which none before him had ventured.

This unfortunate battle took place on the 27th April 1521, which fell on a Saturday, a day chosen by the captain himself, being that which he held most propitious to his enterprise. Eight of our men, and four of the Indians, who had received baptism, presided with him; and few of those who remained regained the ships without being wounded. The men who were in the boats attempted, when they saw us pushed, to assist us by firing the bombards, but the distance was so great from which they fired, that they did us more harm than to the enemy, who nevertheless lost 15 men.

In the afternoon the Christian king, with our consent, caused to be intimated to the people of Matan, that if they would restore the bodies of our dead soldiers, and especially of our captain-general, we would give them whatever merchandise they required; but they answered, that they could not be induced by any consideration, to part with the body of a man like our chief, which they would preserve as a monument of their victory over us.

On learning the death of our captain, those who were left in the town to carry on trade, caused all their merchandise immediately to be transported on board. We then elected in his stead two governors, that is to say, Odoard Barbosa, a Portuguese, and Juan Serano, a Spaniard.

Our interpreter, called Henry, the salve of Magellan, having been slightly wounded in the battle, made this a pretence for going no more on shore, where his presence was necessary for our service, and passed the whole day in idleness extended on his mat. Odoard Barbosa, commander of Magellan's ship, reprimanded him severely on the occasion, and told him, that though his master was dead he was still a slave, and that on their return to Spain, he would deliver him up to Donna D. Beatrix, the wife of Magellan; he moreover threatened to have him beaten with rods, if he did not immediately go on shore for the service of the squadron.

The slave hereupon arose, and seemed to hold no resentment for the reprimand and menaces of the commander. On landing he repaired to the Christian King, whom he told that we intended shortly to take our departure, and that, if his advice was taken, he might render himself master of all our vessels and merchandise. The King turned a favoring ear to his proposals, and conjointly they laid a plot against us. The slave then returned on board, and showed greater activity and more understanding than we had ever notice in him before.

On the morning of Wednesday, 1st May, the Christian King sent to our two governors, to inform them that he had prepared a present of precious stones for the King of Spain, and that he might deliver it into their hands, he begged them to come that day and dine with him, and bring with them some of their suite. They accordingly went, taking with them our astrologer, San Martino of Seville, and, of the different ships companies, as many as made up 24 for the entire number of the party. I was not one on the occasion, my face being swollen by a wound I had received from a poisoned arrow on the forehead. John Carvajo and the provost, suspecting the Indians of entertaining some bad intentions, returned immediately to the ships; it seems their suspicions arose from having seen the nobleman who had been miraculously spared, separate the almoner from the party.

Scarcely had they related thus much to us on board, ere we heard loud cries and moans. Heaving anchor immediately, we laid the vessels close in with the shore, and fired a number of shot at the houses. We then saw Juan Serano, whom they were leading, wounded and tied hand and foot, towards the shore. He entreated us to desist from firing, as otherwise, he said, he should be massacred. We enquired what had become of his companions and the interpreter, and learned that the former had all been murdered, and that the interpreter had taken part with the natives. He conjured us to ransom him with merchandise; but Johan Carvajo, though his fellow gossip, joined with others in refusing to treat his release, and would not allow any of our boats to approach the shore. The reason for this conduct of Carvajo was, in case of the death of the two governors, the command of the squadron developed on himself. Juan Serano continued to implore the compassion of his fellow-gossip, by assuring him he should be massacred the instant we set sail; and finding at length that all his entreaties were vain, he uttered deep imprecations, and appealed to the Almighty on the great day of judgment, to exact account of his soul from Johan Carvajo, his fellow-gossip. He was however disregarded; and we set sail without ever hearing afterwards what became of him.

The Island of Zubu is large; it has an excellent port, with two entrances to it, the one on the west, the other on the northeast. It lies in 10 degrees of latitude north, and in 154 degrees of longitude from the line of demarcation. In this island it was, before the death of Magellan, that we obtained the first intelligence respecting the Molucca Islands.

Book III

From our Departure from Zubu,
to our leaving the Islands of Molucca.

On quitting the island of Zubu, we proceeded to an anchorage off the point of an island called Bohol, 18 leagues distant from Zubu; and, seeing our crews were diminished so greatly by the losses we had sustained as to be no longer adequate to manning the three vessels, we determined on burning the Conception, after taking out of her whatever was serviceable. We then steered south-south-west, coasting along an island called Panilongon, the inhabitants of which are as black as Ethiopians.

Continuing our course, we came to an island called Butuan, where we cast anchor. The King of the island came on board our ship, and, as a symbol of friendship and alliance, drew blood from his left hand, with which he besmeared his breast, and touched the tip of his tongue, a ceremony which we initiated. We then entered a river, in which we saw a number of men fishing, who offered fish to the King. The King, like all the inhabitants of this and the neighboring islands, was naked, wearing nothing but a piece of cloth which concealed his sex, which even he laid aside, as did the chiefs of the island who were with him; after which they seized their oars and began rowing, singing at the same time. We passed by a number of houses built on the side of the river, and at two hours after night fall reached the King's house, which was two leagues distant from our anchorage.

When about to enter the house, we were met by a number of attendants carrying flambeaux made of canes and palm leaves rolled up, and enclosing gum anime. While supper was preparing, the King, with two of his chiefs and two of his wives, who were tolerably pretty, emptied a large vase full of palm wine without eating. They invited me to drink with them, but I excused myself by observing, that I had already supped, and drank only once. In drinking they observed the same ceremony as the King of Massana. The supper was composed of rice, and fish highly salted, served up in China bowls. The rice they ate in lieu of bread. The manner in which they cook their rice as follows: in an earthen pot, similar to our stew-pans, they first put a large leaf, which entirely covers the inside; in this they place the rice and water, and cover the pot; the rice is then suffered to boil till it attains the consistence of our bread, and is taken out in lumps. This is the manner in which rice is cooked in all the islands of these parts.

Supper ended, the King caused a mat or reeds to be brought in, with another of palm, and a pillow made of palm leaves. This was for my couch, on which I laid down to rest with one of the chiefs. The King went to rest in another apartment with his two wives.

The next day, before dinner, I made an excursion into the island; I entered several houses, which were built in the same manner as those before described in the islands we had previously visited, and in which I saw many utensils of gold, but few provisions. I afterwards rejoined the King, and dined with him on rice and fish.

I succeeded, by signs, in making the King comprehend that I wished to see the Queen, and in a similar manner he intimated his consent; we, in consequence, proceeded towards the summit of a mountain where was her abode. On entering I bowed to her, and she returned the compliment. I sat beside her while she was employed in making mats of palm for a bed. Her house was handsomely furnished with vases of porcelain, which were suspended form the sides of the apartments, as were four gongs, one of which was very large, another of a middling size, and two others small. She had a number of slaves of both sexes wait on her. We took our leave and returned to the King's house, and breakfasted on sugar-canes.

We found in this island hogs, goats, rice, ginger, and in short every thing we had seen on the others. What, however, most abounds is gold. Vallies were pointed out to me, in which, by signs, they made me comprehend there were more lumps of gold than we had hairs on our heads; but that, for want of iron, they mines exact greater labor to work than they feel inclined to bestow.

In the afternoon, on my requesting to go on board of ship, the King, with several chiefs of the island, offered to accompany me in their balanghay. As we fell down the river I saw on a small mount on the right three men hanging from a tree. On enquiring the reason of this, I learnt they were malefactors.

This part of the island, which is called Chipit, is a continuation of the same land as that on which Butuan and Calayan are situate: it stretched above Boho. and approaches Massana. The port is a tolerably good one. It is situate in 8 degrees of latitude north, longitude 167 degrees from the line of demarcation, and is 50 leagues distant from Zuba. In the north-west lies the island of Luzon two days sail away. This island is large, and every year there arrive at it six or eight junks from the people called Lequies, for the purpose of trafficking. I shall speak of Chipit in another place.

On leaving this island, steering west-south-west, we came to an anchor off an island almost a desert. The inhabitants, who are very few in number, consist of Moors banished from an island called Burne (Borneo). They go naked like the inhabitants of the other islands, and for their arms use sarbacanes and arrows, for which they have quivers, that likewise serve to hold the herbs with which their arrows are poisoned. They also have poignards, their handles wrought with gold and precious stones, lances, clubs, and small breast-plates made of the buffalo's hide. They looked upon us as gods or saints. In this island the trees grow to a great size, but provisions are scarce. It is situate in latitude 7 degrees 30 minutes north, and 43 leagues from Chipit; it is called Cayayan.

Leaving this island, and continuing the same course, that is to say west-south-west, we arrived at a large island, in which we found abundance of all kinds of provisions; this to us was fortunate, for we were so hungry and so badly provided with food, that we were several times on the point of abandoning our ships and establishing ourselves in some of these countries there to end our days. This island, which is called Palaoan, furnished us with hogs, goats, fowls, bananas of several species; some of these were a cubit in length and as thick as a man's arm; others were but a span in length, while others again, and these were the most excellent, were of still inferior size. It likewise produces coca-nuts, sugar-canes, and roots similar to turnips. They cook their rice in hot embers, placing it in canes or wooden bowls, and find, by this process, that it keeps much longer than when boiled in pots. From the same rice also, by means of an alembic, they extract a wine stronger and superior to palm wine. In one word this island was to us a land of promise. It is situate in latitude 9 degrees 20 minutes north, longitude 171 degrees 20 minutes from the line of demarcation.

We presented ourselves before the King, who contracted an alliance and friendship with us; and to convince us of his sincerity, he begged a knife of us, which he made use of for drawing blood from his breast, with which he touched his forehead and tongue. We repeated the same ceremony.

The inhabitants of Palaoan, like all the other people of these parts, go naked; but they are partial to wearing ornaments, such as rings, small chains of brass, and little bells. What, however, they are most delighted with his brass wire, to which they fasten their hooks for fishing.

Almost every individual cultivates his own lands. They use sarbacanes and large wooden darts more than a span in length, headed with a harpoon; some of them have a fish-bone for a point, others a sharp piece of bamboo poisoned by means of a certain herb; these arrows are not trimmed at the end with feathers, but with a strip of very soft and light wood. To the end of the sarbacane they fasten an iron head when their arrows are expended, and use it as a lance.

They have likewise large tame cocks, which, from superstition, they do not eat; but which they keep for fighting; at mains of these birds considerable wagers are laid, and prizes are assigned to the owners of the conquerors.

From Plaoan, steering south-west, after sailing 10 leagues, we fell in with another island. On sailing along its shores, it seemed to us to ascend. We coasted along it the space of 50 leagues at least before we met with an anchorage. Scarcely had we anchored before a tempest arose. They sky was overcast, and we saw the light of Saint Elme settle on our mast.

The following day, 9th July, the King sent to the vessels a handsome pirogue, the prow and poop of which were adorned with gold. On the prow was a blue and white pavilion, surmounted by a tuft of peacocks' feathers. In this pirogue were musicians who played on the bagpipe and drums, and with them a number of other persons. The pirogue, which is a kind of galley, was followed by 2 almadies or fishing-boats. Eight of the chief people of the island who were in the pirogue came on board our vessel, and took their seats on a carpet spread for the purpose in the hind-caste, where they presented us with a wooden vase full of betel areca, which they continually chew, together with orange flowers and jessamine: the whole was covered with a cloth of yellow silk. The likewise gave to us two baskets of fowls, two goats, three vases of distilled wine, and some sugar canes. To the other vessel they made a similar present, and after embracing us they went their ways.

The wine extracted from rice is as clear as water, but so strong that many of our crew were intoxicated with a very moderate use of the liquor. The name they give it is *arach*.

Six days after, the King sent three other pirogues beautifully ornamented, which were rowed round our vessels, the musicians on board playing all the while on the bagpipe, gongs, and drums. The people on board saluted us by taking off their caps, which are so little they scarcely cover the top of the head. We returned the salute with a discharge of bombards, but without loading them with stones. They brought us several different dishes of rice, variously prepared, now in oblong pieces enveloped in leaves, now in the shape of a sugar loaf, and now made into cakes with eggs and honey.

After these presents on the part of the King, they informed us that he readily granted us permission to wood and water on his island, and that we were at liberty to trade to any extent with the inhabitants. On this intimation seven of us were dispatched with present for the King, the Queen, and their ministries. The present for the King consisted of a Turkish dress of green velvet, a chair covered with violet-colored silk, 5 yards of red cloth, a cap, a glass goblet gilt, and three quires of paper; that for the Queen consisted of three yards of yellow cloth, a pair of shoes embroidered with silver, and a silver etwee full of pins. For the chief minister we carried three yards of red cloth, a cap, and a glass goblet gilt; for the king at arms, or herald, who came with the pirogue, a Turkish dress of red and green cloth, a cap, and a quire of paper; for the seven others personages who came with him, we likewise took presents, some yards of cloth for example, a cap each, and a quire of paper. When all the present were ready, we entered one of the three pirogues.

On reaching the town we were forced to wait two hours in the pirogue for the arrival of two elephants covered with silk, and 12 men, each of which was the bearer of a vase of porcelain covered with silk, to hold our presents. We ascended the backs of the elephants, preceded by the 12 men who carried our presents, and in this manner proceeded to the house of the minister, who had a supper consisting of several dishes served up for us. We slept on mattresses stuffed with cotton and covered with silk, and for coverlids had Cambaian chintzes.

The next day we spent the morning idly at the minister's house; at noon we proceeded to the King's palace. We rode on the same elephant as brought us from the pirogues, preceded by the men who carried our presents. From the governor's house to the King's palace all the streets were lined with men armed with lances, swords, and clubs by special order of the King.

We entered the court of the palace on our elephants, where alighting, we ascended a flight of stairs accompanied by the governor and some officers: we afterwards were ushered into a large saloon full of courtiers, which we should denominate barons of the kingdom: here we seated ourselves on a carpet, and the presents were place near us.

At the extremity of this saloon was another apartment, somewhat smaller, hung with silk, where two curtains of brocade pulled up, exhibited two windows which gave light to the apartment. We saw here 300 of the King's guards armed with poignards, the point of which they rested on their thighs. At the extremity of this apartment was a large door covered by a curtain of brocade, which, as those of the windows, had been before was drawn up, and showed us the King seated at a table with a small child, and chewing betel: behind him there were only women.

One of the couriers then informed us that we were not allowed to address the King; but if we had any thing we wished to communicate to him we might deliver its substance to him; that he should then tell it to a courtier of higher rank, who would repeat it to the brother of the governor's, a minister who was in the small apartment, and who, by means of a sarbacane fixed in a hole in the wall, would impart it to one of the principal officers about the King's person, to be by him reported to the King.

He informed us that we had to make three inclinations to the King, at the same time raising our hands joined together above our heads, and raising first the one and then the other leg. Having complied with these requisite ceremonies, we informed His Majesty that we were subjects of the King of Spain, who desired to live in friendship with him, and asked nothing farther than the liberty of carrying on a commerce with his island.

The King replied, that he was well pleased that His Majesty of Spain sought his friendship; and informed us that we were welcome to wood and water in his dominions, and to follow any traffic we chose.

We then presented to him the different things we had brought; and on each separate article being displayed, he made a slight movement of the head. To each of us was given brocade, with cloths of silk and gold, which were first laid on our left shoulder, and afterwards taken off to preserve for us. A breakfast of cloves and cinnamon was then placed before us, after which all the curtains were let down, and the windows closed.

All those who were in the King's palace had a cloth of gold tied round their waists to conceal their privities, poignards with golden handles, set with pearls and precious stones, and a number of rings on their fingers.

We now again mounted the elephants, and returned to the governor's house. Seven men, who bore the present made us by the King, marched before us; and when we came to the governor's house, the present intended by his Majesty for each of us was, as before, laid on our left shoulder.

We afterwards saw nine men coming to the house where we were, each carrying a tray of wood, with on it 10 or 11 bowls of porcelain, containing different kinds of meat, that is to say, veal, capons, fowls, pea-fowls, and others, with many kinds of fish; of flesh and fowl alone there were upwards of 30 different kinds.

We supped off the floor, seated on a mat of palm. After each mouthful, as was their custom, we sipped some of the spirit distilled from rice out of a porcelain cup, about the size of an egg. We likewise ate some rice and other articles, prepared with sugar, using golden spoons for the purpose, similar to those with us.

We slept in the same place we had done the night before; and in this apartment two wax flambeaux were constantly kept burning in silver candlesticks, and two large lamps supplied with oil, and with four different lights to each. Two men kept watch all night long to attend to them.

The next day we repaired to the sea shore, where we found two pirogues destined to carry us on board our ships.

The city is built in the sea, the King's palace and the houses of the principal persons expected. It contains 2500 hearths, or families. The houses are built of wood upon large piles, to keep them from the water. When the tide rises, the women, who are the chief vendors of necessaries, traverse the town in boats. In front of the King's palace is a large wall, built with bricks of great size, with embrazures, or rather port-holes, as in a fortress; and on the wall are mounted 56 bombards of brass, and six of iron: in course of the two days we passed in the city, they made several discharges from these guns.

The King, who is a Mahometan, is called Rajah Siripada. He is very corpulent, and may be about 40 years of age. He is waited upon by the women alone, the daughters of the chief inhabitants of the island. No one is allowed to address him otherwise than in the manner I have described, through a sarbacane. He has ten secretaries constantly employed on different matters of state, who write on a very thin epidermis of certain trees which is called chiritoles. He never leaves his palace upon any occasion other than to hunt.

On the morning of the 29th July we saw more than a 100 pirogues advancing towards us, divided into three squadrons, with as many tungulis, which is the denomination given to their small barks. As we were apprehensive of some treacherous attack, we immediately set sail, and that in such haste that we left one of our anchors. Our suspicions increased on paying attention to several large junks, which they day before had come to an anchor in the rear of our ships, and which made us fearful of being assailed from all sides at once. Our first care was to relieve ourselves from the junks, at which we fired and killed a number of those on board. We made prize of four junks; four others saved themselves by running on shore. In one of the junks taken by us was the son of the King of Lozon, who was the captain-general of the King of Burne, and who with his junks had come from subduing a large city called Laoe, built on a point of the island opposite to Great Java. In this expedition he pillaged the city on account of its inhabitants preferring obedience to the Gentile King of Java, and disowning the authority of the King of Burne.

Johan Carvajo, our pilot, without consulting us, restored the captain to liberty, having been induced to this measure, as we after-wards learnt, by a bribe of a large sum in gold. Had we retained this captain, the Rajah Siripada would no doubt have given any thing we might have required for his ransom; for he had rendered himself formidable to the Gentiles, who are perpetually at was with the Mahometan king.

In the port in which we were, there was another city, inhabited by Gentiles, like that of the King of Siripada, built in the sea, and of much greater size than the capital of the Mahometan King. The King of the Gentiles is equally potent as his neighbor, but is not so ostentatious; nay, it appears probable that Christianity might with much facility be introduced in this country.

The Mahometan King, on being informed of the damage we had done his junks, caused us to be informed by one of our people settled on shore for the purpose of trade, that his vessels had had no hostile intentions towards us, but were merely on their way to attack the Gentiles; in evidence of which some of the heads of these people who had been killed in battle were shown us. We then sent word to the King, that if this was the case, he had only to sen away the two men who were on shores with our merchandise, and the son of Johan Carvajo, but this the King refused. Thus was Johan Carvajo punished by the loss of his son (born in the Brazils), and whom he undoubtedly would have recovered in exchange for the captain-general, but for his avarice and thirst after gold. We retained on board 16 of the chief men of the island and 3 women, whom we reckoned on transporting to Spain, with intention of presenting these latter to the queen; but Carvajo kept them for himself.

The Mahometans here go naked, like all the other inhabitants of this climate. They are very partial to quicksilver, which they take internally, regarding it not only as a remedy in different disorders, but also as a preservative of health. They adore Mahomet and follow his law, consequently they eat no pork. They wash their posteriors with their left hand, which they never use in eating; and when they void their urine, stoop for the purpose. Their faces they wash with the right hand; but they never rub their teeth with their fingers. They circumcise like the Jews. They never kill either goats or fowls, without first addressing the sun. They cut off the pinions of their fowls, and their feet, after which they sever them in twain. Never do they eat of any animal but such as is killed by themselves.

This island produces camphor, a sort of balsam which exudes by drops from between the bark and the wood of the tree: these drops are as small as particles of bran. If the camphor be exposed to the air it insensibly evaporates. The tree which produces it is called capor. Here also cinnamon grows, ginger, mirabolans, oranges, lemons, sugar-canes, melons, citron, radishes, onions, etc. Among the animals are elephants, horses, buffaoloes, hogs, fowls, geese, crows, and many other birds.

It is said the King of Burne has two pearls as large as pullets' eggs, and so perfectly round that when placed on a polished table, they never remain at rest. When we carried him our presents, I made sign of my desire to see them, which he promised I should do; but this never came to pass. Some of the chiefs told me they knew of them.

The Mahometans of this country have brass money perforated so as to string it. On one side it has four characters of the great King of China. This money is called *pici*. In our commerce with the Borneans for a cathil of quicksilver, they gave us six china bowls. The cathil weighs two pounds. For a quire of paper we received still more. A cathil of brass purchased a small vase of porcelain; and for three knives we obtained one of larger size: for a 160 cathils of brass we obtained a bahar (344 lbs. avoirdupois) of wax. The bahar is a weight equal to 203 cathils. For 80 cathils of brass we purchased a bahar of salt; and for 40 cathils of that metal a bahar of anime, a kind of gum used for paying of ships, for in this country they have no pitch. Twenty tabils make a cathil. The merchandises most in request here are copper, quicksilver, cannabar, glass, woollen cloths, linens, and, prized above all others, iron and magnifying glasses.

The junks we have before mentioned are their largest vessels. They are constructed in the following manner: the sides to within two spans of the dead work are of planking fastened one piece to another by wooden pins, and nicely finished: in the upper part they are formed of large bamboos, which project in a salient angle from the junk to form a counterpoise. These junks will carry as great a burthen as our vessels. The masts are made of the same bamboos, and the sails of the bark of trees.

Having noticed a considerable quantity of porcelain at Burne, I made some inquiries respecting it. I learnt it was formed of a very white kind of earth, which is left for half a century under ground to refine, so that they hence hold as a proverb, that the father buries himself for the welfare of his son. It is pretended, that if poison be put into these vases of porcelain, they immediately break.

The island of Burne is so extensive, that it requires three months to sail round it. It lies in latitude 5 degrees 15 minutes north, longitude 175 degrees, 40 minutes from the line of demarcation.

On quitting this island, we retracted our course to seek a spot fit for repairing our vessels, one of which leaked greatly, and the other, for want of a pilot, had struck on a sand bank near an island called Bibalen; but, thank God, we got it afloat again. We likewise ran a great risk of being blown up: a sailor after snuffing a candle, through inadvertence, threw the lighted wick into a case of gunpowder; but he drew it out again so quickly that the powder did not take fire.

On the way we saw four pirogues. We took one loaded with cocoa nuts destined for Burne; but the crew escaped to a small island. The three others avoided us by retiring behind some other islets.

Between the north cape of Burne and the island of Cimbonbon, in latitude 8 degrees 7 minutes north, we found a very commodious port for careening our ships; but as we were destitute of many things necessary for this purpose, it took us 42 days to finish work. Every one did his best, one taking one part, another a different one. What caused us most trouble was getting wood from the forest, as the whole country was covered with brambles and thorny bushes, and we were barefooted.

In this island there are very large boars. Of these we killed one as it was swimming from one island to another. Its head was two spans and a half in length, and its tusks very long. Here also are crocodiles, which live on land as well as in the water, oysters and shell fish of every description, and turtle of a very large size. We caught two, the meat alone of which weighed, of the one, 26, of the other, 44 pounds. We likewise caught a fish, the head of which, resembling that of a hog, had two horns. Its body was clothed with a bony substance, and on its back was a kind of saddle, but not very large.

What to me seemed more extraordinary was to see trees, the leaves of which as they fell, became animated. These leaves resemble those of the mulberry tree, except in not being so long, their stalk is short and pointed, and near the stalk on one side and the other they have two feet. Upon being touched they make away; but when crushed they yield no blood. I kept one in a box for nine days; on opening the box at the end of this time, the leaf was alive, and walking round it: I am of the opinion they live on air.

On quitting this island, that is to say the port, we fell in with a junk coming from Burne. We made signal to it to lay to; but as it paid no attention to us, we pursued, took, and pillaged it. It had on board the governor of Pulaoan, with one of his sons and his brother, whom we obliged to pay for his ransom, within the space of a week, 400 measures of rice, 20 hogs, a similar number of goats, and 150 fowls. Not only did he give us all we required, but to these he added spontaneously cocoa-nuts, bananas, sugar-canes, and vases of palm-wine. In recompense for his liberal demeanor we restored him part of his poniards and fusils, and gave him a standard, a dress of yellow damask, and 15 yards of linen. To his son we made a present of a cloak of blue cloth, etc. His brother received a dress of green cloth. We, likewise, made presents to the people who were with them, so that we parted in a friendly manner.

We steered to pass on a backward track between the island of Cagayan and the port of Chipit, our course being east by south, and our destination for the islands of Malucho. We coasted certain islets where we noticed the sea covered with herbs, notwithstanding it was here of very considerable depth: we seemed to be in another sea.

Leaving Chipit on the east, we discerned on the west the two islands of Zolo and Tahima, where, as is said, the finest pearls are fished. Here those were taken belonging to the King of Borneo, of which I have spoken; the manner in which he obtained possession of them was as follows: This King married a daughter of the King of Zolo, who one day told him that her father owned these two large pearls. The King of Burne, on hearing it, was anxious to have them, and one night he sailed with 500 vessels of armed men, seized on the person of his father-in-law and his two sons, and made the surrender of these two pearls the price of their liberation.

Keeping now a course east by north we passed by two villages called Cavit and Subanin, and sailed by an inhabited island called Motroripa, 10 leagues from the islets which I have mentioned. The inhabitants of this island build no houses; but constantly live in their boats.

The villages of Cavit and Subanin stand on the islands Bulnan and Caligan, in which the best cinnamon grows. Had we been able to remain there any time we might have loaded our vessel with that spice; but we were unwilling to lose the favorable wind which then prevailed, for we had to double a point and pass some small islands which surround it. Sailing along we saw some islanders who came off to us, and gave us 17 pounds of cinnamon for two large knives we had taken from the governor of Pulaoan.

Having seen the cinnamon tree I am enabled to give a description of it. It is from five to six feet high, and no thicker than one' finger. Never has it more than three or four branches: the leaf is similar to that of the laurel: the cinnamon we use is merely the bark of the tree, which is stripped off twice in the year. The wood itself even, and the green leaves have the same aromatic flavor as the bark. It is called by the natives *cainmana* (whence the name cinnamon is derived) from cain, which signifies wood, and man, sweet.

Changing our course now for a north-easterly direction, we steered for a town called Maingdunao, situate in the same island with Butuan and Calangan, our object in making which place was to obtain precise information respecting the site of the islands Malucho. Meeting a bignaday on our way, a bark resembling a pirogue, we determined on capturing it; but as in effecting this we encountered resistance, we killed 7 of the 18 men she had on board. The prisoners were better made, and more robust than any we had hitherto seen. They happened to be certain chiefs of Maingdunao, and among them was the king's brother, who assured us he perfectly well knew the position of the islands of Malucho.

Upon the account we received from him we changed our direction to the south-east. We were then in latitude 6 degrees 7 minutes north, 30 leagues distant from Cavit.

We were told that at a cape on this island near a river are hairy men, great warriors and excellent bowmen. They have daggers a span long, and when they make prisoners they eat the hearts of them raw with orange or lemon juice. They are called Benaians.

We passed on our way four islands, Ciboco, Beraham, Batolach, Sarangani, and Candigar. On Saturday 26th October, just after the close of day, we experienced a hurricane, during which we took in our sails, and prayed to God for protection. Hereupon we saw our three saints settle on our masts, who dispersed the darkness. They remained there upwards of two hours, Saint Elme on the main mast, Saint Nicholas on the mizen, and Saint Clare on the foremast. In gratitude for the favor they had done us, we vowed them each a slave, and accordingly made them an offering each of one.

Pursuing our course we entered a port about the middle of the island Sarangani, towards Candigar; we anchored here, near a collection of houses in Sarangani, where is abundance of pearls and gold. This port lies in latitude 5 degrees 9 minutes north, 50 leagues distant from Cavit. The people are Gentiles, and go naked like the rest of the inhabitants of these latitudes.

We stopped a day here, and seized forcibly on two pilots to conduct us to Malucho. By their advice we steered south-south-west, and threaded 8 islands partly inhabited and partly desert, which formed a kind of street. Their names are as follow: Cheava, Caviao, Cabiao, Cumunuca, Cabaluzao, Cheai, Lipan, and Nuza; at the end of this street we found ourselves opposite to a tolerably handsome island; but having a contrary wind we were unable to double the point of it, but all night long were constrained to be constantly tacking. On this occasion it was that the prisoners we had made at Sarangani jumped overboard and made their escape by swimming, together with the brother of the king of Maingdunao; but we learnt afterwards, that the son of this prince, not having been able to keep his seat on his father's back, was drowned.

Finding it impossible to double the cape of the great island, we passed to windward of it, by several small islands. This large island, which is called Sanghir, is governed by four kings, the names of whom are as follow: Raja Matandatu, Raja Laga, Raja Babti, and Raja Parabu. It lies in latitude 3 degrees 30 minutes north, 27 leagues from Sarangani.

Continuing the same course, we passed by 5 islands called Chioma, Carachita, Para, Zangalura, and Ciau, the last of which is 10 leagues distant from Sanghir. Here is seen a pretty large mountain, but of no great elevation. Its King is called Raja Ponto.

We reached the island Paghinzara, on which are three high mountains: its King is named Rajah Babintan. Twleve leagues east of Paghinzara we found, beside Talant, two small inhabited islands, Zoar and Mean.

On Wednesday, 6th November, having passed these islands we distinguished four others, pretty lofty, 15 leagues eastward of the last. The pilot, whom we had taken at Sarangani, informed us that these were the islands of Malucho. We now returned thanks to God, and as a signal of rejoicing fired a round from all our great guns; nor will it excite astonishment that we should be elated, when it is considered that we had been at sea now 27 months all but two days, and had visited an infinity of islands in search of those we had now attained.

The Portuguese have given out that the islands of Malucho are situate in midst of a sea impassable on account of shallows which every where abound, and the constant cloudiness and fogs to which the atmosphere is subject; we however found the contrary, and never had we less than 1 100 fathoms water all the way to the Malucho islands themselves.

On Friday, 8th of November, three hours before sun-set, we entered the port of an island called Tadore. We came to an anchorage near the land, in 20 fathoms water, and discharged all our guns.

The next day the King came in a pirogue and made the tour of our ships. We went to meet him in our boats to express our thanks: he caused us to enter his pirogue, in which we seated ourselves by his

201–To America and Around the World

side. He was seated under a parasol of silk, which perfectly shaded him. Before him were one of his sons, who bore the royal scepter, two men, each holding a vase of gold with water to wash his hands, and two others with two small gilt boxes containing betre (betel).

He complimented us on our arrival, telling us that a long time back he had dreamt that some ships would arrive at Malucho from a distant country; and that to be certain whether his dream was true he had consulted the moon, by which he found the vessels would actually arrive, and that it was as he expected.

He next came on board our ships, and we all of us kissed his hand. We conducted him towards the hind-castle, where, that he might not be forced to stoop, he refused to enter otherwise than through the opening at the top. There we caused him to be seated in a chair or red velvet, and threw over him a Turkish vestment of yellow velvet; and the more strongly to mark our respect we seated ourselves opposite to him on ground.

When he understood who we were, and the object of our voyage, he told us, that he himself and all his people would feel happy in the friendship of the King of Spain, and glad to be considered his vassals; that he would receive us in his island as his own children; that we might come on shore and remain there a safe as in our own houses; and that as a token of his affection for the King our Sovereign, his island should no longer bear the name of Tadore but be called Castille.

We then made a present to him of the chair on which he sat, and the dress he wore: we likewise gave him a piece of fine cloth, four yards of scarlet, a vest of brocade, a yellow damask cloth, some other Indian cloths of silk and gold, a very fine piece of Cambayan chintz, 2 caps, 6 strings of beads, 12 knives, 3 large mirrors, 6 pairs of scissors, 6 combs, some glass goblets gilt, and other things. To his son we presented a piece of Indian cloth of silk and gold, a large mirror, a cap, and 2 knives. We likewise made presents to each of the 9 personages who attended him, of a piece of silk, a cap, and 2 knives; and to the remainder of his suite, of each a cap, knife, etc. continuing our fits till the King desired us to cease. He said he was sorry that he had nothing with which to present the King of Spain that was worthy of his acceptance but himself. He recommended us to moor our vessels near the houses, and authorized us, in case any of his people should attempt to rob us during the night, to fire at them. After this he departed highly satisfied with us; but on no occasion would he bend the head, notwithstanding we frequently bowed to him. On his departure we fired a salute form all our guns.

The King is a Moor, that is to say an Arab, about 45 years of age, tolerably well made, and of handsome countenance. His dress consisted of a very fine shirt, the sleeves of which were embroidered with gold; from the waist to the feet he wore a loose drapery; his head was covered by a veil of silk, and over this veil he wore a garland of flowers. His name is Rajah Sooltaun Monzoor. He is an eminent astrologer.

On Sunday, 10th November, we had a second interview with the King, who enquired what our several appointments were, and what our pay; in which articles we satisfied his curiosity. He likewise begged us to favor him with a seal of the King and a royal standard; being solicitous, he said, that his island, as well as that of Tarenate, over which he intended to place as sovereign his grandson, who was called Calanogapi, should henceforth be subject to the King of Spain, for whom he would for the future contend: moreover, he added, if he should be so unfortunate as to be overcome, he would in his own vessels proceed to Spain, and carry with him thither the royal signet and standard. He afterwards besought us to leave with him on our departure some of our people, whom he would hold more dear than all our merchandise, which would not, as he observed, so long remind him, as the sight of these Spaniards, of our monarch the King of Spain.

Remarking our solicitude to hasten the lading of our ships with cloves, he told us, that not having a sufficient quantity in the island in a dry state to answer our demand, he would fetch more from the island Bachian, where he trusted he should find the quantity we needed.

This day being Sunday we made no purchases. The sabbath of these islander is Friday.

It will no doubt be pleasing to you, my lord, to receive information respecting the islands which produce cloves. These are 5 in number: Tarenate, Tadore, Mutir, Machian, and Bachian. Tarenate (Ternate) is the chief: the last King was sovereign of almost the whole of the other four. Tadore (Tidor), where we then were, has its own king. Mutir and Machian are independent republics; and when the Kings of Tarenate and Tadore are at war with each other, these two democratic states furnish soldiers to either party. The last of the islands is Bachian, which has its distinct sovereign. The whole of this district, in which cloves grow, is called Malucho (the Moluccas).

203–To America and Around the World

Upon our arrival at Tadore, we were told that 8 months before a Portuguese died there, of the name of Francis Serano. He was captain-general of the King of Tarenate, who was at war with the King of Tadore. Serano obliged the latter to give his daughter in marriage to the former, and most of the male children of the chief people of Tadore as hostages; by these means peace was effected. From this marriage issued the grandson of the King Calanopagi, of whom we have before spoken; but the King of Tadore never sincerely forgave Francis Sorano, and swore to be revenged: in fact some years after this occurrence, when Serano repaired one day to Tadore to buy cloves, the King had poison administered to him in leaves of betre, and he survived but 4 days. The King wished to have him interred after the custom of his country; but 3 Christian domestics, which Serano had taken with him, resisted his intention. Serano, at his death, left a boy and girl yet infants, the issue of a marriage contracted by him in the island of Java. The whole of his property consisted, almost exclusively, in 200 bahars of cloves (68,800 lbs. avoirdupois weight).

Serano was an intimate friend of, and was even related to our unfortunate captain-general; and him it was who influenced him in undertaking this voyage: for while Magellan was at Malacca, he learnt from Serano that he was at Tadore, where a very advantageous traffic might be carried on. Magellan did not lose sight of this information, when Don Emanuel refused the small increase of pay he solicited of a testoon per month; a recompense which he thought his services to the crown had amply deserved. In revenge, therefore, for the denial of a request so moderate, he repaired to Spain, and proposed to His Majesty the Emperor a voyage to Malucho by a western course, which proposition was listened to, and originated the expedition on which we sailed.

Ten days after the death of Serano, the King of Tarenate, called Rajah Abuleis, who had married the daughter of the King of Bachian, declared was against his son-in-law, and drove him out of his island. His daughter left then her exiled husband to mediate between her father and him, and while with her father for this purpose she administered poison to him, which took him off in the course of 2 days. At his death he left 9 sons: Chechili-Momuli, Jadore-Vunghi, Chechilideroix, Cilimanzoor, Cilipagi, Chialioochechilin, Catar-vajecu, Serich, and Calanogapi.

On Monday, 11th November, Chechilideroix, one of the sons of the King of Tareante whom we have before mentioned, approached our vessel with two pirogues, in which were men playing on gongs. He was dressed in a robe of red velvet. We were afterwards informed that he had with him the widow and children of Serano. Still he did not venture to come on board; and on our part we dared not to invite him without permission from the King of Tadore, who was his enemy, and in whose port we were: we consequently sent to learn his pleasure. His answer was that we had full liberty to do as we pleased. In the mean time Chechilideroix, seeing us hesitate, became suspicious, and kept a greater distance, on which we were induced to send a boat to him, with a piece of Indian cloth as a present, some mirrors, scissors, and knives, which he accepted with reluctance, and afterwards sailed away.

He had with him an Indian who had turned Christian, and was called Manuel; this man was servant to Alphonso de Lorosa, who on the death of Serano had come from Bandan to Tarenate; he understood the Portuguese, and, with the boat we sent, came on board our vessel, and informed us that the sons of the King of Tarenate, though at enmity with the King of Tadore, were well inclined to abandon the King of Portugal for the monarch of Spain. By his means we conveyed a letter to Lorosa inviting him on board, and assuring him of our friendly intentions. In the sequel we shall see that he attended to our invitation.

On enquiry into the customs of the country, I learnt that the King may have as many women as he pleases, but that only one of them is regarded as his queen, the others being reckoned slaves. Without the town he had a large house, in which were 200 of his most handsome women, with an equal number to wait upon them. The King always sits himself, or with his queen, on a sort of elevated platform, which commands a view of all his women, who are seated round him; and after dinner he selects which of them pleases him best for his companion for the night. After the King has dined, provided he allows of it, his women all eat together; otherwise each dines in her chamber by herself. No one is allowed to see the King's women but by express permission from him; and were any daring individual to approach the place of their abode, whether by day or by night, he would instantly be put to death. In order that the King's seraglio may be well supplied, each family is obliged to furnish him with one or two girls. The Rajah Sooltaun Manzoor had 26 children; of which number 8 were boys and 18 girls. In the island of Tadore there is a kind of bishop, who had 40 women and a vast number of children.

205--To America and Around the World

On Tuesday, 12th November, the King caused a shed to be raised for receiving our merchandise, which was completed in a single day. Thither we carried all we designed to barter, and 3 of our men were set to guard the same. The value fixed on the merchandise we meant to exchange for cloves was thus fixed: for 10 yards of red cloth of a fine quality, a bahar of cloves was to be received. The bahar is 4 quintals and 6 pounds, each quintal being 100 pounds. We likewise were to have in barter the same quantity of cloves for 15 yards of inferior cloth, for 15 axes, or 35 glass goblets. After this ratio we disposed of all our glass to the King. Moreover, a bahar of cloves was the price given for 17 cathil of cinnabar, for a similar weight of quicksilver, for 26 yards of linen, or 25 of a finer quality, for a 150 pair of scissors, or as many knives, for 10 yards of Guzzerat cloth, for 3 gongs, or a 100 weight of copper. We should have made great profit of our looking-glass, but most of them were broke by the way, and the residue were almost wholly appropriated to himself by the King. Part of the merchandise I have mentioned was taken out of the junks we captured. We thus carried on a highly advantageous traffic; but we should have made it still more lucrative but for our eagerness to return to Spain. Besides cloves, we every day laid in a considerable stock of provisions, the Indians constantly repairing to us in their barks, bringing goats, poultry, cocoa-nuts, bananas, and other edibles, which they gave us for things of little value. We at the same time laid in a large quantity of an extremely hot water, which after an hour's exposure to the air becomes very cold. It is pretended that this quality of the water is owing to its issuing from the mountain of cloves. In this we recognized the imposture of the Portuguese, who have studied to enforce a belief that there is no fresh water in the Malucho Islands, and that it must be obtained from very distant countries.

The next day the King sent his son Mossahap to the island Mutir in search of cloves, that we might the sooner complete our lading. The Indians, who we had taken on the way, chose this opportunity of speaking to the King, and of interesting him in their behalf. He accordingly begged them of us, in order, as he said, that he might send them home, accompanied by five islanders of Tadore, who by this means would have an opportunity of speaking in praise of the King of Spain, and thus render the Spanish name dear to and respectable among those nations. We delivered up to him in consequence the 3 women we intended to present to the Queen of Spain, as well as all the men we had taken, those only of Burne excepted.

The King begged of us another favor: it was that we would kill all the swine we had on board, for which he offered us ample compensation in goats and poultry. We accordingly complied with his request, and killed them between decks that the Moors might not see them; for such is their abhorrence of this animal, that when by chance they meet one they shut their eyes and put their fingers to their nose, that they may neither see it nor smell the odor it diffuses.

The same evening the Portuguese, Peter Alphonso de Lorosa, came on board our vessel in a pirogue. We were informed that the King had sent to admonish him previously, that, though he was from Tarenate, he must take especial care, as he should answer for a different conduct, to be sincere in his replies to the questions we might put to him. In fact, on his coming on board, he gave us information on every matter interesting to us. We learn from him that he had been 16 years in India, of which he had passed 10 in the Malucho islands, whither he had come with the first Portuguese, who had actually been established there that space of time, though this was kept a profound secret. He added, that a large vessel, 11 months before, had arrived at the Malucho Islands from Malacca, to load with cloves, and had effectively taken in a cargo; but that it had been detained for several months by bad weather at Bandan. This vessel came from Europe; and the Portuguese captain, who was called Tristan di Menezes, told Lorosa, that the most important news at that time was that a squadron of 5 vessels, under the command of Fernandez Magellan, had sailed from Seville, to make the discovery of Malucho in the name of the King of Spain; and that the King of Portugal, who was the more vexed at this expedition from its being a subject of his who sought to do him the injury, had sent vessels to the Cape of Good Hope, and to Cape Sta. Maria in the country of the cannibals, to intercept his passage into the Indian Sea, but that they had not met with him. Having received information of his passing by another sea, and that he was gone to the Malucho islands by a western passage, he had ordered Don Diego Lopez de Sichera, his captain-in-chief in the Indies, to send 6 ships of war to Malucho against Magellan; but Sichera being informed that the Turks were at this time preparing a fleet against Malacca, had previously been obliged to dispatch 60 ships against them to the Strait of Mecca in the land of Judah; and having found the Turkish galleys here cast on shore near the strong and handsome town of Adem, they succeeded in burning them all. This expedition prevented the Portuguese captain-general effecting what he was ordered against us;

but shortly after he prepared a galleon of 2 tier of bombards to attack us, commanded by Francis Faria, a Portuguese. Neither did this galleon proceed to the Malucho Islands against us, for, whether owing to running on the shoals near Malacca, or to currents and contrary winds, it was obliged to return to the port whence it came. Lorosa added, that a few days before, a caravella with 2 junks had come to the Malucho Islands to obtain intelligence respecting us. The junks went in the interval to Bachian to load with cloves, having 7 Portuguese on board, who, notwithstanding the remonstrances of he King, refusing to respect the persons either of the women or the inhabitants, nay, or the King himself, were all of them massacred. On learning this, the captain of the caravella judged expedient to sail as quickly as possible, and return to Malacca, leaving the 2 junks at Bachian, with 400 bahars of cloves (between 70 and 80 tons), and a sufficiency of merchandise to barter for a 100 more.

He likewise told us that a number of us junks go every year from Malacca to Banda, to buy mace and nutmeg, and thence come to the Malucho islands to load with cloves. The voyage from Banda to the Malucho islands is effected in 3 days, and that from Banda to Malacca in a fortnight. This commerce is the most profitable to the King of Portugal of any carried on with these islands, and in consequence the greatest care is used in keeping it secret from the Spaniards.

What Lorosa communicated was very interesting to us; we therefore endeavoured to persuade him to embark with us for Europe, holding out to him the expectation of some valuable appointment from the King of Spain.

On Friday, 15th November, the King told us he was about to proceed to Bachian to take possession of the cloves left there by the Portuguese, and requested presents of us for the King of Mutir, to whom he meant to give them in the name of the King of Spain. He amused himself in the interval of their preparation, while on board our ship, in seeing the exercise of our different arms, that is to say, the cross-bow, the bersil, a weapon larger than the fusil, and the musket. He shot thrice from the cross-bow, but could not be induced to fire the musket.

Opposite to Tadore is a very large island called Ciailolo, inhabited by Moors and Gentiles. The Moors have two kings, one of who, as we were informed by the King of Tadore, had 600, and the other 525 children. The Gentiles have not so many wives as the Moors, nor are they so superstitious. The first thing they meet in the morning is the object of their adoration during the day. The King of the Gentiles is called Rajah Papua: he is very rich in gold, and inhabits the interior of the island. Here are seen, growing among the rocks, reeds as large round as a man's leg which are full of excellent water; of these we purchased a number. The island of Ciailolo is so large that a boat with difficulty can make the tour of it in four months.

Saturday, 16th November, one of the Moorish Kings of Giailolo came, with a number of boats, on board our vessel. We made him a present of a green damask vestment, two yards of red cloth, some looking-glasses, scissors, knives, combs, and 2 glass goblets gilt, which much delighted him. He told us very politely that as we were friends of the King of Tadore he esteemed us also as his friends, since he loved that monarch as dearly as his own son. He invited us to visit his country, assuring us we should be treated with great distinction. This King is very powerful, and much respected in all the neighboring islands. He is of great age, and is called Jussu.

The next morning, Sunday, the same King made us a second visit, and wished to see the manner in which we sought and discharged our bombards; at the exhibition we made in consequence of his request, he appeared to be greatly pleased, for in his youth he had been of a very martial disposition.

The next day I went on shore to see the clove-tree, and to notice the manner in which it fruits; the result of my observations was as follows: the clove-tree attains a pretty considerable height, and its trunk is about as large as a man's body, varying more or less according to its age. Its branches extend very wide about the middle of the trunk, but at the summit terminate in a pyramid. Its leaf resembles that of the laurel, and the bark of it is of an olive color. The cloves grow at the end of small branches, in clusters of from 10 to 20; and the tree, according to the season, sends forth more one side that the other. The cloves at first are white; as they ripen they become reddish, and blacken as they dry. There are annually 2 crops gathered, the one at Christmas, the other about St. John the Baptist's day, that is to say about the time of the two solstices, seasons in which the air is more temperate in this country than at the other periods of the year, though the hottest of the two is that of the winter solstice, when the sun is here at its zenith. When the year is hot, and the quantity of rain that falls is little, the amount of the crop of each island is from 300 to 400 bahars. The clove-tree grown only on the mountains, and dies if transplanted to the plain. The leaf, the bark, and the woody part of the tree, have as strong a smell and a flavor equally potent with the fruit itself. If this last be not gathered just at the proper season it becomes so large and so hard that no part of it remains good but the rind. There are no clove-trees of prime quality but in the mountains of the 5 islands of Malucho; for though some grow in the island of Giailolo, and on the islet Mare between Tadore and Mutir, the fruit of them is inferior. It is said that fogs give them their superior degree of perfection in these islands; however this may be, we certainly did remark every day that a fog, resembling clouds, enveloped first one and then another of the mountains of these islands. Each inhabitant possesses some clove-trees, which he attends to himself, and the fruit of which he gathers, but he uses no species of culture. In different islands cloves bear different names: they are called Bongalavan at Sarangani, at Tadore ghomodes, and in the residue of the Malucho islands, chianche.

This island likewise produces nutmeg-trees, which resemble our walnuts as well in the appearance of the fruit as in the leaves. The nutmeg when gathered is like a quince in shape, color, and the down with which it is covered, but it is smaller. The outward hulk is of the same thickness as the green one of the walnut; beneath, a thin membrane or tissue envelopes the mace, which, of a very lively red color, encloses the ligneous shell containing the nutmeg.

Ginger also grows on this island; in a green state it is eaten in the same manner as bread. Ginger is not, properly speaking, the produce of a tree, but of a sort of shrub, which shoots up suckers about a span in length, similar to the shoots of canes, the leaves, too, like those of the cane, except in their being more narrow. These shoots are of no value, the root only being the ginger used in commerce. Green ginger is not so strong by much as when dried; and to dry it lime is used, for otherwise it could not be preserved.

The houses of these islanders are built in the same manner as those of the neighboring islands, but they are not so high from the ground, and are surrounded with canes so as to form a hedge.

The women of the country are ugly: they go naked, as the females in the other islands, merely covering their sexual parts with a cloth made of the bark of trees. The men in like manner go naked; and, notwithstanding the ugliness of their wives, are very jealous of them. They were especially very angry at seeing us land with our brayettes open, as they were apprehensive this mode of dress might act as a provocative to their women. Men and women alike go unshod.

They make their cloths from the bark of trees in the following manner. They take a piece of bark and soak it in water until softened; they then beat it with sticks, to make it stretch to the length and breadth they think proper; after which it resembles a piece of raw silk, with the membrane interlaced beneath as if it was woven.

Their bread is thus made from the wood of a tree which resembles the palm. They take a piece of this wood, and after clearing it from certain black and long thorns, pound it, and make it into a bread they call fagou. On this bread they lay in store when they go on voyages.

The islanders of Ternate came every day to us in their boats to offer us cloves; but as we expected others from Machian, on the return of the King, we refused to buy of the other islanders, at which those of Ternate were much hurt.

On Sunday night, 24th November, the King returned to the sound of gongs, and passed between our vessels. We saluted him, to show our respect, with several discharges of bombards. He informed us that, in consequence of orders he had given, we should have, in the 4 succeeding days, a considerable quantity of cloves. In fact on Monday we had brought to us a 171 cathil, which were weighed without deducting the tara, or tare, allowed on buying for the consequent diminution of the weight of spices when taken fresh. These cloves sent by the King being the first we took on board, and forming the chief object of our voyage, we discharged several guns as a signal of rejoicing.

On Tuesday, 26th November, the King came to pay us a visit; and told us he had done for us, in leaving his island, what none of his predecessors had ever done for any one before; but that he had resolved on giving this mark of friendship to the King of Spain and to us, that we might the sooner complete our cargoes and proceed home, and the sooner return with additional forces to revenge the death of his father, who had been killed in an island called Buru, and whose corpse had been cast into the sea. He added, it was customary at Tadore, when a vessel received the first part of the cargo of cloves, for the King to give an entertainment to the sailors or merchants of the vessels, and offer up prayers for their happy return. He, at the same time, intended to give a feast in honor of the King of Bachian, who, with his brother, had come to pay him a visit; and for that purpose he had caused the streets and highways to be swept clean.

This invitation generated suspicion, and this the more from our learning that at the spot where we took in water, 3 Portuguese had been murdered a short time before by islanders concealed in a neighboring wood. Moreover the inhabitants of Tadore were frequently seen conversing with the Indians whom we had made prisoners; hence, notwithstanding a difference of opinion among us, some feeling inclined to accept the invitation of the King, the remembrances of what had happened at the fatal feast of Zubu prevailed in causing us to decline being of the party. We, however, sent to return our thanks for his civility to the King, and to excuse our non-attendance on the occasion, beseeching him to repair as soon as possible on board our ships, that we might deliver to him the 4 slaves we had promised, as we intended to sail the first fine weather.

The King came on board the same day, without the least symptom of mistrust. He said he came among us as into his own house; and assured us he felt very much hurt at a departure so sudden and so unusual; as vessels in general are 30 days in taking in their cargoes, though we had completed ours in much less time. He added, if he had assisted us, even by the unprecedented step of leaving his own island, to hasten our lading with cloves, he had no intention thereby of precipitating our departure. He afterwards noticed that this was not a fit season to navigate these seas on account of the shallows near Banda; and admonished us of the probability there existed at this instant of our meeting with vessels of our enemies the Portuguese.

When he saw that all he had said sailed of its effect, "Very well then," added he, "I shall return you the presents made me in the name of the King of Spain; for if you depart without allowing me time to get ready the presents suitable to the dignity of your King, which I am now preparing, all the kings my neighbors will esteem the Sovereign of Tadore one of the most ungrateful of men, in accepting favors from a monarch so powerful as that of Castille, without making a return. They will further say that you went away in this hurry merely from apprehension of some treachery on my part, and thus shall I be stigmatized for the remainder of my life with the odious name of traitor."

After this speech, to remove all suspicion of his good faith, he caused the Koran to be brought to him, devoutly kissed it, and placed it 4 or 5 times on his head, uttering lowly certain words, which were an invocation called Zambiham. Then, in the presence of us all, he observed aloud, that he swore to Allah (God) and the Koran which he held in his hand, that he would constantly remain a faithful friend of the King of Spain. He delivered the whole of this harangue almost with tears in his eyes, and in such an affecting manner that we were induced to procrastinate our stay at Tadore a fortnight longer.

We then delivered him the King's seal and the royal standard. We were afterwards informed that some of the chiefs of the island had advised him to massacre the whole of us, and thus ingratiate himself with the Portuguese, who would be able to assist him better than the Spaniards, in revenging himself on the King of Bachian; but the King of Tadore, faithful and loyal, repelled the proposal with indignation.

On Wednesday, 27th, the King caused an advertisement to be published, bearing that any one was at liberty to sell us cloves, which afforded us an opportunity of purchasing a great quantity.

Friday, the King of Machian arrived at Tadore with several pirogues; but he would not go on shore, as his father and brother, banished from Machian, had taken refuge on that island.

Saturday, the King of Tadore came on board our vessel with the governor of Machian, his nephew, of the name of Hoomai, about 25 years of age; and learning that we had no more cloth remaining, he generously sent home for and gave us 3 yards of a red color, to enable us, with the addition of some other articles, to make a present to the governor, worthy of his rank; this we did; and on their departure saluted them with our artillery.

On Sunday, 1st December, the governor of Machian took his leave; we were informed that, besides what we had given, the King had likewise made him presents, to induce him to expedite the sending us cloves.

On Monday the King understood another voyage with a similar purpose to the preceding.

Wednesday being the festival of St. Barbe, and at the same time that we might show respect to the King who had now returned, we fired a general salute from our great guns, and in the evening exhibited fire-works, with which the King was extremely delighted.

On Thursday and Friday we purchased a large quantity of cloves, which were afforded us at a low rate on account of our being near the time of our departure. We received a bahar (410 pounds) for a few yards of ribband, and a 100 pounds weight for a few small chains of brass, which only cost a marcel. And as every sailor was anxious to carry to Spain as much as he could, every one bartered his property for cloves.

213--To America and Around the World

Saturday, 3 sons of the King of Tarenate with their wives, who were daughters of the King of Tadore, came to our ships. The Portuguese, Pedro Alphonso de Lorosa, was with them. We made a present of a glass goblet gilt to each of the brothers, and gave to the 3 women scissors and other trifles. We likewise sent some trinkets to another daughter of the King of Tadore, widow of the King of Tarenate, who objected to coming on board our ship.

Sunday, being the day of the Conception of the Virgin Mary, we fired, in order to celebrate the same, a number of bombards, three several shells, and let off many rockets.

On Monday, the 9th, the King came on board our ship with three of his women, who carried his betre. I must here observe that kings and the members of the royal family alone have the privilege of taking their wives abroad with them. The same day the King of Giailolo came a second time to see us exercise our guns.

As the day fixed for our sailing drew nigh the King was frequent in his visits, and it was very visible that he felt great concern on the occasion. He told us among other flattering things that he was like the suckling about to lose its mother's breast. He begged of us some bersils for his defense.

He counselled us not to navigate during the night on account of the shallows in these seas; and on our informing him that we intended to sail by night as well as by day in order the sooner to arrive in Spain, he replied, in that case, he could do nothing better than pray himself, and cause prayers to be offered up to the Almighty for the success of our voyage.

In the mean time Pedro Alphonso with his wife came on board our vessel bringing with him all his effects to return with us to Europe. Two days later Chechilideroix, son of the King of Tarenate, came in a boat well manned, and invited him on board; but Pedro Alphonso, who suspected him of some bad intention, declined compliance with his invitation, and at the same time advised us not to suffer him to enter our ships, which counsel we followed. We afterwards were informed that Chechilideroix, being on very friendly terms with the Portuguese captain of Malacca, had formed a plan to seize Pedro Alphonso, and deliver him into his custody. When he found himself prevented, he grumbled much, and threatened to punish those with whom Lorosa had lodge, for suffering him to leave the island without permission from him.

The King had informed us that the King of Bachian was about to make him a visit, with his brother who was to marry one of his daughters, and entreated us to honor their arrival with a salute. In fact on the 15th December he arrived, and we did as requested, not firing however the guns of largest calibre, on account of the heavy lading we had on board.

The King of Bachian with his brother, designed for the husband of the daughter of the King of Tadore, came in a large galley with 3 tier of rowers on each side, in all 120. The vessel was adorned with several pavilions formed of parrots' feathers, yellow, red, and white. As it sailed along, the rowers beat time with their oars to the music of gongs and other instruments. In 2 boats were the young girls to be presented to the bride. They saluted us by making the tour of the vessel and the port.

As etiquette forbids one king setting foot on the territory of another, the King of Tadore paid a visit to the King of Bachian in his galley. The latter, on seeing the King arrive, rose from the carpet on which he was seated in order to give him the seat of honor, but the visitor from civility declined the distinction and seated himself beyond, leaving the carpet between. The King of Bachian then tendered 500 patolles as a sort of compensation for the wife to be bestowed on his brother. These patolles are cloths of silk and gold, manufactured in china, and much sought after in these islands. In barter for each of them 3 bahars of cloves, more or less, are given according to the quantity of gold on the cloth and the value of the workmanship. At the death of any of the chiefs of the country, the parents wear these clothes.

On Monday, the King of Tadore sent a dinner to the King of Bachian carried by 50 women dressed in barments of silk extending from the waist only to the knees. They marched 2 and 2 with a man between them. Each of them carried a large dish in which were small plates containing different ragouts. The men carried wine in large vases. Ten of the oldest women performed the office of mistresses of the ceremony. In this order they proceeded to the vessel and presented the whole to the King who was seated on a carpet beneath a red and yellow canopy. On their return the women fastened on some of our people whom curiosity induced to be present on the passing of the procession, and who were unable to release themselves until they had made them some trifling presents. The King of Tadore next sent provisions to us, consisting of goats, cocoa-nuts, wines, and other edibles.

The same day we hoisted a new set of sails on which were painted the cross of St. Iago de Compostella, with this inscription: *Questa e la figura della nostra buena ventura.*

On Tuesday, we presented to the King some of the musquets we had taken from the Indians when we seized their junks, together with some bersils, and 4 barrels of gunpowder.

On board each of the vessels we shipped 80 tons of water; we had to take in wood afterwards at the island of Mare, near which our course laid, and where the King had sent 100 men to get us a stock in readiness.

The same day the King of Bachian received permission from the King of Tadore to come on shore to contract an alliance with us. He was preceded by 4 men who carried each a poignard raised in their hands. He declared, in presence of the King of Tadore and all his suite, that he should ever be ready to devote himself to the service of the King of Spain; that he would reserve for him alone the cloves which the Portuguese had left in his island until another Spanish squadron should come to take them on board, and would dispose of them to no other person without his consent; and that he should send him, by us, a slave and 2 bahars of colves: he would indeed have sent 10, but our vessels were so deeply laden they could take no more on board.

He likewise presented for the King of Spain 2 beautiful dead birds. They were of the size of a thrush, with a small head, long beak, legs of the length of a span, and thick as a writing pea: the tail of these birds resembles that of the trush also; and they have no wings like other birds, but, instead, long feathers like tufts of different colors; the whole of the feathers, those only excepted which are in lieu of wings, are of a dull color. This bird never flies but when it blows. It is said to come from the terrestrial Paradise, and is called bolondilallah, that is to say, Bird of God.

The King of Bachian appeared to be 70 years of age. A very strange matter was related to us concerning him: whenever about to combat his enemies, or to undertake any thing of importance, he previously submitted himself 2 or 3 times to the enjoyment of one of his servants, destined for this purpose, in the same manner as, according to Suetonius, Caesar was wont to submit himself to Nicodemus.

One day the King of Tadore sent to advise the people who kept the warehouse in which our merchandise was lodged, not to leave their home during the night, because, as he observed, there were islanders who, by means of certain ointments, assumed the figure of men without heads, and who, if they chanced to meet any one they disliked, laid hold of them by their hand and anointed the palm of it with their unguents, in consequence of which the person so anointed became ill and died in 3 or 4 days time. Whenever they meet with 3 or 4 persons together, they do not touch but possess the art of stupefying them. The King added that he found it requisite to keep watch for them, and that he had already caused many of them to be hung.

Before any new house is inhabited it is customary to surround it with a large fire, and give several entertainments; afterwards a specimen of every good thing produced in the island is fastened to the roof, and the people are then persuaded that the person about to swell in the house will never know want of any thing.

By Wednesday, in the morning, every thing was made ready for our departure. The kings of Tadore, Giailolo, and Bachian, as well as the son of the King of Tarenate came to accompany us as far as the island of Mare. The ship La Vittoria sailed first, and stood out for sea awaiting the Trinidad; but this vessel was a long time in raising the anchor, and when this was effected the sailors perceived she leaked fast in the hold. The Vittoria then returned to her anchorage. Part of the cargo of the Trinidad was unshipped, to allow of searching for and stopping the leak; but notwithstanding for this purpose the vessel was laid on her side, the water still entered rapidly, as from a spout, but the leak could not be found. The whole of this and the next day the pumps were kept going but without the least success.

Upon intelligence of this, the King of Tadore came on board to assist us in discovering the leak, but his efforts in this view were ineffectual. He ordered 5 divers, accustomed to remain a long time under water, to examine the ship externally: they continued under water more than a half an hour, but could not find the leak; and as, notwithstanding the pumps were kept continually going, the water still increased on us, he went to the other side of the island for 3 men capable of keeping a longer time under water than those who had dived before.

The next morning early he returned with them. These men dived into the sea, with their long hair loose, in expectation that the water streaming through the leak, by bearing their hair with it would point out the spot; but after an hour spent under water, in a vain search, they came up again to the surface. The King seemed much affected at this misfortune, so much so indeed that he offered to go himself to Spain to acquaint the King with what had befallen us; but we informed him, that as we had 2 vessels we might complete our voyage in the remaining one, which however must sail shortly, to take advantage of the east winds which began to blow; that in the mean time the Trinidad might be careened, and afterwards under favor of the west winds reach Darien, which is on the other side of the sea, in the land of Diucatan. The King then remarked that he had 250 ship-wrights, who should be employed in refitting the vessel under direction of our people; and that such of our crews as remained for the purpose should be treated as his own children. This promise he made in a manner so truly affecting, as to draw tears from our eyes.

We who were on board the Vittoria, apprehensive of her being too heavily laden, which might occasion her foundering at sea, determined on landing 60 quintals of cloves, and caused them to be transported to the house in which the crew of the Trinidad were lodged. Some of our party, however, resolved on remaining in the Malucho Islands, either from fear of our vessel being unable to sustain a voyage of such length, or from remembrance of what they had already endured before they reached these islands, and dread of perishing of hunger in midst of the ocean.

On Saturday, 21st December, St. Thomas' day, the King of Tadore brought us 2 pilots whom we paid beforehand to take us through the channels of the islands. They told us the season for beginning our voyage was excellent, and that the sooner we sailed the better it would be; but being under necessity of waiting for the letters of our comrades, who remained at the Malucho islands, to their friends in Spain, we did not weigh anchor till noon. The two vessels then bade adieu to each other by a reciprocal discharge of artillery. Our comrades followed us as far as they were able in their boat, and we parted in tears. Juan Carvajo remained at Tadore with 53 Europeans and 13 Indians.

The governor, or minister, of the King of Tadore, accompanied us as far as the island Mare; and scarcely had we arrived there before 4 boats came alongside our vessel, laden with wood, which in less than an hour was taken on board.

All the Malucho islands produce cloves, ginger, fago (the tree of which bread is made), rice, cocoa-nuts, figs, bananas, almonds of larger size than ours, pomegranates sweet as well as acidulous, sugar-canes, melons, cucumber, pumpkins, a fruit called comilicai, extremely refreshing, and of the size of a water melon, a fruit resembling a peach, and called guava, besides other vegetables good to eat; oil is likewise extracted form the cocoa-nut and gengili. As for useful animals, here are goats, fowls, and a species of bee, not larger than an ant, which builds its hive in the trunks of trees, in which it deposits its honey, of excellent flavor. There is a great variety of parrots, among others white ones, called catara, and red ones denominated nori, which are the most valued, not only on account of the extreme beauty of their plumage, but also for their speaking more plainly the words they are taught than the others do. A parrot of this species costs a bahar of cloves.

Scarcely 50 years are past since the Moors first came to and subdued the Malucho Islands, and introduced their religion. Before this they were peopled by Gentiles, who paid but little attention to the clove-tree.

The island Tadore lies in latitude 27 minutes north, longitude 161 degrees from the line of demarcation. It is 9 degrees 30 minutes south-east by south of the first island of this archipelago, called Zamal.

The island Tarenate lies in latitude 40 minutes north. Mutir is exactly upon the equinoctial line.

Machian is situate in latitude 15 minutes south. Bachian is latitude one degree south.

Tarenate, Tadore, Mutir, and Machian have high and cone-shaped mountains on which the clove-tree grows. Bachian, though the largest, is not distinguished from the 4 other islands. Its mountain of clove-trees is not so much elevated nor so pointed at its summit, as those of the other islands, but its base covers a larger area.

Keeping on our course we passed several islands, the names of which are as follow: Caioan, Laigoma, Sico, Giogi, Cafi, Laboan, Toliman, Titameti, Bachian, of which we have already spoken, Latalata, Iabobi, Mata, and Batutiga. We were told that in the island of Cafi, the inhabitants are small as pigmies: they are subject to the King of Tadore.

We steered westward of Batutiga, on a course west-south-west. Southward we saw several small islands. Here the pilots from the Molucha Islands recommended we should anchor in some port, that we might not be subject to run ashore on the numerous islets and shallows. We consequently tacked to the south east, and made an island situate in latitude 3 degrees south, distant 53 leagues from Tadore.

This island is called Sulach. The inhabitants are Pagans, and have no king: they are anthropophagi, and, both men and women, wear no other clothing than a small piece of cloth, made of the bark of trees, 2 fingers broad, which conceals their sexual parts. There are in the neighborhood other islands, the inhabitants of which feed on human flesh. The names of some of them are: Silan, Noselao, Biga, Atulabaon, Lertimor, Tenetum, Gonda, Kaiabruru, Mandan, and Benaia.

We afterwards coasted along the islands Lamatola and Tenetum.

After a run of 10 leagues in the same direction from Sulach, we came to an anchorage on a large island called Buru, where we found provisions in abundance; for example, hogs, goats, fowls, sugar-canes, cocoa-nuts, sago, a dish composed of bananas called canali, and chiacares, known here by the name of nanga. Chiacares are a fruit resembling water melons, but of which the rind is full of knobs. Internally it is full of small red seeds, similar to the seed of the melon; they have no ligneous rind, and are of a medullary substance, similar to that of our white beans, but larger; they are very tender, and in taste resemble chestnuts.

We likewise found here another fruit similar in its exterior to pine cones, but of a yellow color; internally it is white, and when cut bears some resemblance to a pear; it is however much more tender than that fruit, and is of exquisite flavor: it is called comilicai.

The inhabitants of this island have no sovereign: they are gentiles, and, like the people of Sulach, go naked. The island of Buru lies in latitude 3 degrees 30 minutes south, 75 leagues from the Malucho islands.

Ten leagues eastward of Buru there is a still larger island, which is little distant from Giailolo, and is called Ambon. It is inhabited by Moors and Gentiles; the former dwell near the sea, the other in the interior. The latter are anthropophagi. The productions of this island are the same as those of Buru.

Between Buru and Ambon are 3 islands surrounded by shallows: to wit, Vudia, Kailaruru, and Benaia. Four leagues south of the island of Buru lies the little island Ambalao.

At a distance of 35 leagues from Buru, in the direction south-west by south, is the island of Banda, with 13 other islands. In 6 of these islands mace is grown, and nutmeg. The largest is called Zoroboa; the smaller are Chelicel, Saniananpi, Pulai, Puluru, and

Rasoghin; the other 7 are Univeru, Pulan, Barucan, Lailaca, Mamican, Man, and Meut. In these islands nothing is cultivated but sago, rice, cocoa-nuts, banana, and other fruit trees. They lie very near each other, and are all of them inhabited by Moors who have no sovereign. Banda is situate in latitude 6 degrees south, longitude 163 degrees 30 minutes, from the line of demarcation. As it laid out of our course, we did not go thither.

Steering south-west by west from Buru, after traversing 8 degrees of latitude, we found ourselves off 3 islands, contiguous one to the other, called Zolot, Noumamor, and Galian. While sailing between these islands we experienced a tempest, which made us apprehensive for our lives; so that we made a vow to go on pilgrimage to our Lady of Guida, provided we escaped the threatened danger. We went direct before the wind, and made for a tolerably lofty island, called Mallua, where we anchored, but before we came to anchorage, we suffered much from the currents and squalls which came from the gullies in the mountains.

The inhabitants of this island are savages, and resemble beasts from than men; they are anthropophagi, and wear no other clothing in common than a narrow slip of cloth made from the bark of trees, to hide their privities; but when they go out to fight they cover their breasts, back, and sides, with pieces of the buffla's hide, ornamented with corniole, and the teeth of swine: behind and before they attach tails made of goat's skin. Their hair is turned up and fastened with combs, having large teeth. Their bear they wrap up in leaves, and enclose it in boxes made of reed, a custom which made us laugh immoderately. In one word, they are the ugliest people we met with in the whole course of our voyage.

They have bags made of leaves of trees, in which they place their food and drink; Their bows as well as their arrows are made of reeds. When their women first perceived us, they advanced towards us with their bows in their hands in a menacing attitude, but on our making them some trivial presents we became good friends.

We passed a fortnight on this island in repairing the sides of our vessel, which were much strained in the storm: we found on it goats, poultry, fish, cocoa-nuts, wax, and pepper. For a pound of old iron we received in barter 15 pounds of wax.

There are here two kinds of pepper: long and round; the fruit of the long pepper-tree resembles the flowers of the hazel. The plant, like the ivy, is a climber, which adhered to the trunks of trees; but its leaves are similar to those of the mulberry. This pepper is called luli. Round pepper grows on a like climber, but its fruit, as maize, is in ears, and is beaten out as that grain; this species of pepper is called lada. The fields of the country are covered with pepper plants, formed into bowers.

At Mallua we took a man on board who engaged to conduct us to an island more abounding in provisions. The island Mallua lies in latitude 8 degrees 30 minutes south longitude, 169 degrees 40 minutes from the line of demarcation.

Our old pilot from the Maluccas related to us on our way that in these parts is an island called Arucheto, the inhabitants of which, men as well as women, are not more than a cubit high, and have ears as long as their body, so that when they lied down to rest one serves as a mattress to lie upon, and the other for coverlid. Their hair is shorn, and they go entirely naked: their voice is harp, and they run with much swiftness. Their dwellings are caverns under ground, and their aliment fish and a kind of fruit they obtain from between the back and ligneous body of a certain tree. This fruit, which is white and round as comsits made of coriander, is called by them ambulon. We would willingly have visited this island, but were prevented by the shallows and currents.

On Saturday, 25th January, 1522, at 22 o'clock (half past 2), we sailed from the island Mallua, and after a course south-south-west of 5 leagues, reached a tolerably large island called Timor. I went on shore alone to treat with the chief of a village, called Amaban, for hogs. He offered me buffalos, hogs, and goats; but when the merchandise to be given in barter was mentioned we could not agree, as he required much, and we had little remaining to give. Upon this we determined on retaining the chief of another village, called Balibo, who had come on board of his own accord, bringing his son with him. We told him if he wished to recover his liberty he must procure for us 6 buffalos, 10 hogs, and as many goats. This man, who was apprehensive of being put to death immediately, gave the necessary orders for all we required to be brought to us; and as he had but 5 goats and 2 hogs, he gave us 7 buffalos instead of 6. This effected, we sent him again on shore, well satisfied, as on releasing him we have him some linen, a piece of Indian cloth, silk, and cotton, some axes, Indian cutlasses, knives, and mirrors.

The chief of Amaban, to whom I first went, had none but women to wait on him, who went naked like those of the other islands.

In their ears they wear small gold earrings, to which they fasten small skeins of silk. On their arms they wear so many bracelets of gold or brass, as to cover the arms to the elbow. The men are likewise naked, but round their neck they have a collar of round plates of gold, and their hair is fastened up with combs of bamboo, ornamented with gold. Some, in lieu of golden rings, wear in their ears circles made form the neck of the pumpkin dried.

White sandal is found in this island alone. I contains, as we have shown, buffalos, hogs, and goats, besides fowls and parrots of different plumage. Here, likewise, grow rice, bananas, ginger, sugarcanes, oranges, lemons, almonds, and French beans; and wax is also abundant.

We cast anchor off that part of the island on which are some villages inhabited by their chiefs. In another quarter of the island are the residences of 4 brothers, who are its kings. The villages where these residences are, are called Orbith, Kichsana, sinai, and Cabanaza; the first of them the most considerable. We were told that a mountain near Cabanaza produces abundance of gold, and that the inhabitants purchase with the grains of it they collect, whatever articles they stand in need of. Here it is that the people of Malucca carry on a traffic in sandal wood and wax. We found there, likewise, a junk newly come from Lozon, to load with sandal wood.

These people are Gentiles. They told us that when they go to cut sandal wood a demon presents himself under different forms, and asks them in a very courteous manner what it is they want. But notwithstanding his civil demeanor the apparition frightens them so much that they are always ill in consequence for several days together. They cut sandal at particular phases of the moon, at which alone it is good. The merchandise best suited for bartering for sandal is red cloth, linen, axes, nails, and iron.

The island is wholly inhabited; it extends considerably from east to west, but from north to south is very narrow. It lies in latitude 10 degrees south, longitude from the line of demarcation 174 degrees 30 minutes.

In all the islands of this archipelago visited by us, and in this more than any other, the malady of Saint Job is very prevalent. It is called, Fro Franchi, that is to say, the Portuguese disease (venereal disease).

We were told that at a day's sail west-north-west of Timor is an island called Ende, where much cinnamon grows. The inhabitants of it are Gentiles, and have no king. Near it is a chain of islands stretching as far as Java Major and the Cape of Malacca, the names of which are: Ende, Tanabuton, Crenochile, Birmacore, Azanaran, Main, Zubava, Lumboch, Chorum, and Java Major, which the inhabitants call Jaoa, and not Java.

The largest villages of this part of the world are in Java, and the chief one is called Mugepaher, the King of which, while living, was reputed the greatest monarch of the islands of this part; his name was Rajah Patiunus Sunda. Much pepper is gatherd here. The other islands are: Dahaduma, Gaciamada, Minutarangam, Ciparisidain, Tubancressi, and Cirubaia. Half a league distant from Java Major are the islands of Bali, called Little Java and Madura: these two islands are of similar dimensions.

We were told that it is customary in Java to burn the bodies of the chiefs who die; and for the wife cherished most to be burnt alive in the same fire. Adorned with garlands of flowers, she causes herself to be carried by 4 men on a seat through the town, and, with a tranquil and smiling countenance, comforts the relations who bewail her approaching end, telling them, "I am going this evening to sup with my husband, and shall sleep with him tonight." On her arrival at the funeral pile she again comforts them with similar speeches, and throws herself into the consuming flames. Were she to refuse to act thus, she would no longer be regarded as a reputable woman, or a good wife.

Our old pilot related to us a still more extraordinary practice: he affirmed that when the young men are amorously inclined, and wish to obtain the favors of any particular female, they fasten small round bells on them between the glands and the prepuce, and thus dance under the window of their mistress whose passions they excite by the sound of these bells. The lady constantly insists on the lover wearing these trinkets.

He told us moreover that an island called Ocoloro, below Java, is peopled by women alone, who are rendered pregnant by the wind. Should they produce a boy they kill him immediately; if a girl, it is preserved. If a man at any time presumes to visit the island, they put him to death.

Other tales were likewise related to us. North of Java Major, in the Gulf of China, called by the ancients Sinus Magnus, there is said to be a very large tree, called campanganghi, on which certain birds roost, called garuda, of such immense size, and so strong, as to be able to fly away with a buffalo or an elephant, when they carry it to a part of the tree called puzathaer. The fruit of the tree, which is called buapanganghi, is larger than a water melon. The Moors of Burne told us they had seen two of these birds, which their sovereign had received from the King of Ciam. This tree cannot be approached on account of the whirlpools about the island, which extend 3 or 4 leagues form shore. To this account was added that the history of this tree became known in the following manner: A junk was drawn in by these whirlpools, and shipwrecked on the shore near the tree, and the whole of those on board perished on the occasion, a small child only expected, who was miraculously saved by means of a plank. On reaching the tree he climbed up, and concealed himself under the wing of one of these large birds, without being perceived. The next day the bird flew to the main to seize upon a buffalo, when, on its touching the ground, the child slipped from beneath the wing, and escaped. By this means the history of these birds was known, and of the fruit of such considerable size so often found in these seas.

The Cape of Malacca lies in latitude 1 degree 30 minutes south. Eastward of the cape are many villages and towns, of which these are the names: Cingapola, situate on the Cape itself; Pahan, Calantan, Patani, Bradlini, Benan, Lagon, Chireyigharan, Trombon, Joran, Cium Brabri, Banga, Iudia (residence of the King of Ciam, called Siri Zacabedera), Jandibum, Laun, and Langonpisa. These towns are all of them built after our manner, and belong to the King of Ciam.

We were likewise told that on the banks of a river of this kingdom there are large birds which live on dead carcasses only; but which never devour the carrion until some other birds have made their prey of the hearts of them.

Beyond Ciam lies Camoyia. The king of this country is called Saret Zacabedera; next follows Chiempa, the king of which is the Rajah Brahami Martu. In this country it is that rhubarb grows, which is found in this manner: a company of 20 or 25 men go together into the woods, where they pass the night in trees, to be secure from the attacks of lions and other wild beasts, and at the same time the better to distinguish the rhubarb, which they seek by the smell, the odor of it being borne by the wind. Rhubarb is the putrid wood of a large tree, and acquires its smell from the putrefaction it undergoes: the best part of the tree is the root, though the trunk, which is called calama, possesses equal medicinal virtue.

To Chiempa succeeds the kingdom of Couhi, the sovereign of which is called Rajah Siri Bummipala. After this follows Great China, the king of which country is the most powerful monarch upon earth. His name is Santoa Rajah. Seventy sovereigns wearing crowns are dependent on him, and each of these have from 10 to 15 others subject to him. The port of this kingdom is called Guantan, and among its numerous cities the two principal are Nakin and Comlaha: the king resides in this last. In his palace he has 4 prime ministers, each of whom gives audience in one of the 4 fronts of it, which look towards the cardinal points. All the kings and lords of Greater and Upper India are obliged to erect in the middle of the square, as a mark of dependence, the image of an animal stronger than the lion, called chinga, which image is also engraved on the royal signet, and all vessels entering the port of this monarch have the same image in ivory or wax on board. Whenever any of his lords show signs of disobedience, they are slayed alive; and their skins, dried, pickled, and stuffed, are placed in some conspicuous part of the square, the head bent, and the hands tied over the head in the act of making the zongu, or reverence to the king. This monarch never shows himself to any one; and whenever desirous of seeing any of his subject, he causes himself to be carried on a peacock, made with much ingenuity, and richly ornamented, accompanied by 6 women dressed entirely like himself, so that one cannot be distinguished from the other. He then places himself in the hollow image of a serpent, called Naga, superbly decorated, which has a glass window in its breast, through which the king sees what he pleases, without being seen himself.

He marries his sisters, that so the royal blood may not be intermingled with that of his subjects. His palace is surrounded by 7 walls, and to every wall are 10,000 guards, which are relieved every 12 hours. Each wall has its gate, and every gate likewise its guard. At the first gate is a man with a large whip in his hand; at the second, a dog; at the third, a man with an iron club; at the fourth, another with a bow and arrows; at the fifth, again another with a lance; at the sixth, a lion; and at the seventh, 2 white elephants. In the palace of this monarch are 79 halls, which contain women alone for the service of the king, and which are constantly lighted with flambeaux. It takes an entire day to make the tour of the palace. At the extremity of the palace are 4 halls, whither the ministers repair when they wish to speak to the king. The walls, the vaulted roof, and even the floor of one of these halls, are ornamented with bronze; in the second, the ornaments are of silver; in the third, of gold; and in the fourth, of pearls and precious stones. In these halls are deposited the gold and other valuables given in tribute to the king. I have seen nothing of all this which I now related, but merely repeat the account of a Moor, who assured me that he had himself been witness of what he delivered.

The Chinese are fair, and wear clothing; like us they eat off tables. With them corsses are likewise seen, but of the use they put them to I am wholly ignorant.

From China it is that musk is brought: the animal which produces it is a species of civet, which feeds entirely upon a soft wood of the thickness of the finger, called chamaru. In order to extract mush from this animal a leach is fastened on it, which, when well filled with blood, is crushed, and the blood received on a plate that it may be dried in the sun the space of 4 or 5 days, in order to perfect it. Every one who keeps one of these animals is bound to pay a certain tribute. The grains of musk brought to Europe are no other than small pieces of goat's flesh steeped in real musk. The blood is sometimes clotted, but it is readily purified. The cat which produces musk is called the castor, and the leach is termed linta.

Coasting along China many different nations are found, to wit: the Chiencis, who inhabit the islands near which pearls are fished, and which produce cinnamon. The Lecchii inhabit the main opposite to these islands. The entrance into the port of these people is under a large mountain, whence all junks and vessels on going into or leaving the port, are obliged to lower their masts. The king of this country is called Moni, and is subject to the King of china, but he has 20 sovereigns under his command. His capital is called Barunaci, and here it is the Eastern Cathay is situate.

Han is an island very lofty and cold, productive of copper, silver, and silk: it is under the dominion of Rajah Zotru. Mili, Jaula, and Gnio, are 3 countries on the continent, of rather cold temperature. Friagoula and Frianga are two islands which yield copper, silver, pearls, and silk. Bassi is a low country on the main. Sumbdit Pradit is an island very rich in gold, in which the men wear a ring of gold round the leg at the ankle. The neighboring mountains are inhabited by people who kill their parents after they have attained a certain age, in order to prevent their suffering the maladies incident on old age. The whole of the people we have described are Gentiles.

On Tuesday, 11th February, at night, we quitted the island of Timor, and entered the great sea called Laut Chidol. Bending our course west-south-west, we left north-ward on our right, from dread of the Portuguese, the island of Zumatra, anciently called Taprobana;

Pegu, Bengal, Urizza, Chelim, inhabited by Malays, subjects of the King of Narsinga; Calicut, dependent on the same monarch; Cambuia, inhabited by the Guzzarats; Cananor, Goa, Armus, and the whole of India Major.

In this kingdom there are 6 classes of people, to wit: the Nairi, Panicali, Franai, Pangelini, Marcuai, and Poleai. The Nairi are the chiefs; the Paniculi, citizens; these two classes converse together: the Franai collect palm-wine and bananas; the Macuai are fishermen; the Pangelini sailors; and the Poleai sow and gather in rice. These last constantly inhabit the fields, and never enter towns. When any thing is given to them, it is put on the ground for them to take. When on their journey any where they constantly keep exclaiming, po, po, po; that is to say, take care of me. It was related to us that a Nairi who accidentally had been touched by a Poleai, caused himself to be put to death, unable to survive so great an infamy.

In order to double the Cape of Good Hope we ascended as high as 42 degrees south; and we were obliged to remain nine weeks opposite to the Cape with our sails lowered, on account of the west and north-west winds which constantly blew, and which terminated in a dreadful tempest. The Cape of Good Hope lies in latitude 34 degrees 30 minutes south, 1600 leagues distant from the Cape of Malacca. It is the largest and the most dangerous cape known.

Some of our men, especially the sick, were desirous of making the shore at Mozambique, where is a Portuguese establishment, as our vessel was very leaky, the cold we endured extremely severe, and above all, as we had no other than rice and water to live upon; for all the meat which, for want of salt we had been unable to pickle, had become putrid. But the major part of the crew being still more attached to honor than to life, we determined on using every exertion to return to Spain, however great the perils we might have to undergo.

At length, by the help of god, on the 6th of May we doubled this terrible cape; but to effect this we were forced to approach within 5 leagues of it, as otherwise, from the constancy of west winds, we could never have effected this end.

We afterwards steered north-west for 2 whole months together (May and June) without any rest, and in this interval lost 21 men, including Indians. We made a singular observation on throwing them into the sea; the corpses of the Christians floated with the face towards heaven, but those of the Indians with the face downwards.

We were now almost wholly destitute of provisions, and had not heaven favored us with fine weather, we should all have perished with hunger. On the 9th of July, on a Wednesday, we distinguished Cape Verd Islands, and anchored off that called Sant Jago.

As we knew we were in an inimical country, and expected we might excite suspicion, we had the precaution of enjoining the men in the long boat, whom we sent on shore for provisions, to say that we had touched at this port on account of our foremast being split on crossing the line, which occasioned us to lose so much time, that the captain-general, with 2 other vessels, had continued his course to Spain without us. We moreover spoke in such manner as to cause them to imagine we came from the shores of America, and not from the Cape of Good Hope. We obtained credit, and our longboat was twice laden from shore with rice, in exchange for different merchandise.

In order that we might discover if our journals had been regularly kept, we enquired on shore what day it was, and was answered Thursday; this occasioned us much surprise as, according to our journals, it appeared to be Wednesday. We could not be satisfied of having lost a day; and for my part I was still more astonished at the circumstance than the rest, for I had enjoyed so perfect a state of health as to be able, without interruption, to mark the days off the wee, and the months. We afterwards found that there was no mistake in our calculation; since, having constantly travelled westward and followed the course of the sun, on our return to where we departed from we ought naturally to have gained 24 hours on those who remained on the spot; this, to be convinced of, requires but a moment's reflection.

The long-boat on its third trip, we perceived, was detained, and we had reason to suspect by the movements of certain caravels, that a design was meditated against our ship; in consequence, we resolved on immediate flight. We afterwards were informed that it had been stopped on account of one of the sailors having divulged our secret, by relating that the captain-general was dead, and that our ship was the only one of the squadron of Magellan which had returned to Europe.

Thanks to Providence, on Saturday, 6th September, we entered the bay of San Lucar; and of 60 men of which our crew consisted on our leaving the Malucho Islands, but 18 remained, most of whom were sick. The residue had either ran away from the ship at the island of Timor, had for different crimes there been punished with death, had died of hunger, or become prisoners to the Portuguese at Sant Jago.

229--To America and Around the World

From our departure from the bay of San Lucar to the day of our return, we reckoned to have sailed upwards of 14,600 leagues, having circumnavigated the globe from east to west.

On Monday, 8th September 1522, we cast anchor near the Mole of Seville, and fired the whole of our artillery.

On Tuesday, we repaired in our shirts, barefooted, and carrying a taper in our hands, to the church of our Lady of Victory, and to that of Sta, Maria de Antigua, as we had vowed to do in the hour of danger.

On leaving Seville, I went to Vagliadolid, where I presented to His sacred Majesty Don Carlos (Charles V) neither gold nor silver indeed, but things far more precious in his eyes: among other articles, I presented him a book written with my own hand, in which, day by day, I had set down every event on our voyage.

I left Vagliadolid as early as I was able, and repaired to Portugal, to present to King John a narrative of what I had seen. Afterwards I traveled through Spain to France, where I presented different articles from the other hemisphere to the Queen Regent, mother of the Most Christian King, Francis I.

At length I returned to Italy, where I devoted myself for ever to the service of Signor Philippe de Viller l'Ile-Adam, Grand Master of Rhodes, to whom also I gave the narrative of my voyage.

Il Cavagliero Antonio Pigafetta.

Amerigo Vespucci
(Spaniers Illustrirte Weltgeschichte, 1894)

The Name

America

by Marco Giacomelli

Translated by Fiona Dalziel

Christopher Columbus and Amerigo Vespucci are linked to one another by the name *America*. Over the centuries it has been bitterly disputed as to whether they should be united in common glory or opposed in an unresolvable disagreement. It is not only logical but historically necessary to discuss their relationship.

At the end of the 15th century, while the Portuguese were attempting to sail eastward round Africa to reach Asia--the land of spice, some astonishing news was received: Asia and its precious spices could be reached by sailing westward. All one had to do was to cross the Atlantic Ocean. On March 15, 1493, two Spanish ships, the *Nina* and the *Pinta* had returned to Palos. They were under the command of Christopher Columbus, who, on August 3, 1492, had actually sailed westward and on the 12th of October had arrived at an island, *Guanahami*, which he renamed San Salvador.

With this feat, the Atlantic was no longer mysterious and forbidden. In fact, it immediately became the object of contention between Portugal and Spain. To put an end to the dispute, a line of demarcation--the *RAYA* was decided upon and established in 1493, more or less along meridian 39W. It was moved in 1494 to roughly along the meridian 45W. The Portuguese zone lay to the east of the RAYA and that of the Spanish to the west.

The Atlantic was confronted once again by Columbus, who, on the third of his four voyages, on the August 1, 1498, landed on the continent 10 degrees above the equator: near the mouth of the Orinoco, opposite the island of Trinidad, on a coast named Parias. And in the north, the Venetian, Giovanni Caboto (John Cabot) reached Newfoundland in 1497.

Amerigo Vespucci was completely unconnected with these vents. It was well-known to the scholars of the day that he had sailed a lot later than Columbus and that the discovery of the new lands was attributable to Columbus.

The very well-informed Turkish navy also knew that Columbus was the discoverer. In Constantinople, at the Topkapi palace, there exists a fairly large fragment (discovered in 1929) of a man of 1513, the work of Piri Reis, Solyman the Magnificent's cartographer. In the lower left hand corner, he wrote: "These coasts are called the Antilles... it is said that a faithless Genoese, by the name of Columbus, discovered the place."

Although voices of scholars remained unheeded, and although Columbus discovered the new lands, nevertheless the north and south American continents are named not after Columbus, but after Amerigo. Why such a gross miscarriage of justice?

In 1504, in many European cities, there appeared in print a short work in Latin (with a note saying that it had been translated from Italian). It was entitled *Mundus Novus* (The New World). Albericus Vespucius, in a letter to the distinguished Florentine, Lorenzo Pierfrancesco de' Medici, cousin of Lorenzo the Magnificent, referred to a voyage of 1501, on behalf of the King of Portugal, westward to unknown countries. "E lecito chiamarlo un mondo novo"--(It is permissible to call it a new world).

In 1507 a 52 page book in Latin appeared, printed at Sancti Deodati Oppidum (identified after long controversies as St. Die' in the duchy of Lorraine). This book included Amerigo Vespucci's *Quatuor Navigationes* (The Four Navigations) and the universal cosmography with the addition of places discovered recently which Ptolemy had not known about.

233--To America and Around the World

The *Quatuor Navigationes:*
a) The first took place between May 10, 1497 and October 15, 1498 with the Spanish, during which Vespucci landed on the continent at Paria (thus preceding Columbus by one year);
b) The second between May 16, 1499 and September 8, 1500 with the Spanish;
c) The Third between May 10, 1501 and October 15, 1502 with the Portuguese (corresponding to the voyage described in *Mundus Novus*);
d)The fourth between May 10, 1503 and June 6, 1504 with the Portuguese.

In St. Die' Jean Basin, a linguist by the name of Martin Waldseemuller Hylacomylus, a 27-year old geographer, member of the Gymnasium Vosgianum, had decided to publish Ptolemy's cosmography enriched with Amerigo's descriptions of his four voyages which Vespucci had personally went to Duke Rene in a letter written in French: this was according to Basin, who declared himself the author of the translation from French into Latin. The name *Amerigo* was translated as *Americus*. In chapter VII, Waldseemuller, dealing with the quarta orbis pars (fourth part of the earth), maintained that it was permissible to call this the land of Americo or America since Americus had discovered it. In chapter IX, he was insistent; and close to the margin, he wrote "America". He also wrote America next to the Brasilian coast in the planisphere he drew up. The name was immediately welcomed and everything discovered south of the equator became America. Subsequently it was realized that South America and North America constituted a single land mass. In 1538 Mercator drew the single continent and wrote in the north AME, RICA in the south. And so it was from that day onwards.

The desire for an indigenous origin of the name gave rise to the assertion, not supported by historical fact, maintained some years ago by the Jamaican Jan Carew in an essay, "The Caribbean writer and exile". He stated that America derives its name from the Indios Ameririques and the Sierra Amerrique to the north-east of Lake Nicaragua in the area of Chontalegna cordillera; and that the name Amerigo was invented for convenience: however, at Ognissanti's Church (All Saints' Church) in Florence one can see the tombstone of 1471 of an ancestor of Vespucci, also called Amerigo.

Christopher Columbus is not even mentioned in the St. Die' publication. Only Vespucci's portrait is deemed worthy of appearing next to that of Ptolemy: there is no sign of Columbus.

In the 16th century, Vespucci was the discoverer or rather the *Amplificator Mundi* (Amplifier of the World).

But Bishop Bartolomeo Las Casas, who disembarked in Haiti in 1502 and lived in America until 1547, turned up in defence of Columbus. He returned to Spain and died there when he was 90. In Valladolid in 1559, at the age of 85, he began to write his *Historia general de las Indias* (General History of the Indies). Columbus "was the first to open the doors of that ocean which had remained closed for so many centuries"; and he was the first to land on the continent at Parias on the 1st August, 1498 during his third voyage. But in the *Quatuor Navigationes* it is stated that Amerigo had reached the content at Parias in 1497, a year before Columbus. Las Casas reveals that Vespucci had been to America in 1499 and not 1497 and accuses him of passing himself off as the discoverer of the new continent in foreign books.

In 1601, Herrera--having seen Las Casas' as et unpublished text--made a slanderous condemnation of Vespucci. In 1627, Fray Pedro Simon proposed the prohibition of the use of maps and works where the name America appeared. It was for this reason that in Spain up until the 18th century the name West Indies was used, never the name America. The scholars of the era--including Voltaire--showed contempt for Vespucci, who was no longer considered the Amplifier of the World, but a common fraud, at Columbus' expense.

But little by little, documents and information have been emerging from the archives which allow his personality to be outlined more clearly and give reason for the discussion to be re-opened.

Vespucci's family was cultured, not wealthy; and he himself was cultured. He was born in Florence in Borgo Ognissanti and died in his late fifties (on the February 22, 1512, six years after Columbus). He was on very good terms with the Medici family. In 1491, he went to Seville as an official in Juanoto Beraldi's company, a branch of a shipping agency owned by the Medici family. In his will, signed on December 15, 1495 (published in 1891), Beraldi nominates him as his testamentary executor, demonstrating extreme trust in him. There is no doubt that Vespucci participated in the Spanish voyage of 1499 and participated in it as an "expert in cosmographic and nautical science": according to Hojeda, who participated in the voyage of 1499 and testified in the proceedings for the acknowledgement of the rights of discovery of the land of Parias brought against the treasury of the heirs of Columbus. In 1501 and 1502 he was in Portugal. At the end of 1502 he returned to Spain. In spite of his previous connection with the Portuguese and although he was a foreigner, he was consulted by the Spanish court in matters related to sea voyages. From a letter written by Columbus on February 5, 1505 (published in 1829) we know that he participated authoritatively in the royal hearing of February 1505. The "cedula real" on the 5th or 25th April 1905, declared him a Castillian citizen "for the good services he has rendered and will continue to render to the crown." He is mentioned in official documents with the title "captain".

When the post of Piloto Mayor was created, the first person to take office was Vespucci on the March 28, 1508 by deed of Queen Joan. From this document (published in 1839) it is known that among others the hob included--in view of the numerous "padrones de cartas" (registers of nautical maps) of the discovered lands--organizing the preparation of a general register called the *padron real* for the use of all sea captains, who were obliged to report back to the Piloto Mayor on returning from voyages. Vespucci held office until his death (February 22, 1512). The importance of the Piloto Mayor is also proven by the significance of his successors: Juan Diaz de Solis--then Sebastiano Caboto, the son of Giovanni.

As Piloto Mayor, Vespucci planned a voyage round the southern tip of the new continent in order to land in Asia (an aim fulfilled eight years after his death). In 1508, the Venetian delegate Francesco Corner informed his government that 19,000 duchies had been given to Amerigo and to Juan Bistaim (Giovanni de la Casa, Biscaglino) for the discovery of new islands which they called mainland; and that Vespucci had to provide good ships "and go westward to find the lands that the Portuguese find by sailing eastward". The cartographer Nuno Garzia de Toreno would provide written evidence of these. Sebastiano Caboto remembered him as a great expert *en las alturas* (in the navigation of the high seas) and praised him. Vespucci himself disclosed a method, which he had discovered, to determine longitude--a very difficult task in those days because of the lack of precise instruments for measuring time.

But all this is not enough to give us a clear picture of the man. Until 1502, the cartographical representation of the new lands retained Ptolemy's great Asiatic inlet: the Atlantic Ocean went as far as Asia.

But in the *Carta Marina Portogallensium* of 1502, the representation is correct. In that map many names are written in Italian. The Caribbean and the Atlantic coasts of South America correspond to what Vespucci expounded in two letters. And there is no information about the Portuguese voyages or any others before 1502 along the eastern coast of South America apart from Vespucci's voyage for the King of Portugal in 1501-1502, narrated by him in a letter of 1502. The map--which is of the greatest importance--leads one to believe that the coasts belong to a land mass which is clearly separated from Asia.

Peter Martyr, a member of the *Consiglio dell Indie* (The Indies Council), gave an account of the utmost importance. After asserting Vespucci's skill in cartography and nautical science, he says that in order to get an idea of the discovered lands, he went to Bishop Fonsecain whose study he saw a great number of navigational maps, to one of which, drawn up in Portuguese, it was said that Vespucci had contributed; who--under the auspices of the Portuguese and with their financial support--had himself sailed several degrees beyond the equator. In order to be by the Portuguese with Vespucci's contribution, the map must date back to before his return to Spain at the end of 1502. And it is symptomatic that later, in 1511, the Portuguese (according to Herrera) asked Vespucci for maps with much insistence. As well as the above mentioned Carta Marina Portugallensium (studied by Hamy in 1896), there is an entire series of maps which show or hint at existence of land mass independent of Asia: they were all produced after 1502. Among them is Waldseemuller's map of 1507, included in the *Quatuor navigationes*, discovered in 1901 at Wolfegg Castle in Wurtemberg, Germany. The cartographer cites Vespucci as his source. Here, South America appears isolated from Asia as a fourth part of the world. One can affirm that the cartography of the period was based on the works of Vespucci, who drew a map of South America whose general outlines are correct. He was not therefore a mediocre man as the Viennese historian Stefan Zweig maintains in his book, *Amerigo*. Vespucci appears to have been an exceptionally talented geographer; and few have influenced the history of geography as much as he did: thus concludes the Turinese geographer Alberto Magnaghi (who died in 1945), after having provided an irreplaceable service by collecting, reordering and systematically assessing all the above data.

Therefore, the basic question becomes more difficult to answer: honest in his personal relationship, cultured, expert, even brilliant, is

237--To America and Around the World

Amerigo Vespucci the pride of humanity: Or was he a refined usurper who stole Columbus' glory? Is the name America the result of Amerigo's deceit? Or not?

Among the documents discovered, a printed booklet of 1504, in Italian, ignored for centuries, is of great importance. The title is: *Amerigo Vespucci's letters about the re-discovered islands of four of his voyages*. The addressee is not indicated; but in subsequent editions, the name of the greatest authority in Florence, Gonfalonier of Justice Pietro Soderini, is mentioned. Three letters addressed by Vespucci to Lorenzo di Pierfrancisco de' Medici are of equal importance, the texts of which were copied by a certain Piero Vaglienti in 1514 in one of his manuscripts. Thus, six accounts of voyages attributed to Vespucci are obtained: three in printed works and three copied by Vaglienti in his manuscript.

The three in print:

1) *Mundus novus* (The New world), a letter in Latin of 1504, with the note saying that it has been translated from Italian, addressed to Medici, about the voyage of 1501 along the Atlantic coasts of South America on behalf of the Portuguese, with the promise of an account of other voyages.

2) *Quatuor Navigationes* (The Four Navigations), in Latin (with the note that Basin had translated a letter written by Vespucci in French to Duke Rene' into Latin), printed in St. Die' in 1507 with the account of the two Spanish and two Portuguese voyages.

3) *I Quattro Viaggi* (The Four Voyages): a letter in Italian of 1504 with the account of the same Spanish and Portuguese voyages.

The three copies, all in Italian:

4) The letter of 1500 to Medici (published in 1745) with the account of a voyage on behalf of the Spanish;

5) The letter of 1501 to Medici (published in 1827) with the account of the voyage with the Portuguese as far as Cape Verde where Vespucci met some of Cabral's ships returning from the India;

6) The letter of 1502 to Medici (published in 1789), a continuation of the previous letter with the account of the voyage of 1501 along the Atlantic coasts of South America setting off from Cape Verde, the same as the narrated in *Mundus Novus*.

In the manuscript of 1500 (4), the accounts of the two voyages for the Spanish described in the *Quatuor Navigationes* (2) and *I Quattro Viaggi* (3), appear united into the account of one single voyage. Here the continental landing at Parias is described but the voyage is set in

1499, one year later rather than one year before Columbus' landing there in 1498. In the manuscript of 1502 (6), about the voyage along the South American coasts, there is basically the same information as that published in *Mundus Novus* (1); but--unlike the later--no mention is made of two previous Spanish voyages.

Therefore, Vespucci himself seems to have denied the existence of the so-called first Spanish voyage, that of 1497. For this reason there arose the accusation that Vespucci had a double personality: an honest informant in his private letters to Medici, a fraud in print, creating two voyages from a single Spanish voyage, inventing one in 1497. But a comparative study of *I Quattro Viaggi* (3) and the *Quatuor Navigationes* (2), reveals that the latter is a translation of the Italian text: Basin, in homage to his Duke, invented a non-existent original letter written by Vespucci in French. And in *I Quattro viaggi*, the landing place of 1497 is in fact mentioned, but is described as a landing at Lariab (a place which has not been identified), not at Parias as in the *Quatuor Navigationes*: thus Las Casas' fundamental accusation wavers. In the map of 1507--only discovered in 1901--Waldseemuller professes to have followed Vespucci's description; but it differs from the account in the *Quatuor Navigationes*, to which it is attached, in many details; from this we can deduce that he did not follow the text of the *Quatuor Navigationes*, but a different narration by Vespucci.

The three manuscript copies are certainly incompatible with the three printed works. An extremely lively polemic broke out between the accusers and defenders of Vespucci. In this century, at the height of the polemic, there occurred a *coup de theatre*. Its author was Alberto Magnaghi. He resolved the problem: in praise of him, we can say (paraphrasing one of his own comments) that he "links Amerigo to Columbus". Magnaghi allots great importance to the post of Piloto Mayor in his studies. Being a geographer, he devotes all his attention to the "Carta Marina Portogallensium" and to Waldseemuller's map: he does not limit himself to observing how this differs from the description in the *quatuor navigationes* and *I Quattro Viaggi*, but stresses, on the other hand, that it adheres to the descriptions in the manuscript copies. Above all--and this is *the coup de theatre*--he upturns the order of inquiry. This had always left off from the preconceived idea that the printed works were true; and with this basic assumption attempts had been made to assess the manuscript copies and to judge Vespucci. Magnaghi states that the printed works are false and should be ignored whilst examining the truthfulness of the contents of the manuscript copies. Magnaghi's investigation is convincing. One should ignore the three printed works which are false. One should believe the three manuscript copies which are true. The conclusion: not four voyages, but only two: in 1499--partly with Hojeda--for the Spanish; and in 1501 for the Portuguese. This is known from the statements of the Spaniard, Hojeda and the Portuguese, Alvarez. Vespucci never claimed to have completed the so-called first voyage of 1497 with the Spanish or the so-called fourth voyage of 1503 with the Portuguese. Vespucci landed on the coast of Parias in 1499, one year after Columbus; he never pretended to have preceded him there in the non-existent voyage of 1497.

And what about the printed letter of the *Four Voyages*? The voyage of 1497 was fabricated from the letter of July 1500 about the voyage of 1499 by altering facts and names: thus Parias becomes Lariab as Haiti becomes Ifi. The fourth voyage was fabricated from the letter concerning the Portuguese voyage of 1501. Thus a work describing four voyages, equally as important as those of Columbus, was obtained. The letter, composed in this way ("stretched" according to Stefan Zweig), has all the requirements for editorial success.

(Fabricating false works by famous authors is not and was not a new thing. A sensational forgery attributed to Vespucci himself was discovered at the end of the 19th century when a report of a fifth voyage, edited by a Dutchman, was found: but it was revealed that the report was of the Tyrolese Sprenger, whose opening "Ego Balthasar Sprenger", had been altered by the editor to "Ick Albericus").

The letter of *I Quattro Viaggi* had been an unforeseen consequence: with the invention of the voyage in 1497, preceding Columbus' landing on the continent by one year, it brought about Waldseemuller's christening in Amerigo's glory and also caused Vespucci to be considered a fraud and usurper for centuries. Such an impact was insured by the correction of the name Lariab to Parias in Basin's Latin Translation of the *Quatuor Navigationes*.

The name America was, therefore, born by chance. Amerigo cannot be blamed for the fact that he was not in any way related to this baptism.

One question remains: The relations between the Spanish and the Portuguese were very hostile, as both were extremely jealous of the other's new discoveries. How was it that Vespucci was entrusted with the Portuguese voyage of 1501 after his spanish voyage of 1499? And why was he later welcomed back again by the Spanish who not only forgave his defection but went on to nominate him Piloto Mayor? In the voyage of 1499, Vespucci sailed along the northern coast of south America as far as Cape S. Rocco (6); having returned northwards he went westward along the Caribbean coast, where the place-name Valdamerigo is situated, as far as the gulf of Venezuela (and perhaps further). In the course of this exploration, he had the opportunity to study the constellation of the Southern Cross (which reminded him of the tercets in Dante's Purgatory); he reached Brasil and the Amazon, landed on the coast of Parias, discovered one year before by Columbus; in the extreme west, he arrived at the Gulf of Venezuela and saw the island of Arruba, where there were "houses built on the sea like at Vinegia with much skill and wonder": from whence the name Venezuela. Vespucci discerned the continental nature of the coastline but believed he had arrived in Asiatic land: "I say it is on the border of Asia". He declared to have hoisted sails first of all southward in the hope of "heading for a cape which Ptolemy called the Cape of Cattegara" "which is joined to the *Sino Magno...*". Amerigo remained anchored, as did columbus, to the erroneous data of Paolo del Pozzo Toscanelli, who set a very much smaller distance than the real one between Spain and Asia. The discovery of land at the distance indicated by Toscanelli convinced Columbus that he had actually reached Asia; likewise Vespucci, who concluded: "In my opinion, I wasn't very far from it (Ptolemy's Sino Magno) according to the degrees of latitude and longitude". From whence came his hope of managing to reach, in a following voyage, "the island of Taprobana, which lies between the Indian sea and the Gangetico sea", namely the island of Ceylon. In this first voyage Vespucci violated the line of demarcation between Spain and Portugal which allotted the eastern part of South America (namely Brazil) to the Portuguese zone: with Spanish ships he advanced far into the Portuguese zone.

To continue his research into Cattegara and to reach the island of Taprobana, he had no choice but to turn to the Portuguese. They were very glad and made his second voyage of 1501 possible. During this voyage, Vespucci, having reached from Cape Verde the American coast at 5 S, pushed forward towards the South-west and reached 50 S less than three degrees (200 miles) from the Straits of Magellan. Fernao de Magalhaes confirmed this. The discoverer of the passage in the south-west entered the port of San Giuliano situated at 49.15 south on the 31st of January 1520. Given the custom of naming places discovered with the name of the saint venerated on that day and the fact that the day dedicated to San Giuliano is the 28th of February and not the 31st of January, one must conclude (as does Magnaghi) that the name of that port was given by a discoverer preceding Magellan. Who could it have been? Magellan, compelled to stop at San Giuliano in terrible conditions, appealed to his crew: it was necessary to go at least as far as Amerigo's had gone. Therefore, the latter had gone beyond the latitude 49.15 S and advanced much further south than every known or believed limit: much further than 34 S, the extreme southern limit of Africa; much further than 33 S, the extreme southern limit-- according to Ptolemy--of the Chersoneso aurea (the peninsula of Malacca), namely of Asia. During this second voyage, sailing towards the south-west, Vespucci crossed the line of demarcation once more, traveling westward over it and thus entering the Spanish zone with Portuguese ships. Therefore, having completed the journey, he returned to Spain where the news of his voyage was gratefully received.

Vespucci should be praised for his exceptional navigation along almost the entire length of the Caribbean coast and the Atlantic coast of South America. But his true glory lies in the fact that he realized that he was dealing with a new world: "In short, I was at the antipodes; which for my navigation was *a fourth part of the world*". (The original text: "in conclusione fui alla parte degli antipodi; che per mia navichazi- one fu *una quarta parte del mondo*"). Therefore, he directed Spanish expeditions to go around the southern cape of the new continent in order to reach Asia. Eight years after his death the Spanish expedition headed by the Portuguese Magellan (of which we have the accounts of the sea-captain Francesco Albo, Antonio Pigafetta, and Leone Pancaldo from Savona) managed to do so.

This is the logical justification of the name America: a fortuitous name but utterly deserving and valid. Magnaghi, with a clever scientific synthesis concludes that "Vespucci links Columbus to Magellan".

Columbus and Vespucci are not only united for scientific reasons. They were also united by their esteem for one another, or rather, by personal friendship: and whoever utters the name America evokes the memory of both: of the discoverer and of the one who enhanced the discovery, understanding the individuality of the new continent. In a letter of February 5, 1505 (found in 1829), Christopher Columbus writes to his son Diego: "... I have spoken to Amerigo Vespucci, who is going to the court to be consulted on certain matters relating to a sea voyage. He has always had the desire to please me. He is going with the hope of obtaining, if he can, some benefit for me. He is a great gentleman."

Vespucci is well worthy of being honored together with Columbus and Magellan.

With the words of Christopher Columbus, one must conclude that the new world, *America* bear the name of a "great gentleman".

Christopher Columbus
(Unknown artist)

John Cabot departing from England
(Unknown artist)

Sebastian Cabot
(Unknown artist)

Giovanni da Verrazzano
(National Gallery of Art)

"8 Goths and 22 Norwegians on [this] discovery voyage from Vinland over [the] west we had camp by 2 skerries one days journey north from this stone we were and fis[hed] one day after we came home found 10 men red with blood and dead AV[e] M[aria] preserve from evil have 10 men by the sea to see after our ship[s] 14 day journeys from this island year 1362." from *The Kensington Rune-Stone Is Genuine* by Robert A. Hall.

The Vinland Map, ca. 1440
(From 1973 edition of Heimskringla)

Toscanelli's 1474 Map
(Spaniers Illustrirte Weltgeschichte, 1894)

Columbus
Mass Media and
Scholarly Pursuits

Having found the South and North American Continent, together with new routes to the Orient, Columbus accomplished the unexpected. Those being the facts, Columbus' persona, as a result, has come under tremendous scrutiny: either he was a scoundrel or traitor of the worst kind, or one of our greatest heros. Maligned or loved, Columbus has generated some very bizarre reactions. The following is an attempt to expose some of this vast amount of literature.

The Forged Vinland Map and Leif Ericson

Yale University scholars have done a great injustice to the Italian Americans and to erudition through their shoddy and irresponsible publication of the false Vinland Map.

And by proclaiming October 9, Leif Ericson Day, *Jimmy* Carter has done no less to the spirit of all Americans including those of Italian descent, who must neither forget nor forgive.

A greater harm to Columbus, however, has and continues to come by way of unscrupulous hackers in the mass media and from would-be scholars.

The following is an exposé of the manner in which Columbus and his descendents, through the controversy over the banality of who discovered America, are being maligned and denigrated:

*****

Aside from a "tiny village at the northern tip of Newfoundland", an island off of the northeastern coast of Canada, where "three pieces of rusted iron were found", according to the editors of *Many Nations--One Nation* (a textbook for fifth and sixth graders), there are three other pieces of evidence normally used to back up Mr. Carter's and similar type proclamations:

1) The Kensington Stone (discovered in 1890 in
   Kensington, Minnesota), which many people
   still believe in the authenticity
   of this forgery, with Professor Hall
   seemingly one of these,

2) The Vinland Map of 1965, which has created the
   biggest stir because of the timing, and
   manner in which it was promulgated,

3) A Viking coin "found in 1961
   by an amateur archaeologist
   digging in Blue Hill Bay",
   as reported by the *Boston Herald*,
   February 8, 1979, and possibly,

4) Various *one of a kind* items as ax heads, and
   other items of the type spoken by
   Professor Horsford.

The Kensington Stone and the Vinland Map have been proven forgeries. Concerning the "coin", which was struck in Norway, some 60 to 80 years after the supposed discovery of America on the part of Leif Ericson, no witnesses to the find have come forth. No Indian artifacts have been found in Norway, although, according to German, English, and American scholars, the Vikings traveled back and forth between North America and Norway for over 100 years. Columbus, of course, on his first voyage, brought back artifacts as well as living specimens of the Indian race.

It is obvious that Columbus and his crew brought *real* items back to Europe, while his detractors bring *badly forged* items to America.

It is incredible, therefore, that the American people in general--together with the mass media representatives in collaboration with individuals of questionable scholarly backgrounds, continue to up-grade Leif Ericson at the expense of Christopher Columbus.

251--To America and Around the World

There is no reason for this situation other than to irritate the Italian Americans. Unfortunately for all Americans, this crazy game has had, and will continue to have, severe ramifications in forms of backlash bickering, acute anger and strong feelingsof suspicion on the part of the Italian Americans against those who insist on carrying on with what is obviously a perpetration of historical facts--a perpetration that comes in many forms and under many guises as evidenced by the following examples.

Irving Robbin

In his textbook, *Explorations and Discoveries* (designed for upper elementary and junior high school students and published by Grosser & Dunlap in 1961--and by other publishers as well), Irving Robbin sets the stage concerning the discovery of America, with the obvious comparison between Leif Ericson and Christopher Columbus. To the question, "What discovery did Eric the Red make?", and "Who discovered North America?"--here is what he says:

"Eric the Red gathered his family and servants and set sail to the west in the year 982. On that voyage he discovered Greenland. He spent the rest of his exile in exploring the many small islands in the area and when the three years ended he returned to Iceland. There he immediately equipped an expedition of over 700 people and 25 ships. These people became the original colonizers of Greenland. The fierce Eric the Red ruled over them as a self-appointed king.

"The next step in the spread of the Vikings was to the mainland of North America itself.

"By the year 1000, Leif Ericson, son of Eric the Red, was old enough to continue the exploring tradition of his father. Leif became the first to set foot on North America. His expedition consisted of a single ship manned by 35 Vikings. The ship itself had a tradition. It was purchased from Bjarni Herjulfsson, a Viking explorer who may or may not have discovered America before Leif. Herjulfsson made his voyage in 985, but the written account of his trip and the places he claimed to have visited do not seem to be accurate. Most historians do not accept his claims. There is, however, little doubt that Leif Ericson did land in North America.

"He called the land of his discovery "Vinland the Fair".

Vinland means Wineland, and presumably Leif referred to the great number of grapes he found growing along the eastern coastline. He described and mapped areas that many people recognize today as

Cape Cod, Massachusetts and the island of Nantucket and Martha's Vineyard. Historians have made many claims about possible landing sites of the Vikings, which include Newfoundland, Nova Scotia, Maine, Massachusetts, and Virginia, to name a few, but the true identity of Leif Ericson's Vinland has never been accurately established.

In spite of the above 'facts', Mr. Robbin nevertheless concludes that "Leif Ericson returned to Greenland a year later with the news of his discovery. It was a great voyage and one of the most important in man's history."

Mr. Robbin further states that there is "little doubt that Leif Ericson did land in North America", and that "He called the land of his discovery "Vinland the Fair".

The weather of northeast America and Canada does not allow for grapes to grow in abundance, not even under scientific cultivation. If Leif had come upon a land with a "great number of wild grapes", it must have been a land other than Cape Cod whose "true identity... has never been accurately established." Yet, Mr. Robbin goes on to conclude that "Leif Ericson returned to Greenland a year later with the news of his discovery." The final statement, though absurd, nevertheless has a certain impact on the young: "It was a great voyage and one of the most important in man's history." Having said this, here is how he then treats Columbus on the very next page of his book. Notice the emphasis on the word "Rediscovery":

"Columbus and the Rediscovery of America
"By the 15th century the western world was in earnest about finding a sea route to the Far East. It was the age-old problem--not enough goods were arriving from the faraway lands. This time it was due to two powerful groups. The Turks had become extremely powerful and managed to blockade many of the overland caravans, while the Arabians controlled the waters of the eastern Mediterranean and the Red Sea. It seemed as though every time a new contact was established with the Orient, some nation turned up to block further exchange. So once more the explorers went forth."

Having told the students that Columbus had rediscovered America, Mr. Robbin now states that Columbus was not alone in believing the earth was round.

"In the 15th century most people had forgotten that it was possible to sail around Africa. A notion had been growing for a long time that China, India and the East Indies could be reached by sailing westward across the Atlantic. The notion was correct, but no one knew that two mighty continents--almost stretching from pole to pole--blocked the way. They were the Americas.

"To believe that one could sail to the East by sailing west, one must also believe that the earth is a sphere. A Genovese sea captain named Christopher Columbus believed this, but he was not alone. He was not alone by many centuries, for as far back as 500 B.C., A Greek scholar, Pythagoras, asserted that the earth was round. A Norwegian textbook written in 1250 not only said the same thing, but also gave the reasons for the varying climates of the earth, the angle of the sun at different times of the year and the prevailing winds. Not all ancient knowledge had been lost. It was just out of favor for a while."

Columbus "believed" the word was round, "but [of course] he was not alone." In other words, in believing something that Columbus alone proved to be correct--that is, that the world was round, Columbus "was not alone." But, according to Mr. Robbin, Columbus was alone when he made a "great mistake":

Columbus seemed to have dedicated his life to just one purpose--that of making a trip across the Atlantic to the East Indies. He studied astronomy, map making, navigation, and even sailed to England and Iceland where he heard about the Viking voyages. He did, however, make a great mistake. He assumed the world to be much smaller than it really was, and he thought that Asia was much larger than we know it to be. But he was determined to make the voyage. Columbus had a mission, not for any country or monarch, but for himself."

Yes, Columbus "did, however, make a great mistake." The individual who had arrived at this conclusion was not Mr. Robbin, but Samuel Eliot Morison, who, in his *Christopher Columbus, Mariner*, (Mentor Book, NY, 1942) reported that Columbus had overestimated his distance which "did not prevent his finding the way home, because the mistake was constant, and the time and course were correct." The "mistake" was that, having received the calculations of his contemporary scientist--with the distances so measured by other navigators--Columbus, by using those figures, made the "mistake" every other navigator had made. It was Columbus, however, who uncovered that mistake wherein the earth had been assumed "to be much smaller than it really was", causing the scientists to re-figure, and to come up with the right measurements. Mr. Robbin emphasized the "mistake"; Mr. Morison, on the other hand, had simply observed with accuracy and proper perspective the mistake of overestimation.

Mr. Robbin makes other statements that are incorrect. He says that "Isabella decided to back the expedition, even with her personal fortune": the Queen's jewels. The fact is that Columbus financed one ship and the city of Palos supposedly the other two. In the transaction, there also figured other Italians.

C. Giardini, in his *The Life and Times of Columbus*, (Curtis Books, NY, 1967) makes this statement:

"Half of the two million 'maravedis' ($14,000) was put up by Genovese and Florentine friends of Columbus, the other half by Luis Santangel--a prominent and influential Spanish Jew--and by Francisco Pineli, joint treasurers of the Santa Hermandad, a sort of military brotherhood which defended the Crown. Pineli was actually from Genoa. Three quarters of the sum (or, if we count Santangel a mere go-between, the whole of it) necessary for the expedition that was to give Spain a world empire was of Italian origin."

Ernle Bradford, in his *Christopher Columbus*, (The Viking Press, NY, 1973) makes the following statement concerning the financing of the voyage:

"There were others who were prepared to invest their own money in the Enterprise of the Indies, among them his original backer Medina Celi, as well as a Florentine banker, Berardi, who was resident in Seville."

In a subsequent chapter, Irving Robbin, not satisfied with downgrading Columbus, picks on John Cabot: "John Cabot Follows the Path of the Vikings," as if the voyages of Ericson, and not those of Columbus, were known in England.

Outside of Mr. R. A. Skelton, who wrote in 1965, pursuant to the publication of the forged Vinland Map, Mr. Robbin is about the only one who speaks of Cabot as having followed in the footsteps of the Vikings. But Skelton, at least, had the Vinland Map from which to draw his conclusions.

The arrogance of American Heritage:

In the proud article, "Vinland the Good Emerges from the Mists", the unkind editors of the prestigious *American Heritage*, October 1965, above the bold bow of the symbolic Viking ship, printed the following introduction:

255--To America and Around the World

"American Heritage takes part in announcing an astonishing discovery at Yale--the earliest map ever found that shows any part of America. Traced to a copyist in Basel about 1440 A.D., it shows, long before Columbus, the new world lands discovered by the Norsemen. Authenticated by painstaking scholarly detective work at Yale and the British Museum, it opens the door to tantalizing historical speculations..."

In their Introduction, the editors of the magazine emphasize the "astonishing discovery...of the earliest map ever found", and the fact that "it shows, long before Columbus, the New World." The third item of emphasis is devoted to the "painstaking scholarly detective work at Yale and British Museum."

Certainly the latter, the readers should know that it took eight years for Yale and British Museum scholars to authenticate their map--eight years, from October 1957, when Lawrence Witten showed the map to the *scholars* Alexander O. Vietor and Thomas E. Marston of Yale, to October 11, 1965, when they made the map public. In those eight years of *painstaking scholarly detective work*, without making the obvious and amateurish tests of "ink and paper" so that they could date with fair precision the fabrication of the map, the Yale and British Museum scholars chose the vigil of America's Columbus Day to make public the forged document. In their machinations, they enlisted the willing support of the mass media, whose members thrive especially when the news covers the Italian Americans. Here is how the Editors of *American Heritage* showed their privilege:

"*American Heritage* is privileged not only to take part in announcing the news of the Vinland Map discovery but to publish the first extended magazine treatment of the studies that have been made of it. The Yale University Press is publishing the entire work this month as a book under the title *The Vinland Map and the Tartar Relation*, with texts by R. A. Skelton, George D. Painter, and Thomas E. Marston. This massive, complicated, but intensely interesting volume, which costs $15, includes facsimiles of the map and the Tartar Relation, translations, commentaries, and a foreword by Alexander Orr Vietor, Curator of Maps at the Yale University Library and editor and organizer of the project. We wish to thank Mr. Vietor and Chester Kerr, director of the Yale University Press, for making our presentation possible."

In their article, "Was There a Lasting Colony?", Skelton and Painter do make, however, interesting observations about other fraudulent ironware that may well have been brought from Scandinavia and planted in modern times--the so-called "small ballards".

"Such finds sometimes show a suspicious correlation with areas of 19th century Scandinavian immigration, and genuine known to have been manufactured in the 1890's for cutting plug tobacco! Finds made in Minnesota and other districts far inland have been used to substantiate the fraudulent runic inscription on the Kensington Stone and the fantastic theory of a 14th century Norse land expedition through the heart of the continent. On the other hand, it would not be surprising if Norse ironware acquired by Indians from trading settlements on the Vinland coast should have passed from tribe to tribe far inland. The whole rather scabrous question of these finds perhaps deserves more serious investigation than it has hitherto received."

The Kensington Stone, the American Goliath, the Vinland Map, and many other similar items, were all purposefully forged. Instead of taking part in the Vinland Map scheme, Skelton and Painter should have spent time in discovering and in telling truths; they should not have waited for others to do so. In the above caption, they conclude the paragraph with what, at the very least, is a contradiction: "The whole rather scabrous question of these alleged finds perhaps deserves more serious investigation than it has hitherto received."

In his article, "Did Columbus or Cabot See the Map?", Skelton, after much speculation on the parallel course to the West taken by the two Italian mariners, concludes that there was a possibility of their having seen the map, but surely they had heard about it from Icelandic and Bristol fishermen:

"A phrase in John Say's letter describing the Cabot voyage of 1497, which must have been written at the end of 1497 or beginning of 1498, indicated that its recipient already had knowledge of the earlier Bristol discovery of 'mainland' in the North Atlantic. The letter is addressed to the 'Almirante Mayor', whom (as Dr. Vigneras has shown) there are grounds for identifying with Christopher Columbus, Admiral of the Ocean Seas. Acceptance of this identification admits the possibility that news of the English discovery may have been in Columbus' possession before he sailed in 1492 and have contributed to his 'conviction that there was land to be found within the range of distances which he anticipated.' It may be added that, if Columbus in fact visited Iceland in 1477, it was very probably in a Bristol vessel; that he made the trip, and if so, he could have shared the Icelandic information picked up by Bristol seamen. We do not go so far in skepticism as Admiral Morison, who writes: 'the Vinland story was not likely to come [Columbus'] way, unless he had learned Icelandic and attended saga-telling parties ashore' (S. E. Morison, *Admiral of the Ocean Sea*...

"To amplify the argument, let us make the improbable assumption that Cabot had seen some version of the map itself. Comparison of its representation of the North Atlantic with the courses and distances logged by the Bristol pilots would undoubtedly have led him to identify the lately discovered *Brasil* with the southern part of Vinland as shown on the map. This would have provided him with mutual confirmation of the reliability of his two sources. He would have seen that Vinland extended, on the map, little south of the latitude of Bristol and that, if it were an island (as it is depicted) and not mainland, it would not bar an onward voyage to Cathay on a course changed slightly south of west."

The Vinland Map story was obviously a news-worthy item. Everyone picked it up; many made hay.

Conclusions based on false documents are themselves false:

The New York Times printed front page articles. Magazines published full page copies of the map. All the while, Italian Americans became more and more furious. The reason for their attitudes was understandable.

Though they had no way of proving the Map a fraud, they felt it was so due to the manner in which the announcement had been made. The editors of the *New Haven Register*, October 13, 1965, pinpointed the problem:

"The Yale map demonstrates the excitement of scholarship, while its announcement and display on the eve of the national day of tribute to Columbus displays the sideshow weakness for publicity which even lofty scholarship sometimes embraces.

"Having invited reaction and outraged orthodoxy Yale must now weigh the results. Having wedded the historian's search for truth to the huckster's search for attention it must assess the cost. Will a brisk sale for Yale's new map and book, for instance, outweigh the possible loss to Yale of even a single husky Italian American football player who's been outraged by all the talk? Who knows? But Yale is going to find out!"

In the same issue of the *Register*, the Editors publish two contrasting letters: "Recognizing Leif" by George Wyman, and "Glory of Discovery" by Stelvio Papetti. The two letters easily show the divisiveness the *map* created.

Recognizing Leif [--] Now that the Yale map has become public, which shows that the Norsemen discovered America about 500 years before Columbus, why go on with the farce every year of observing Columbus Day? If memory serves me right Columbus never set foot on mainland North America, but instead landed on some islands around Cuba.

I know there has been some pressure in Congress to have Columbus Day, Oct. 12, designated a national holiday. This effort should be emphatically opposed. The only motivation the politicians have in this endeavor is to carry the Italian ethnic vote--and nothing else.

Let us press, instead, for a national holiday in memory of the Norsemen Bjarni, and Leif who was the son of Eric. While we are at it how about the city of New Haven canceling its annual Columbus Day parade and celebrating Leif Ericson Day instead? Give credit where credit is rightly due. Of course the Scandinavian ethnic vote in New Haven is small, and for that reason I doubt if City Hall has anything even resembling the courage to give public credit to Leif Ericson. Such is the stuff politicians are made of.

Glory of discovery [--] Columbus or Ericson? Certainly this Yale scholar is trying very hard to obtain notoriety by making this finding public the eve of Columbus Day. This is quite an unorthodox way of bringing up a new discovery without any of the ethics involved in pro-claiming a scientific fact.

I would like to point out that the claim of any discovery is awarded only to a person or persons who have the personal initiative to find, describe and evaluate a new thing. It is from the discovery of America by Columbus that Europe learned about the continent and became interested.

Everyone was taught in elementary school that there was a probability that the Scandinavians reached the

northern part of the American continent prior to Columbus on their fishing trips. This was all that was
known. One can't call this a discovery any more than one
can call the finding of more land on the other side of the
Bering Straits by the Indians a discovery.

It is a historical fact that the Scandinavians did
not bring America to world attention. They themselves
have been unsuccessful in finding evidence much less the
contribution given by a map found in 1957, in a manuscript called the 'Tartar Relations.' It is my opinion that
if the Norwegians can claim the discovery of America
around the year 1000, then by the same token the Asians
can do the same at a much earlier date.

It is hard to believe that Columbus undertook a
trip which he thought would bring him to the Far East
'knowing' that he would arrive in a new continent to the
finding of Ericson. In conclusion, far more evidence than
that presented will be needed to prove that anyone but
Christopher Columbus is worthy to be singularly honored
on the discovery of America.

Mr. Papetti, of course, raises an important point: Would
Columbus, and his followers, have taken the initiative to go to Cathay
by a westward ocean route if he had known that a land mass stood in
the way?

The *Saturday Evening Post*, in an editorial, talks about a "trivial
quarrel" whose "attitudes..are not so trivial." Then it tells about the
"Melting Pot" being a "false image", failing to note, however, that when
a group of people is victimized by another, there cannot be a melting
pot. If Americans haven't achieved a real "melting pot", the cause may
be shown over the manner in which the victimization of the Italian
Americans has taken place. "Who discovered America?", is the title
question of the article. Should the question be asked at all?

"The ridiculous controversy over Yale University's Vinland Map
has finally died down, yet the unsettled question that remains is not
who discovered America but what America is.

"In brief, Yale University proudly announced just before
Columbus Day that it had acquired a map dated 1440 and showing an
outline of North America, based on the explorations of Leif Ericson-
-long before Columbus' celebrated voyage. There had never been much

doubt that the Vikings reached America before Columbus, but the publication of the map, which should have been a scholarly achievement, was treated like a crime.

"One, John Lacorte, head of the Italian Historical Society of America, began fulminating against Yale and announced that he wouldn't send his son there. Congressman John V. Lindsay, campaigning for mayor of New York, claimed that any denigration of Columbus was comparable to the denigration of Arturo Toscanini or Joe DiMaggio. Senator Clifford Case (R. NJ) declared that 'Leif Ericson is just an upstart, as far as I'm concerned.' While all these self-appointed defenders of Italian honor held forth, the Spanish began rumbling about their own role as Columbus' financial backers. The Madrid newspaper *ABC* accused Yale of 'a gesture of methodical and incredible belligerence, designed, if possible, to pulverize Spanish glory for the discovery of the New World.'

"It was all a trivial quarrel, of course, but the attitudes involved are not so trivial. The original idea of this country was that it would provide a haven for all nationalities and all faiths, and that they accepted in coming here the idea of a mixed society. 'Melting Pot' was the popular cliché. It was a false image, since people do not melt like so many iron ingots, and America would not be what it is if everyone were identical to his neighbor."

Richard J. H. Johnston, in his article on Amintore Fanfani, then Foreign Minister of Italy and President of the United Nations General Assenbly, presents his article in *The New York Times*, December 11, 1965, with this headline: "Fanfani, Supporting Columbus, Drags Isaac Newton Into Act." With the words "drags...into act", Johnston and the editors of the *Times* show how much respect they had for Mr. Fanfani--the man, and Mr. Fanfani--the representative of Italy and of the United Nations.

"**Italian Diplomat Says Vikings Were 'Pre-Newtonian' in Discovery of America [--]** A scholarly defense of Christopher Columbus as the true discoverer of the New World was offered last night by Italy's Foreign Minister, Amintore Fanfani.

"Mr. Fanfani, who is President of the United Nations General Assembly, carefully disassociated his vigorous support of his fellow countryman from his diplomatic position, however. He spoke here in his long-standing role as professor of economic history at the University of Rome.

261--To America and Around the World

"Mr. Fanfani likened Columbus' discovery to that of Isaac Newton's discovery, of the law of gravity. He suggested that Viking adventurers might be considered 'pre-Newtonian' in so far as finding America was concerned.

"'In physics, for instance, we may say that Newton had millions of forerunners who had an apple fall on their head from an overhanging tree...

"'But he had no forerunners in the real sense of the word, in as much as we justly attribute to him not the fact that an apple fell on his head but rather the discovery of the cause and the laws of such a fall.'

"Mr. Fanfani, speaking in Italian, addressed 250 members of the Italian diplomatic corps, their friends, and a sprinkling of college and university professors at the Institute of Italian Culture, 686 Park Avenue. His subject was: 'The Vinland Map and the New Controversy Over the Discovery of America'.

"The controversy erupted on Columbus' birthday [sic], October 12, when Yale University announced the publication of a Vinland it had acquired.

"The map, drawn 52 years before Columbus sailed for 'India', was said to show that Leif Ericson, the Viking adventurer, had beat Columbus to the New World and had reached land somewhere in the vicinity of the Gulf of St. Lawrence around the year 1000.

"Mr. Fanfani said he deplored the 'ink storm' that had been whipped up by the Yale announcement and by the 'very timely publicity' coinciding with the celebration of Columbus Day here.

"'As might have been foreseen, the day after the yearly Columbus Day parade dawned upon a raging controversy', Mr. Fanfani said.

"'Scandinavians exulted, Latins protested, professors clashed and reporters assumed the mantle of scholarship.'

"He said the map's publication had made a significant contribution to knowledge, but he deplored what he called the publication's 'aggressive timing'."

In his article entitled, "Columbus vs. Ericson--What Science Says", *Science Digest* (January 1966), Daniel Cohn seems tired over the question on the priority of America's discovery, and is now sure to have the answer, although he calls to the attention of the reader that such items as the Kensington Stone, and the "so called Viking stone tower in Newport, Rhode Island... [are] highly questionable."

"It's proven again, for the umpteenth time, that the Vikings really did discover America before Columbus. This time proof is so solid that it will probably end the argument.

"For hundreds of years, there has been a strong suspicion that the Vikings or Norsemen landed on the North American continent around 1000 A.D. The suspicion was based on Norse sagas telling how the Vikings, sailing westward from their colonies in Greenland or Iceland, came upon a new land that they named Vinland. If the tales were to be believed, Vinland could only have been North America. The Vikings were among the greatest sailors the world has ever known, and the voyage would not have been an impossible or even an unusually difficult one for them. But there was little supporting evidence for the tales, and the stories themselves were so filled with obviously mythical events, that the case for the Viking discovery of America had to be regarded as unproven.

"Archaeologists, historians and enthusiastic amateurs searched for tangible evidence of the Viking landing. And they found some, like the so-called Viking stone tower in Newport, R.I., and the Kensington Stone in Minnesota. Such evidence, however, was highly questionable...

"The Italians, who claim Columbus as a native son, are unhappy. And the Spanish, who say that the discovery of America is their glory because Columbus sailed for the King of Spain, are absolutely furious. But aside from national pride they have been able to raise no solid objection to the map. So the Vinland map seems to have finally settled the question of whether or not the Vikings landed in America before Columbus."

Cohn, like other authors, surely could not have known the *map* to be fraudulent or authentic. And he is right in stating, in January 1966, that "aside from national pride they [the Italians and Spaniards] have been able to raise no solid objection to the map." But now that the map has been found to be a fraud, what have Cohn and the other authors done to correct the mistake they made. Mr. Robbin has stated that Columbus had made a "great mistake", because Columbus had accepted, as true, the information given him. Columbus, however, proved that much of it was wrong; in that case, there was no need for apologies. In the case of Mr. Cohn, there is a need, still, to correct the information he so scientifically declaimed. Where is his correction?

One thing is certain: any glory belongs to Spain alone, for the simple results of the discovery of the first westward ocean route by

263--To America and Around the World

Columbus, and the eventual circumnavigation of the earth by Magellan, and surely not to Italy, Portugal, and least of all, Scandinavia.

American Heritage again:

The editors of *American Heritage* (February 1966) continue to cover the reactions of the Italian Americans over the Vinland Map.

Under the heading, "Postscripts to History", they published a lengthy editorial on those *tutti frutti* Italian Americans with their threats of enlisting the help of the Pope, of historians, etc., to prove that the "new map meant nothing". What irony! Those who supposedly knew from nothing had the right answer all along and were ridiculed for it; those who didn't were acclaimed. This is how the editors wrote and illustrated it:

"*Pride Followeth A Landfall [--]* But if devout dissent is what can be expected from associations given to the vindication of famous men who have long been considered cads, it is nothing to fuss aroused when a veritable folk hero like Christopher Columbus is thought to have suddenly had his reputation dimmed. In our October issue we were proud to share with the Yale University Press the announcement of the finding of the now widely known Vinland Map of 1440, which furnishes indisputable evidence that the Norse discovery of America at the turn of the 10th and 11th century was not (despite long belief to the contrary) unknown to pre-Columbian scholars. Public reaction to the announcement was quick and surprising. Every newspaper carried the story, many to the accompaniment of amusing cartoons...; but what astonished us was the roar of outrage that went up from partisans of Columbus all over the country, and particularly from many Italian-Americans. Now, this fascinating map, though it indirectly adds substance to the reputation of Leif Ericson, certainly takes little from that of Columbus, whose rediscovery of America was an independent triumph and the beginning of the permanent development of the New World.

"Yet all over the country, Italian-Americans hit the ceiling, shedding a tutti-frutti of charges against the map, Yale, and the Norsemen themselves. On a wall in the Italian section of Boston someone scrawled, 'Leif Ericson is a fink'. Across the river in Cambridge a city councilor named Alfred E. Vellucci cried that Yale was making an attempt to 'disgrace the Italian race of America', and demanded that Harvard suspend all athletic contests with Yale until that institution apologized.

"Down in New York, girding itself for the vast annual Columbus Day parade, the Vinland Map put a Yale man on the spot. Mayor (but then candidate) John V. Lindsay, facing an Italian audience, shrugged off Alma Mater and declared, 'Saying that Columbus did not discover America is as silly as saying that DiMaggio doesn't know anything about baseball, or that Toscanini and Caruso were not great musicians.' Lindsay's host at the rally, John Napoleon La Corte, general director of the Italian Historical Society of America, could not contain himself. He would not send his son to Yale, he announced. 'Many good American families will not sent their children to Yale', he added. Having thus dashed the university's hopes, Mr. La Corte said that he would enlist the help of 'Vatican, world historians, and the National Geographic society' in proving that its new map meant nothing. 'We're going to put Yale University against the wall', he said.

"In Chicago, where putting people against the wall is more or less traditional, the chairman of the local Columbus Day parade, a lawyer named Victor Arrigo, called the map 'a Communist plot.' Referring no doubt to *The Tartar Relation*, one of the manuscripts accompanying the map, he added that 'You can almost see the Russian influence in the title.' How could Mr. Arrigo know that the *Relation* was written some six centuries before the birth of Karl Marx? How could Mr. La Corte know what the National Geographic Society sponsored the dig that recently found the archaeological evidence of Norse settlement in Newfoundland?

"Well, one group concerned with the discovery of America remained magnificently calm, their claim to priority completely beyond contest. 'You will forgive me for saying,' observed Mr. Richard Halfmoon, a chief of the Nez Perci Indians, 'that this controversy does not interest me or my people.'"

Two cartoons appear on this page: "Hey--America Has Discovered Me!" exclaims Leif Ericson to a bewildered Columbus. The more important cartoon is of two monks, with one holding the plume and jesting, "I'll throw in a couple of extra islands on this map, just for laughs!"

The readers of *American Heritage* must have laughed a great deal too. After all, the Italian Americans, it is assumed, scrawled on a Boston wall, "Leif Ericson is a fink." To think that *American Heritage* is a keeper of America's heritage!

Though the joke is on the Yale and British Museum *scholars*, and those editors and writers of newspapers the likes of *The New York*

Times and of *American Heritage*, there are still many who believe the joke is on such individuals as Alfred Vellucci, John Lindsay, John N. La Corte, Victor Arrigo, and others. These individuals, who reacted as they did, and rightly so, have not yet been vindicated. But justice for all the Italian Americans was on the way.

The editors of *The New York Times*, of *Time* Magazine, and much of the rest of the mass media, began to print brief messages on the inside pages concerning certain possibilities--yes, possibilities that the Map was not authentic.

On April 11, 1966, the editors of *Newsweek* introduced their article with the title, "The Map Flap":

"Forgery was the ugly word circulating in the normally sedate precincts of antiquarians and cartographers last week. It was being applied to none other than Yale University's Vinland Map, hailed as dating from around the year 1440 and showing part of North America.

"Released in a great burst of publicity--and with perfect timing--the Yale University Press on Columbus Day eve last year, 'The Vinland Map and the Tartar Relation' delighted scholars who believed that the Vikings were first to reach the New World--and also outraged Columbus' supporters. George Painter of the British Museum, one of the group who studied the map, called it 'the most tremendous historical discovery of the twentieth century.' Even by trade-book standards the Vinland Map has had a big success: 10,000 copies have been sold, most of them at $15.

"The credentials of Painter and his associates are impeccable. But so are those of the skeptics who suspect that the Vinland Map may be a fake, a cartographic Piltdown man. Eighty-five-year-old Eva G. R. Taylor, the most prominent critic of the map, is professor emeritus of geography at the University of London. Professor Taylor's main argument, published in part in the Journal of the Institute of Navigation, goes as follows:

"'1--The outline of the northern coast of Greenland in the Vinland Map is far too accurate to have been drawn in the fifteenth century. Up until that time, she says, the Vikings had not sailed beyond 76 degrees north latitude.

"'2--The relative positions of Ireland, Iceland and the Shetland and Faroe islands on the map correspond precisely to those shown (inaccurately) on Mercator's world map of 1569.

"'3--Whoever made the Vinland Map could have derived the formula for its elliptical boundaries from Plate V in Deetz and Adams'

Elements of Map Projection, a 1945 publication of the U.S. Coast And Geodetic Survey. The outlines of the two maps, when compared in scale, Professor Taylor claims, match within nearly one-tenth of an inch. Her suggestion: someone who had seen the 1945 book could have drawn the '1440' Vinland Map.'

"G. R. Crone, librarian and map curator of the Royal Geographic Society, questions the Vinland Map from another angle: 'How such a document could have escaped notice for so long is difficult to understand,' Crone says. Crone believes the Vinland Map was probably drawn after Columbus' voyage and therefore is 'not of exceptional significance.'"

"For their part, the Vinland Map scholars stand by the evidence of the map's validity; but, says R. A. Skelton, superintendent of the British Museum's map room, 'no artifact whose history is unknown is immune from the hypothesis of perfect or near perfect forgery.' Skelton and the others admit the relatively accurate rendering of Greenland is puzzling. Perhaps, they speculate, Vikings did explore the northern part of the islands. Or the mapmaker may have guessed at the coastline.

"The Big Gap: Skelton discounts the Taylor theory that the position of the Shetlands and other islands bears a striking resemblance to the Mercator map. 'In small-scale maps,' he argues, 'measurements' may be extremely misleading if used to deduce affinity, influence or copying.' Other scholars brush off the close fit of the map's elliptical boundaries as coincidence. Finally, the 500-year gap in the Vinland Map's history does not disturb Alexander Vietor, curator of maps at Yale. The 'Speculum Historiale,' which the map accompanied, he explains, 'did not usually have illustrations, so no one would look there. It would be like looking for a dollar bill in an encyclopedia.'

"Academic opinions seems convinced by the watermarks, binding, writing and other evidence of age. But no one makes a categorical statement. Perhaps the memory of Piltdown is too strong."

Will the arrogance of American Heritage ever subside?

The editors of *American Heritage*, (April 1966) in an article by Robert Larson that has nothing to do with Columbus, nevertheless introduces his piece with the question, "Was America the Wonderful Land of Fusang?" Then the editors add the following preamble:

"How many men, from how many nations, voyaged to the American continents before Columbus? Norsemen certainly, around

1000 A.D. Possibly other Europeans, by design or accident. And, it seems quite likely, a Buddhist named Hwui Shan, in 458 A.D. He left a written record. After the ludicrous uproar last October over the Vinland Map (which we published jointly with the Yale University Press) it seems wise to remind the ethnically sensitive that this is not a new story, although modern archaeological studies in Mexico seem to be adding new evidence to back up old conjectures."

The pretentious editors want "to remind the ethnically sensitive" that even a Buddhist may have landed in North America in 458 A.D. The "ethnically sensitive" are the Italian Americans. That the editors should continue to berate a large number of Americans is astonishing, in view of the fact that news of the forgery had already broken. From 1965 to 1979, the editors of this otherwise revered magazine have yet to apologize to the "ethnically sensitive", whose millions of members have surely shown a greater nobility than those who have perpetrated the fraud. Obtuseness, unfortunately, does not allow for apologies. It does not even allow for corrections of facts. Surely, the false materials that have been published should be recalled, just as cars and tires, and anything else that is dangerous. Or is the body more important than the spirit? Surely, Jimmy Carter, before proclaiming October 9, Leif Ericson Day, must have consulted *American Heritage*.

Again in August 1972, the editors of *American Heritage* published an article by Gerard L. Alexander, **'Viking America; A New Theory:** Was Columbus motivated by Norse discoveries, concealed over the centuries in misinterpreted maps?" The article starts with the insinuation that the Vinland Map is still authentic:

"In 1965 widespread interest was excited by the first publication of a fifteenth-century map showing 'Vinland' and purporting to be the earliest cartographic representation of any part of the North American continent. [See 'Vinland the Good Emerges from the Mists,' *American Heritage*, October, 1965.] The Vinland Map tended to reinforce the conclusion long held by many historians that Leif Ericson (or Erikson) and other Vikings landed on the northeast coast of the continent around A.D. 1000. It did little if anything, however, to encourage the idea that this Norse discovery of America was more than an isolated event, one that led neither to permanent settlement nor to important historical consequences."

In 1966, at the time when forgery charges were being directed against the "scholars" of the Vinland Map, John R. Hale published a two-page copy of the map in the well written, *Age of Exploration*, Time

Inc. In 1967, a revised edition came out, with the Map unaltered. Yet, Mr. Hale had plenty of time to make corrections. One, therefore, is to question the sincerity of the author.

The *scientific* observations of Mr. Ceram:

In another book, *The First Americans*, (Harcourt Grace Jovanovich, 1971), C.W. Ceram, the author, continues to talk about Italian Americans and Columbus in a book that is supposed to report on scientific research. Of all the books, Ceram's is probably one of the worst--an opinion grown out of sheer exasperation!

In his first chapter entitled, "Columbus, the Vikings, and the Skraelings", Mr. Ceram comments on the reaction of Italian Americans pursuant to *The New York Times* publication of Yale University's discovery of the Vinland Map. "Yet the article," he observes, "made no attempt at a sensational tone. It began with a simple statement..." The sententiousness of this man should be evident in the following passages, all from his first chapter:

"Where had this extraordinary map suddenly come from?

"That the Vikings discovered North America some 500 years before Columbus has been in the schoolbooks [his is one of those books] for many decades. And there is a certain irony in the fact that some 10 million to 15 million Americans of Italian descent continue to dismiss the Viking voyages as a myth and go on celebrating Columbus' discovery every year. For, in the first place, it is not at all certain that Columbus was even an Italian, and, in the second place, it is a matter of sober history that Columbus did not so much as glimpse the North American continent, let alone set foot on it. He discovered only the island off Central America. In fact, he did not even see South America until his third voyage in 1498. But a year before, on June 24, 1497, John Cabot of England had actually rediscovered North America. He had landed at Cape Bauld, Newfoundland, and sailed around Cape Race. He did not, as historians believed up to a few years ago, explore the coast of North America as far as Cape Hatteras. According to the most recent researchers (as Admiral Samuel Eliot Morison has informed the author in a letter dated December 3, 1969), he found his time running short and had to turn back.

"In any case, if anyone should be hailed as the discoverer of North America (aside from the Vikings and obscure later explorers), that man is certainly Cabot, not Columbus. To further compound the irony, Italian pride is in no way compromised by this acknowledgement.

269--To America and Around the World

For John Cabot's real name was Giovanni Caboto and he was undoubtedly an Italian who was merely employed by the English.

"As far as Columbus' descent is concerned, there are many obscurities. It was probable that he was born in Genoa, but it is by no means certain that his parents were Italians. The first event we hear of in connection with him is his participation, probably at the age of fifteen, in a naval battle off Cape St. Vincent, Portugal--and here he fought on the side of the Portuguese against Genoa! The name he gave himself was always Colon, which is distinctly Spanish; he never used the Italian form Colombo. Moreover, among all his writings there is not a single line in Italian. Even his letters to his brothers and to Genovese officials are written in Spanish, and his brothers also called themselves by the Spanish names Bartolome and Diego. There is even a theory, though the evidence for it is rather weak, that he was the son of Spanish Jews who fled, to Italy from the Inquisition's persecutions then raging in Spain. [The expulsion of the Jews from Spain was set for the end of July 1492].

"But let us be careful: none of all this is certain, and these remarks are not intended to rob our schoolbooks and the Italian Historical Society of America of their Columbus. Even though he never saw the North America continent and believed until the end of his life that he had discovered India, the fact remains that he and no other inaugurated the 'Age of Discovery'. To that extent his accomplishment stands far above that of the Vikings in the history of civilization. In order to clarify this matter we must say something here about these 'Norsemen'. But now a last word about Columbus, to make it clear why we began a book on 'the First American' with him. Columbus was--and this, alas, is undeniable--the first slave hunter on the outlying islands of the American continent. The most deprecating thing that has been said about him is that he introduced slavery to America and syphilis to Europe. (Syphilis was a relatively mild disease in Central America. It became a frightful plague only after it had been imported into Europe by Columbus' sailors.)"

Among the many things told by Mr. Ceram, several stand out: "it is not at all certain that Columbus was even an Italian". But Columbus wrote, in his own hand, that he was born in Genoa, Italy. No one has yet proven the writing to be a forgery.

Mr. Ceram states, observedly, that Columbus' "was the son of Spanish Jews." With the Inquisition raging in Spain, and the expulsion of 1492, Columbus, a Jew, would not have gone to Spain much less remain there? No! "Let us be careful", Mr. Ceram commands, for "none of all this is certain, and these remarks are not intended to rob our schoolbooks and the Italian Historical Society of America of their Columbus." Right! Let's not rob the American school children of their ideal hero, Columbus, even though Columbus, "alas, is undeniably--the first slave hunter on the outlying islands of the American continent. The most deprecating thing that has been said about him is that he introduced slavery to America and syphilis to Europe."

Enough said on Columbus--back to the Vinland Map:

"Back to the Vinland Map. The discovery of this map was the outcome of pure chance. As Thomas E. Marston of Yale University has recorded: 'In October, 1957 the antiquarian bookseller Lawrence Witten of New Haven showed to my colleague Alexander O. Vietor and myself a slim volume, bound in recent calf, which contained a map of the world, including Iceland, Greenland, and Vinland, and a hitherto unknown account of the mission of John de Plano Carpini to the Mongols in 1245-47. Mr. Witten told us that he had acquired it from a private collection in Europe...

"...Bjarni and Leif Erikson discovered a new land, extremely fertile and even having vines, which island they named Vinland.

"In his foreword to the 1965 edition of *The Vinland Map*, Vietor writes: 'The Vinland Map contains the earliest known and indisputable cartographic representation of any part of the Americas, and includes a delineation of Greenland so strikingly accurate that it may well have been derived from experience. If, as Mr. Skelton supposes, this part of the map originated in the North, and probably in Iceland, it represents the only surviving medieval example of Norse cartography. These conclusions, if accepted, have far-reaching implications for the history of cartography and of the Viking navigations."

"If accepted" are the key words of Mr. Ceram, whose book appeared in 1971. Could there still be doubts after an eight-year examination of the Vinland Map?

After having reported that the "Vinland Map contains the earliest known and indisputable cartographic representation of any part of the 'Americas', Mr. Ceram guardedly says that his "conclusions, if accepted, have far-reaching implications..."

"If accepted", he emphasizes. "Could there still be doubts after an eight-year examination of the map?" Mr. Ceram asks in the year 1971--some six years after the forgery charges had been published.

271--To America and Around the World

Let's see now: Yale and British Museum *scholars* began to study the map in October of 1957, and continued until October 1965 which totals about eight years. Mr. Ceram is right. His book, however, came out in 1971. From 1965 to 1971, there are another six years? So, eight plus six makes fourteen. And of course, can "there still be doubts"? Let's be cautious, nevertheless. After all, the Kensington Stone even embarrassed the curators of the Smithsonian Institution.

Mr. Ceram and the Kensington Stone:
"There is sound reason for scholars to move with extreme caution especially in the field of Viking research. For it was a forgery (or was it not, after all?) that once created the first great sensation in this field and gave rise to a scientific dispute that went on for decades: the so-called Kensington Stone.

"Although the fact that the Vikings reached America before Columbus had already been accepted in the last century, this thesis rested upon the Old Norse sagas, which were passed on orally and not set down in writing until the thirteenth century.

"There was therefore a sensation when a new 'document' was suddenly added to these sagas, a testimony literally in stone that Northmen had been on the North American continent long before Columbus."

The Kensington Stone has long been shipped back to Minnesota by the Smithsonian, and indications are that it was filed for good--but not destroyed--as it shouldn't be. The Minnesotans of the next century must not be robbed of their unearthing. Mr. Ceram continues:

"The present situation is this: by far the greater number of scholars in the field consider the Kensington Stone a forgery. They do not believe it dates to the year 1362 but to the late nineteenth century. Their arguments are good and persuasive. But--and this must be mentioned--they are based on circumstantial evidence. What might be called juridical proof of the forgery has not been offered even by a scholar so thorough as Wahlgren, for he too has not been able to answer the questions: Who forged the stone and why? And it remains highly interesting to reflect upon the whys, the possible motivations for such a forgery.

"Whatever the truth of this matter, today we are in the happy position of being able to file this dispute away. For we can now actually prove by archaeological methods that Vikings landed and settled in North America before Columbus and Cabot. But first of all let us take a brief glance at what the sagas have to tell us..."

"Who forged the stone and why?" Let's reflect on it, for this is "highly interesting!" In other words, until the culprit comes forward with a confession, we should continue to reflect on it, and assume the Stone is not a forgery. Then, rubbing his hands in satisfaction, he concludes: "Whatever the truth of this matter, today we are in the happy position of being able to file this dispute away." From here on out, therefore, the dispute is filed. There are more important statements to make about the Vikings. Specifically, the German-born author C. W. Ceram must ask: who were and where did the Vikings come from? He gives the answer.

At least one was German:

"It was Leif, who, according to the sagas, first discovered the 'New World' after it had been previously sighted by another man, Bjarni Herjolfsson. With 35 men, among them a 'southlander'-- probably a German, or at least a German-speaking man--named Tyrkir, Leif sailed westward in A.D. 1000 on a voyage of exploration. He came first to a stony coast, for which he called 'Helluland' (Flatstone Land), present-day Baffin Land. Sailing southward, he discovered a richly wooded coast and called the land 'Markland' (Woodland), present-day Labrador. Continuing on to the south, he reached a country which--but the name he gave it deserves a more detailed account. After the Vikings had arrived in this third region, it seemed to them so beautiful and fruitful that they stayed, built houses, and soon went on further explorations inland. One day the 'German', the man named Tyrkir, was missed. Leif set out to look for him. He had not searched long when Tyrkir came staggering toward him. He made faces and behaved foolishly; in short, he acted as if he were drunk. Asked the meaning of his behavior, he offered an astonishing piece of news: he had found wine grapes [from which he must have gotten drunk]. He was highly indignant when his companions doubted his story. After all, he said, he had been born in a southern country where the vine was cultivated! Leif thereupon named the country Vinland." Amazing scientific research and conclusions!

Could Tyrkir have gotten drunk from having eaten grapes? An impossibility! Or, had he secretly built the first *still* of the New World. Had Mr. Ceram observed or made wine or beer, he would have known that grape juice becomes wine after a period of fermentation.

273--To America and Around the World

Having learned form Mr. Ceram how the name Vinland scientifically came about, it is important to know its location. Vinland, as shown in Mr. Ceram's map, is east of Canada, on Newfoundland. He then makes a very perceptive observation: "unlike Columbus, they [the Vikings] reached the New World by a succession of leaps from island to island."

Now, if Columbus knew all about the vikings, and their factual sagas, why didn't he follow in the footsteps of the Vikings when he sailed westward looking for a route to the East? After all, out there on the Atlantic, weren't there still those giant sea monsters and precipitous water falls?

Mr. Ceram's Cardiff Giant:

In his 17th chapter, entitled, "The American Goliath", Mr. Ceram published a picture of the *Goliath* being buried, while seven men with their hats off, and their right hands held on their hearts, bid the "biggest forgery" to final rest. Mr. Ceram apparently revels in and is pleased by the scene. He obviously is a willing participant and as desirous in burying the "fake" once and for all. How strange!

The *Cardiff Giant*, or, the "American Goliath" is to be buried, but not the Kensington Stone, the Vinland Map, the Dighton Stone, the Norse penny, and so on. Why?

The answer may be found in the following ingratiating long passage necessarily included here so the reader can have a better measure of Mr. Ceram's *scientific* writing:

> In this book we have laid considerable stress on the wrong paths science has taken, as well as the right ones, to illustrate the point that science is in the most literal sense a quest for knowledge. In the same spirit, therefore, we shall tell 'the True, Moral and Diverting Tale' of the Cardiff Giant, also known as the American Goliath. The story has its humorous aspects, for it is concerned with a gigantic hoax; but inasmuch as it happened in America the hoax was on a larger scale than elsewhere, and the forged fossil involved was also larger than life...
>
> The story opens in 1866, and oddly enough begins as a theological dispute between a tobacco farmer and a minister in a small town in Iowa. The Reverend Turk

obstinately insisted that there were giants in the old days, for so it was written in the Bible, and whatever was in the Bible had to be true. George Hull, farmer and cigar manufacturer, regarded both the assertion and the reasoning as sheer nonsense. In present-day terminology we might call the antagonists a Fundamentalist and an agnostic--names unknown to the persons involved. Views such as Hull's were first characterized as agnosticism in 1870 by Thomas Henry Huxley, and Fundamentalism as a conservative religious movement did not really begin to rally significant numbers of followers in the United States until after the First World War.

In any case, the agnostic Hull became so riled at the minister that he decided on a stupendous act of revenge. If Turk believed in giants, Hull would give him one!

Hull took his time. In June, 1868, he and a friend were seen at the gypsum quarries near Fort Dodge, Iowa, where they cut a gigantic block and with extreme care and many security measures carted it away. To inquiries of what it was for, he said either that it was for a Lincoln Memorial or that he was bringing it to Washington, where it was to be exhibited as a sample of the 'best building stone in the world.'

Hull went to an enormous amount of trouble to transport this five-ton block. He broke several wagons just on the forty miles of poor road to the nearest railroad station and caused one bridge to collapse under the weight. There were further difficulties at the railroad station, but Hull succeeded in bringing the block intact to Chicago, where the stonemason Edward Burckhardt went to work on it. The result was a recumbent figure 10 feet 4 1/2 inches long, weighing a mere 2,900 pounds.

Hull then 'treated' the sculpture. With a special hammer studded with spikes he pounded 'pores' into the huge body. Then he washed the stone in acids to give it the appearance of venerable age and transported it farther by railroad, in an iron-bound chest, and by wagon, by way of Detroit and Syracuse to the small town of Cardiff, south of Syracuse, New York. He took it to the farm of his relative, William C. Newell, who was in on the conspiracy. There the giant was buried. This whole affair, springing from the quarrel with the minister, had so far cost Hull no less than $2,200.

On the morning of October 16, 1869, one year after the 'burial,' Mr. Newell casually ordered two of his hired hands to dig a well behind the barn. At a depth of three feet the men came across a human foot, and ran terror-stricken into the house. Within a few hours the whole neighborhood had heard about the find; within a few days thousands, literally thousands, of persons poured into the area to see the giant, which had been unearthed and was now presented to view in all its great size and bleached beauty.

From the very first moment opinions were divided. But by and by the rather vague views of a respected businessman prevailed: 'This is not a thing contrived by man, but the face of one who lived on earth, the very image and child of God.' Someone else opined that it was a forgotten monument to George Washington. A third suggested that it was a statue put up by the first Jesuits in the country and meant to frighten the Indians. But more and more persons maintained that it was undoubtedly thousands of years old and the fossilized body of a gigantic primitive man, which, of course, was what Hull wanted them to think. Controversy broke out among the learned when James Hall, the respected director of the New York State Museum, declared the giant 'the most remarkable object yet brought to light in this country.' That was true enough. Two Yale professors categorically sneered: 'Humbug!' All this provided a field day for newspapers. And Hull and Newell found themselves in business overnight. They charged admission fees for the privilege of seeing the 'American Goliath.' Booths sprang up around the farm, and an extra horse omnibus had to be placed in service from Syracuse to bring all the curiosity seekers. On one day alone there were 3,000 visitors! A man from New York offered $100 for 'a very small piece of the giant.' Within a few weeks two new restaurants were opened in the area, the Giant Saloon and

Goliath House, where three different broadsides were sold, each offering the 'only authentic and reliable' descriptions of the giant.

To make a long story short, it cannot be said that American science, young though it was, was altogether deceived by the giant. From the start sharp questions were asked, and after a relatively brief period serious people came to the conclusion that the giant was a giant humbug. But the amazing fact is: when Hull broke down and revealed the true story, the voices of those who insisted that the giant was a fossilized primitive man were by no means silenced. No less a personage than Oliver Wendell Holmes, the great physician and essayist, bored a hole behind the ear of the gypsum figure and reported that it displayed marvelous anatomical detail. The philosopher Ralph Waldo Emerson announced that the giant was beyond his depth, 'very wonderful and undoubtedly ancient.' Perhaps neither had heard of Hull's public confession. And the same may be true for the Yale student who wrote a seventeen-page paper arguing that the giant was an ancient image of the Phoenician god Baal. He had even discovered hieroglyphs between the elbow and shoulder, though no one else ever saw these.

The end of the story sounds like something from the *Commedia dell'Arte*. Phineas T. Barnum, the great circus tycoon, offered $60,000 for the gypsum giant. After some spirited bidding, another impresario won the contest. He brought the giant to New York and exhibited it on Broadway--only to discover, a few days later, that the clever Barnum had the effrontery to present in Woods' Museum, a few blocks away, an exact copy of the giant, a forgery of the forgery, which he shamelessly billed as 'the original of all Cardiff Giants.' Naturally, the owner of the first figure tried to sue. But the outraged public now turned against both giants; the pavements of New York became too hot for the exhibitors, and the 'genuine' giant began his travels. He was put on show until interest faded. Then he was forgotten for decades, 'dug up' once more for a movie, *The Mighty Barnum* (1934), and finally

277--To America and Around the World

found a well-deserved rest in the Farmer's Museum in Cooperstown, New York.
Anyone seeing him resting there (a few years ago a tractor and ten men were needed to move him into another room) may have his laugh..."

Although Italian Americans are absent in the process of these frauds, Mr. Ceram does show his erudition, for he likens the buffonery of the protagonists of the hoax to the *Commedia dell'Arte*--an Italian institution of world renown.

Through the *Commedia dell'Arte*, Italy created for the western world what is considered the modern theatre. It was the Italian troupes of the late Renaissance that went to France, England, Spain, Germany, Portugal, etc., to revive and to launch the new theatrical forms. It is a well documented fact that the Italians made a rather substantial contribution to the world of the theatre. Moliere, for instance, was an actor as well as a student of the *Commedia*; then he became the great Moliere.

So, in the words of Mr. Ceram, who deprecated the Italian Americans over their reactions to the "timely" announcement of the Vinland Map fraud, nevertheless likens the story of the American Goliath hoax to "something from the *Commedia dell'Arte*" whose "impresario" [another Italian word], P. T. Barnum "had the effrontery to present... an exact copy of the giant, a forgery of the forgery, which he shamelessly billed as the original of all Cardiff Giants."

The American Goliath was a hoax, and he readily associates the *Commedia dell'Arte* with this type of hoax. But why is Mr. Ceram so willing to bury--yes, bury this hoax and not the others? Perhaps, at the writing of his book, he may have been suffering from a concomitant atrophy of the brain and diarrhea of the mouth--words that should not appear in this book. But, enough is enough!

Professor Hall and the Kensington Stone:
With the title, *The Kensington Stone Is Genuine*, published in 1982, professor Robert A. Hall Jr. comes to the following conclusion: "There is nothing in the language of the Kensington Stone that indicates the influence of nineteenth-century English or Scandinavian languages. Certain of its features, both linguistic and graphemic, are specifically ancient, and unlikely to have been known to any except a most learned nineteenth-century forger. The assumption of improvisa-

tion on the part of one or more runographers, who were not professional rune-masters, in a group of fourteenth century voyagers stranded far from any source of detailed runic knowledge, and who were recording their own every-day speech, fits the observable facts best."

There may not be any doubt that he who wrote the text on the Stone must have been a schooled person. Likewise, whoever sculpted the stone was a skillful craftsman with proper tools in hand, as the one who did the Cardiff Giant. Looking at a picture of the Stone--herein reproduced from Professor Hall's book, it becomes difficult to believe that a sculptor would have traveled a few thousands of miles to an unexplored Kensington deep in Minnesota, around the year 1362 just to sculpture **one** single stone, in that area only, and not leave traces of other similar pieces elsewhere en route to or from Kensington.

Professor Hall, however, may have overlooked the retro cuneiform. Under glass, it says: 5 of 10 (signature unreadable as it was in pencil) made in Taiwan.

A question and the proof as to how the Vikings got to Minnesota may be found on page 590 of *Urantia Book* (Chicago, IL 1955). The Vikings must have run into the last of the pterodactyls of North America. "These enourmous birds [were] able to carry one or two average-sized men for a nonstop flight of over 500 miles." Unfortunately, for the Vikings, those *birds* must have been running one way flights only.

In 1988, Governor Rudy Perpick of Minnesota proclaimed October Lief Ericson Day, while overlooking Columbus Day. As reported in the *Italo Americano* (July 27, 1989), several Italian American organizations went on the offensive against Perpick. He responded by stating that a proclamation *also* on Columbus was "only a request away", having been "reminded that 70,000-odd Americans of Italian descent call Minnesota their home, and that the nation's largest repository of Italian Americana, the Sons of Italy Archives, are housed at the university in the state's capital city."

Sad that the governor had to be convinced via the ballot threat rather than by the evidence on hand. Certainly, for a governor in whose state the Kensington Stone fraud is very much alive, it is difficult to accept that kind of behavior. It does not make sense politically for his career; it doesn't make sense historically, in view of the abundant verifiable documentation on behalf of Columbus and the frauds perpetrated on behalf of Ericson.

In 1972, Mr. Fleming learns who *really* discovered America:

In his article, "Who Really Discovered America?", *Reader's Digest*, (March 1973), Thomas Fleming shows "startling evidence... that the American continent drew many early visitors, including some more than 2000 years before Columbus." These "visitors"--(that is how easily they traveled in those days) actually came and went without problems: "The story of seafarers from the Mediterranean city of Sidon landing in South America 2023 years before Columbus is not science fiction; it is sober scientific facts." What other facts does he present to illuminate the reader? Here are some:

"Most controversial of Leif's place names is Vinland, which has been variously identified as Newfoundland, the mouth of the St. Lawrence River, Nova Scotia, Northern New England, Cape Cod and Virginia. In 1965, Yale University entered the controversy, publishing a medieval world map which had been confirmed by scholars to be genuinely pre-Columbian. It showed a land called Vinland west of Greenland. Stirred by the Yale map and the many unexplained aspects of the Norsemen's North American history, James Enterline, a former computer technologist, devoted six years to a search for old maps from libraries all over Europe and on field trips to Greenland, Iceland and the Northwest Passage. He describes his findings in his book, *Viking America*, (published in 1972 by Doubleday). Since the early Middle Ages, most scholars had translated "Vinland" to mean 'wine land.' Enterline established that the word should be translated as 'pasture land.' By studying the reports of explorers of the coasts of Baffin Island and northern most North American, he demonstrated that Vinland lay somewhere along the west shore of Ungava Bay of northern Quebec...

"Students of maps and literature have combined to study the transatlantic adventures of another sea-fearing race, the Vikings. These fierce warriors established themselves in Iceland as early as 874. From here a daring sailor named Erik Thorvaldsson Rauda--Eric the Red-- sailed westward and discovered an island that he named 'Greenland.' He persuaded others to join him in colonizing the southern end of this land, where hills and valleys rich in grass and flowers were ideal for dairy farming.

"Two colonies, eventually numbering several thousand people, flourished on Greenland's southwest coast for more than 400 years, and from these bases generations of Norsemen explored the continent of

North America. Their sagas, vivid spoken histories written down some 200 years later by Icelandic scribes, tell us that Ericson's son, Leif the Lucky, sailed west from Greenland about the year 1000 and discovered Helluland, Markland and Vinland.

"Helluland (flat rock land) has a place where meadows are covered with a deep growth of lichen and grass and where reindeer herds thrive.

"Recent archaeological evidence supports long-held theories that the Norsemen penetrated deep into the North American continent. Near lake Nipigon in Ontario in the early '30s, for example, a grave containing the remains of a Norse sword, shield and battle-ax was discovered by a gold prospector.

"Do these findings mean that Christopher Columbus should be dumped on history's junk heap? Not at all[!]..."

American Heritage had already talked about James Enterline's book, *Viking America*. Now, *the Reader's Digest* corroborates the story: "by the Yale map... James Enterline, a former computer technologist... established that [Vinland]... should be translated as 'pasture land.'" Mr. Fleming also states that there were "several thousand" Vikings in Greenland alone, and that a gold prospector discovered **one** Viking sword, **one** shield, and **one** battle-ax, and that because of items as these as well as the Yale Map which stirred Enternline to new conclusions, Christopher Columbus, therefore, "should [not] be dumped on history's junk heap... Not at all!'" Fleming is remindful of Mr. Ceram. (After having made Columbus and his crew syphilis carriers who also introduced slavery and other *goodies*, Mr. Ceram declares Columbus the Father of American anthropology.)

Harvard University's E. N. Horsford:

In the September/October 1988 issue of *Harvard Magazine*, Richard R. John, an instructor in history and literature at the University, wrote a telling *Vita* on Eben Norton Horsford.

A highly praised German-trained professor of chemistry (unlike Mr. Ceram, who was born in Germany), upon his resignation from that position in 1863, he became an avid antiquarian. In no time, it seems, he acquired the skills if not the art of his new endeavor.

Combining the skills of a chemist to the zeal of an antiquarian, Horsford wrote "five densely argued books" proving that the Northmen had lived for many generations in and around the Charles River basin, his main intention to prove that the "Norse voyagers had landed in

281--To America and Around the World

America half a millennium before Columbus... [having] calculated that Leif Ericson's Vinland could only have been located along the banks of the Charles River, which was conveniently located a mere three blocks from Horsford's Craige Street home.

"Testing his hypothesis," Mr. John goes on to state, "Horsford made a remarkable discovery. Wherever he looked--in Cambridge, in Weston, and especially in Watertown--he uncovered traces of the Norse colony of Norumbega founded by Leif Ericson around A.D. 1000. Horsford was exultant: 'There is not a square mile of the whole basin of the Charles for fifty miles from its mouth that does not contain incontestable monuments of the presence of the Northmen.'"

In fact, there is a Northmen tower on the beautiful campus of Regis College in Weston (said to have been used during World War II as a Civil Defense sight). In Cambridge, a granite tablet marks the site of Leif Ericson's house.

"Both of these monuments remain today to tempt the curious. Horsford's theories have fared less well," concludes Mr. John. "Riddled with logical inconsistencies and errors of fact, they were discredited soon after his death. For historians of science, they have come to be regarded as an embarrassing chapter in an otherwise distinguished career. While understandable, this attitude is in at least one respect unfortunate."

It is difficult to understand the need for so much negative zeal on behalf of the Vikings, whose travels even to Cambridge, true of imaginary, are not challenged. Is this zeal something that would please the real Leif Ericson and his true descendants?

Would Leif Ericson want this kind of apotheosis?

Perhaps Mr. Ceram may have done his research in Professor's Horsford five tomes. With the idea of Vinland so alive in Horsford, could not his books be the repository of so much fraud?

Harvard University and Massachusetts Institute of Technology (MIT) have been accommodating themselves along the banks of the Charles River in Cambridge whose Mayor is Alfred Vellucci. Mr. Vellucci has often been an outspoken critic of those who make statements without backing, or at least, with some logical arguments, especially when scientific proof may be lacking.

From the editors of Time:

The Editors of Time, (February 4, 1974) in the article below, talk of "A $1 Million Forgery?" A copy of the forged map is also printed:

"In 1965 scholars called it "the most exciting cartographic discovery of the century. The map acquired by Yale's library was the first to show the Western Hemisphere as it was discovered by the Vikings centuries before Columbus. It became known as the "Vinland map because it bore a Latin inscription declaring that Bjarni and Leif Ericson had discovered a new land, extremely fertile, and even having vines, the which island they named 'Vinland.'

"A New Haven Conn. antiquarian bookseller named Lawrence Witten purchased the map, which had been bound with 13th century narrative of a Central Asian voyage from a European dealer in 1957. Later Witten was given a fragment of a medieval encyclopedia that appeared to be written in the same hand as the narrative. Wormholes for all three documents--map, fragment and narrative--matched perfectly. Convinced of the map's authenticity, Witten in 1959 sold all three reportedly for nearly $1 million, to an anonymous buyer, who in turn donated them to Yale. There, scholars determined that the map had been drawn about 1440, [--] probably by a monk in a Swiss scriptorium.

"Last week Yale announced that the map may be the work of a skilled 20th century forger. Using an intricate form of small particle analysis that employs techniques developed since 1957, a Chicago firm found that the map's ink contained traces of anatase, a form of titanium dioxide whose properties were not known before the 1930s. Said Witten, 'I have always said that the Vinland map was controversial and that arguments about it were likely to continue for generations. I could not feel any other way than sad.' About the way the 10,000 others--who paid $15 each for copies of the map published by Yale--must also feel."

The Editors of *Time*, (October 1965) carried a big spread on the Yale Map, saying, among other things, that "the map throws further doubt on the legend that Columbus was sailing into completely mysterious and uncharted seas when he set out with his small fleet in 1492. Instead, it appears possible that the Viking voyages may have served as an incentive to Columbus and Cabot and other rediscoverers of America in the 15th century."

The editors emphasize the word "legend" in connection with Columbus and not with the Vikings. Still, after their derogatory descriptions of Italian Americans, the same editors should have entitled their article of February 4, 1974, *The Vinland Map Is A Forgery.* But they didn't.

In the above article, it is interesting to note the reaction of Mr. Witten, the antiquarian who presented the Map to the so-called Yale *scholars.* He feels sad: "I always said the Vinland map was controversial and that arguments about it were likely to continue for generations. I could not feel any other way than sad."

Sad! About what! Sad that he was no longer making money on the Map? Surely he was not sad about the treatment of Italian Americans let alone honesty in scholarship. The effrontery of this man, who dares say that he "always said the Vinland map was controversial", even now that the "Chicago firm found that the map's ink contained traces of anatase, a form of titanium dioxide whose properties were not known before the 1920s."

The Map and textbooks:

In the textbook for fifth and sixth graders, *Many Americans-- One Nation*, (Noble and Noble, 1974), the authors make the following statement:

"WHAT THE EVIDENCE TELLS [--] One of the most important pieces of evidence is a map. It is called the Vinland Map, drawn around 1440. The map was made more than 300 years after Bjarni and Leif described their new discovery. But it is the earliest known map to show a realistic, or true-to-life, outline of Greenland and a large land mass west of Greenland. Could they have gotten the information to draw the map if they had not been there?

"Another piece of evidence is a tiny village at the northern tip of Newfoundland. It contains nine buildings and a primitive blacksmith shop. Experts say it is the remains of an early Viking settlement. And in Ontario, Canada, three pieces of rusted iron were found. Experts have identified them as a broken sword, an axhead, and a 'rattle' belonging to the Vikings.

"But some evidence is not quite so clear. In 1898, a stone slab was uncovered in Kensington, Minnesota. It was carved in an old alphabet used by the Vikings. But experts are not sure that the stone was left by the Vikings.

"Historians are not certain about all the evidence they have found. But most historians do believe that the Vikings explored parts of North America nearly 500 years before any other Europeans. What were they looking for? And why didn't they stay? Do you have any ideas?"

In 1974, eight years after word had come out about the forgery of the Vinland Map, the writers of *Many Americans* say that "One of the most important pieces of evidence is a map. It is called the Vinland Map, drawn around 1440."

"Another piece of evidence is a tiny village..."

"But some evidence is not quite so clear. In 1898, a stone slab was uncovered in Kensington, Minnesota. It was carved in an old alphabet used by the Vikings. But experts are not sure that the stone was left by the Vikings."

The following letter was sent to the Editors of Noble and Noble:

"We are using your book, *Many Americans--One Nation*, as our text for fifth and sixth graders. On pages 56-57, 1974 edition, you state that the Vinland Map provides one of the proofs that Ericson was in America. I would like to know the source behind this statement. Some of the students would like to know."

The reply is as follows:

"Thank you for you letter of January 4, 1979... Now to your question. I was a little perplexed when I looked on pages 56-57 in one of the books. A tear sheet is enclosed for you and your class. From what I can gather, in 1974, the Vinland Map once thought to be authentic was declared by scholars to be a fraud. Now, the social studies program was published in 1974, probably before the fraud was discovered. You undoubtedly are using one of the early printings of the book. In subsequent printing the error seems to have been accounted for, as the tear sheet indicates. I hope this clears up the problems for you and your class. I'm glad you wrote to question it. Your students must be good thinkers. If you aren't satisfied with this explanation, we'll try again, though it seems the answer to me."

The tear sheet shows the following changes:

"WHAT THE EVIDENCE TELLS [--] Scientists thought that one important piece of evidence was a map. They called it the Vinland Map. They thought that it was the earliest known map to show a realistic or true-to-life outline of Greenland and some land area west of Greenland. However, after years of study, scientists now believe that the map is a forgery..."

A second letter to the Editors of Noble, dated 31 January 1979, is as follows:

"I wish to thank you for your prompt reply to my letter of 4 January 1979, but more so for the information you included regarding the 'fake' Vinland Map. In doing further research, I have learned that the news of it being a forgery began to spread as early as April 1966. I believe that in the same year, between one test and another, the map was a definite fake. My question to you is this: in writing the 1974 edition of *Many Americans--One Nation*, what was the source material used by the authors in making the statements about the Map? In other words, I would like to have, if possible, the bibliographical information that was used..."

The answer came back as follows:

"In answer to your question, I can't tell you what source was used by the people who wrote *Many Americans--One Nation*. I can't tell you because I don't know..."

And from Norway in 1973:

In his, *From the Sagas of the Norse Kings* (first published in 1967 and again in 1973), Snorri Sturluson nevertheless ends his book with a copy of the Vinland map. The whole page is reproduced so the reader may better contrast the language and other context of this and similar documents herein mentioned. Is it outright gall or simple ignorance?

Mr. Carter proclaims October 9 Leif Ericson Day:

In the late Italian language newspaper from New York, *Il Progresso Italo Americano*, 6 October 1978, its editors, in a front page editorial, announced that the White House had declared October 9, Leif Ericson Day, with the title, "An affront to the Italians for Columbus--Affronto agli italiani per il 'Columbus Day'". Outside of this newspaper, hardly any other of Italian American interest, and of general American interest, said much on the new proclamation. How strange, especially if one remembers the clamor, the difficulty, and the embattlements to establish October 12 as Columbus Day. For Leif Ericson, no clamor, no difficulty, no embattlements of any kind. On the other hand, it has been made to see that Americans of Italian descent are against a Leif Ericson Day. However, having been announced as it was, it became another blow to Italian American sensibility.

The editors of the above newspaper ask themselves why the White House acted in such a sinister way, and why Governor Carey, of all people, "acted with so much zeal in confirming, in propagandizing, and in guaranteeing such a singular initiative which, to say the least, mixes legend with history, in the attempt to 'piggyback' Ericson onto Columbus..."

In the issue of 15 October 1978, the same editors report on the "ferment within the community against Carter," calling it a veritable "casus belli". Italian Americans acted just as vehement against Carey for having also proclaimed October 9 Leif Ericson Day. The article goes on to explain that there are hardly any authentic documents on behalf of Leif Ericson that satisfy to his enterprises. The fact is that no one knows who Ericson was, or when he was born or when he died. It is understandable, therefore, to see how Italian Americans reacted, especially those of New York. After all, so much of the important evidence has turned out to be forged. This time, however, as the editorial points out, Italian Americans, because of their large numbers, do have a weapon in their hands--their votes!

The New York Times (June 6, 1979) published an article by E. J. Dionne Jr., with the following title: "Ethnic Voters Get New Attention":

"In the old Italian American neighborhoods, 'Vote the vowel' meant casting a ballot for 'one of your own.' But Italian Americans are not looking for the vowel enough any more, according to some scholars and politicians who gathered here today under the aegis of the Italian American Legislators Club.

"The club, traditionally a social group bringing together legislators of Italian background from both parties for food and spirits, decided to bring together scholars and community activists from around the state to discuss how Italian Americans could make their influence felt in New York politics.

"Governor Carey did his part, too, announcing the creation of an Italian American Institute to 'conduct and stimulate study of the experience of Italian Americans in American culture.' The institute will get $500,000 in state money."

And it seems those Italian Americans--instead of rejecting the *tribute* money with an accompanying note with choice words from their immigrant forefathers telling the Governor to use that money for other projects--may have accepted it. Does this mean that politicians can do what they wish with the Italian American vote--that it can be bought without difficulty! But, aren't Italian Americans always accused of

voting the 'vowel"? The fact is that Italian Americans do not; otherwise, there would be a few vowel-ending names in key and appointed
political positions in this nation. Look at Bush's cabinet and of other
key positions in 1989--hardly any name with an Italian vowel ending!
And Bush seems to have received heavy support from the Italian
Americans.

Judge Montemuro:
Perhaps the strongest letter of protest was written by Judge
Frank J. Montemuro, Jr., Supreme President of the Order Sons of Italy
in America, dated October 3, and published on October 9, 1978, on the
front page of the *Sons of Italy Times* of Pennsylvania:

> Dear Mr. President: I am writing to you in my
> capacity as the Supreme Venerable of the Order Sons of
> Italy in America, the largest fraternal organization of its
> kind in the United States--both in terms of numbers (over
> a quarter million members) and geography (Grand Lodges
> in 22 states and 2 Grand Lodges in the Dominion of
> Canada).
> During the early part of September 1978, an
> article appeared in the *Washington Post* captioned in large
> black letters 'Leif Erikson Day joined to Columbus'...
> The immediate, and quite understandable, reaction of
> millions of Americans of Italian descent was one of shock,
> disbelief and anger. Year after year we have tolerated the
> innuendos, suppositions and theories--without any support-
> ing evidence--that perhaps Columbus did not, after all,
> really discover our beloved America. If not Columbus--
> then who? The ancient Phoenicians? The Romans? The
> Chinese? A band of fifth century Irish monks? The 12th
> century Welsh King Madoc? Jews fleeing Romans in the
> Middle East? Or the Norsemen led by Leif Erikson?
> For all except the last mentioned the evidence is
> nebulous and completely fragmentary and circumstantial.
> However, with the 'discovery' of the so-called Vinland
> Map, which was purchased by Yale University for a sum
> reportedly in the area of a million dollars, it was an-
> nounced to the world on October 11, 1965 that America

was actually discovered by Norsemen some 400 years before Columbus.

Although angered that the University had waited eight years after first seeing the map to make the announcement the day before the annual Columbus Day celebration, most Americans of Italian descent were content to believe the words of the indomitable and beloved Jimmy Durante, who declared with Ciceronian eloquence, 'When Columbus got here he played for nobody but the Indians. There were no Norwegians in the Audience.'

You know, I am sure, that the famous proof--the wormeaten piece of vellum only eleven by sixteen inches--could not stand the test of spectrum analysis and was subsequently declared a fraud. The analysis done by the use of an electronic device showed that the wax used contained a large quantity of anatase which was not discovered before 1920. Imagine Yale's embarrassment! It was the late Justice Michael A. Musmanno of the Supreme Court of Pennsylvania, the son of Italian immigrants, noted throughout the world for his legal brilliance and literary genius, who shattered into pieces the arguments of all those who deny that Columbus was the discoverer of America.

But for all the excitement of a mystery, the question would seem to be largely academic. The important fact is that Columbus actually explored the new areas and he and only he led the first successful discovery. It was his discovery which led to the immediate further exploration and colonization of America.

Future discoveries may prove that some stray adventurer, storm-driven sailor or nomadic tribes did indeed reach America's shores before Columbus. But it was the discoveries of Columbus--the Bahamas, which he took in the name of Christ and named San Salvador; Cuba; the Lesser Antilles; Puerto Rico; Haiti; Santo Domingo; Panama; the east coast of South America and the mouth of the Orinoco River just thirty miles from the Pacific Ocean--that forever changed the face of the world.

In view of all of the above, we Americans of Italian descent were saddened to read that the President of the United States issued a proclamation designing Leif Erikson Day the same day as the statutory Columbus Day. Can we expect that before long Columbus Day will officially be known as 'Columbus-Erikson Day?' Your declaration recognizing Leif Erikson as the original discoverer and explorer of North America has tremendous historic impact coming as it does from the President of the United States.

To dilute the importance of the discovery by the courageous Genovese navigator, the Admiral of the Ocean Seas, is insulting to millions of Americans of Italian descent. We would most respectfully suggest that if there are those who want to honor Erikson it should be done on the day Erikson allegedly discovered America. I recognize that the difficulty with that is that there is no such date which can be supported by credible evidence. The alternative, of course, is to pick any date; but in the interest of fair play, a characteristic which made you beloved by all of us, it should not be on the same day we celebrate the discovery by Columbus.

With sincere esteem and best wishes for your continued good health, I remain, Sincerely yours, Frank J. Montemuro, Jr."

The same paper, without even inferring that the President of the United States had involved himself in a fraudulent scheme, and without mentioning possibilities of boycott, also carried the UPI release of President Carter's Proclamation. Of interest, in view of the materials and controversies presented herein, is Mr. Carter's rationalization for his act:

"Leif Erikson Day Joined to Columbus [--] Every school child knows that in 1492, Columbus sailed the ocean blue to discover America.

"Actually, many historians contend the new world was discovered almost 500 years earlier by a Norseman named Leif Erikson.

"Americans observe Columbus' feat on the second Monday in October. This year, thanks to President Carter, Americans can honor both explorers on the same day.

"Carter Tuesday designated Oct. 9 as Leif Erikson Day in recognition of his discovery of North America and the Scandinavian characteristics of 'imagination, courage and perseverance.'

"Oct. 9 is the second Monday this October and, therefore, also is Columbus Day--a federal holiday.

"In making his proclamation under a 1964 congressional resolution, Carter said:

"'Stories of brave men battling fearful odds fire our imaginations. We honor such men long after the memories of their adventures have been dimmed by time.

"'So it is with Leif Erikson. His original discovery and exploration of North America was the supreme achievement of a race of men who truly were the masters of the sea. His voyage enlarged mankind's horizons and pointed the way for the others who were to follow.'"

Sons of Italy gives President Carter a hero's welcome:

During the Sons of Italy Convention, held in Baltimore, Maryland during the week of 6 August 1979, President Carter appeared before the members of the Order, surrounded by Mr. Civiletti, Judges Sirica and Montemuro and other dignitaries. Needless to say, *Jimmy* Carter, the President of the United States of America, received an overwhelming reception. (A few week before, Mr. Carter accepted the "resignation" of Mr. Joseph Califano. Earlier, he had also accepted the "resignation" of Midge Costanza.) At the Convention, however, he announced the promotion of Mr. Civiletti to Attorney General, to the wild cheers of the Italian American audience.

Will the Americans of Italian descent ever learn?

The National Italian American Foundation:

In the Special Edition, Vol. 2, Fall 1978, *Washington Newsletter*, there appeared three pictures of Mr. Mondale, Vice President of the United States, and of Mrs. Rosalyn Carter, wife of the President of the United States. (It should not be forgotten that in his campaign, Mr. Mondale singled out the name of Segretti in conjunction with the Watergate scandal, as though Segretti--an Italian American, had been the cause of it all.) In the Special Edition, the editors reprinted, with apparent pride, *Jimmy* Carter's Proclamation which changed Columbus Day from the traditional October 12 to October 9. The editors make no comment whatsoever on the event. They don't even suggest to refute October 9 and retain October 12 as it originally was. They could have remembered a certain Italian American by the name of Angelo Noce, who, in 1907, succeeded in establishing "Columbus Day" in the State of Colorado--in 1907. Some 415 years after having discovered the Americas, Columbus was being recognized by someone, but only because of Mr. Noce. In 1934, Columbus Day was proclaimed for the nation. In essence, therefore, Carter's proclamation is no proclamation at all. What is worse is that the editors of this Italian American paper are completely silent about Mr. Carter's proclamation on Leif Ericson. Here is the Proclamation:

The White House **Columbus Day,** 1978 By The President of the United States of America A Proclamation [--] Nearly five centuries ago an Italian navigator in the service of Spain gazed beyond the wisdom of his time and sailed west to rap at the portals of the New World. Yearly, in gratitude, we celebrate this incomparable achievement of Christopher Columbus. We honor too the courage, self-sacrifice, and perseverance that propelled him on that voyage.

These qualities can fairly be held as a standard for the people of the United States of America. When they have been foremost in our spirit, they have produced the finest moments in the history of our Republic. Let us continue to hold them fast so that we may always be open to new wisdom, but courageous and persevering in defense of the ideas we hold dear.

On October 9 we again honor the memory of Christopher Columbus and the ever-young promise of the New World.

In tribute to his achievements, the Congress of the United States, by joint resolution approved April 30, 1934 (48 Stat. 657), as modified by the Act of June 28, 1968 (82 Stat. 250), asked the President to proclaim the second Monday in October of Each year as Columbus Day.

Now, Therefore, I, Jimmy Carter, President of the United States of America, do hereby designate Monday, October 9, 1978, as Columbus Day. I invite the people of this Nation to observe that day in their schools, churches, and other suitable places with appropriate ceremonies to commemorate his great adventure.

I also direct that the flag of the United States be displayed on all public buildings on the appointed day in memory of Christopher Columbus.

In Witness Whereof, I have hereunto set my hand this seventeenth day of August, in the year of our Lord nineteen hundred seventy-eight, and of the independence of the United States of America the two hundred and third. **Jimmy Carter**

The following letter was sent to the Foundation on October 19, 1978:

"I am in receipt of your Newsletter, Fall 1978, in which you reprint President Carter's Proclamation that makes the ninth rather than the "second Monday in October of each year as Columbus Day." From the various pictures and the accounts of activities reported in this Volume, I would have to conclude that the Italian Americans adhering to the Foundation are very happy with the Proclamation. In reading the *Progresso Italo Americano*, 8 October 1978, I learned that besides Hugh Carey of New York, that the White House has recently taken the initiative of declaring October 9 also Leif Ericson Day. No historian has been able to establish the date of birth or of death of Ericson let alone the time and sequence of his voyages to the North American Continent. Of course, we all know now that the Vinland Map was a forgery, as was the "Viking" stone from Minnesota which was removed from the Smithsonian Institution. Although I can understand and accept the "political" goals of the Foundation, if my observations are right, I must protest against the Foundation for placing politics above integrity and dignity--physically and spiritually--of the Italian American Community. I should like to look at the Foundation as the guardian against all those who in any way attempt to slander or denigrate the people of the Italic race. Mr. Carter's proclamation is no proclamation at all. Columbus Day, thanks to the efforts of Mr. Angelo Noce, was already proclaimed in 1934. Mr. Carter's proclamation, therefore, takes away; it does not add."

The editors answered through a pre-printed card stating the correspondence had been received.

Children who break their toys receive new ones; those who conserve them receive none more.

A lesson from Garibaldi:

In his book, *Garibaldi*, Viking Press, 1974, Jasper Ridley tells that Abraham Lincoln invited Garibaldi to fight, as a general, in the United States Army. Although Garibaldi received permission from King Victor Emanuel to fight on behalf of America, nevertheless, he refused. Garibaldi refused because the United States would not make him Commander-in-Chief so as to be able to fight for the emancipation of the slaves.

An appointment as Commander-in-Chief was not a serious obstacle, Mr. Ridley observes. The abolishment of slavery, however, was the insurmountable problem, and the real reason why Garibaldi did not accept Lincoln's offer.

On page 532, Mr. Ridley reports the following correspondence: "His Scottish friend, John McAdam, who had lived for fourteen years in the United States, wrote to him that the American Civil War being fought, not for Negro emancipation but for 'dollars and cents-- and trade protection', and told him that he would have been 'despised' if he had been 'entrapped by the poor spirited wretches, who dare not come out boldly and honestly for the entire abolition of Negro Slavery.' 'You may be sure,' replied Garibaldi, 'that had I accepted to draw my sword for the cause of the United States, it would have been for the abolition of Slavery, full, unconditional.'"

Garibaldi's lesson and Machiavelli's observations on the nature of *man* have served little lesson. Columbus, likewise, with his feat wherein he changed the course of western history--which is no small contribution, has fared badly. Still, everyone wants to claim his kinship--Germans, Jews, Spaniards, Portuguese, etc.

Columbus was neither Jewish nor anti-Semitic:

Mr. Ceram, as has already been shown, pointed out the possibility of Columbus having been of Spanish-Jewish background. The editors of *Picture History of Jewish Civilization*, Massada Press, 1970, not only claim that Columbus was Jewish, but that the voyage of 1492 was financed for the most part by Jews.

Concerning his ancestry, the editors of the book state the following:

"One of the great events which made the period of the Renaissance a major dividing line in human history was the series of important maritime discoveries culminating in the discovery of America by Christopher Columbus, which at this time extended the boundaries of human knowledge and changed the perspective of the world. According to the latest investigations, it is highly probable that Columbus himself was of Marrano origin; in fact, the name, both in this form and in the alternative form, Colon, was well-known among Jews, and there was a famous rabbi named Joseph Colon among his Italian contemporaries. It is certain, however, that Jews did do much to make the great maritime discoveries possible."

How great was the participation can be seen in the following statement from page 136:

"The expedition to discover the New World was made possible chiefly thanks to the large loan to Their Catholic Majesties advanced by Luis Santangel, the chancellor and comptroller of the royal household of Aragon, from his own pocket. Santangel was of Jewish extraction, as was Gabriel Sanchez, the Finance Minister of Aragon. He and a number of other Marranos were the most loyal supporters of Columbus.

"Accompanying Columbus on his expedition were the following men of Jewish origin: Alonzo de la Calle, Rodrigo Sanchez, the physician Bernal, the surgeon Marco, as well as Luis de Torres..."

On the same page, the editors quote with evident pride directly from Columbus' diary--its very first paragraph:

"In the same month in which Their Majesties issued the order to expel the Jews from the kingdom and the lands belonging to it, in that same month, they gave me the order to board a properly outfitted vessel on an expedition of discovery to India."

In tracing the dispersion of the Jews, the editors point to the fact that throughout history, many have found haven in several parts of the Italian peninsula. Many, in fact, were prosperous in southern Italy until they were expelled once again by the conquering Spaniards. Even in recent times, Italians have risked their lives to save a few hundred thousands from the various pogroms and German holocausts. To corroborate the above statement, one needs only to see the 1988 documentary, *The Righteous Enemy*.

When Columbus set sail, there were many Jews on similar embarkations, "pitiful refugees" in search of a home and tolerant neighbors. Admiral Morison draws a very human and pointed analogy between the two events, and makes the following comment:

"Columbus in all his writings dropped no word of pity for the fate of this persecuted race, and even expressed the wish to exclude them from the lands he discovered. But if there had been a new prophet among the Spanish Jews, he might have pointed out the

Columbian fleet to his wretched compatriots on that August morning and said, 'Behold the ships that in due time will carry the children of Israel to the ends of the earth.'"

That his feats were greater than Columbus himself is generally accepted, with ample proof from Columbus' own writings (which expressed his attitudes only)--and not reports resulting from action taken by him or his crew. That he was anti Semitic, therefore, does not seem to be the case. That he adhered to the policies of the Spaniards is true.

Mr. Katz and the "final solution":

William Loren Katz, (author of "'Ill Winds' Drove Columbus", *New York Times*, October 8, 1979), because Columbus did not refuse to set sail in protest of Spain's expulsion of the Jews, suggests that America should drop Columbus Day altogether. What is startling about the editorial-type article is not so much its content, as much as the practice of the editors of this newspaper, to publish around the time of Columbus Day, this type of article. Perhaps, if Garibaldi had come to America, and seen how, as men and women, we allow ourselves to be so mentally enslaved, he might have organized a worldwide crusade. Still, surely, he would have failed. Human nature, as discovered by Machiavelli, has not changed, and Mr. Katz, a teacher of American history, is not untypical:

'Ill Winds' Drove Columbus", except for the surrealistic-type cartoon by Anita Siegel, is reproduced herewith:

Columbus Day poses a dilemma for me as an American and a historian. Despite both major and minor criticism about how matters are run here, I am thankful that my great-great-grandparents, fleeing European pogroms and conscriptions for senseless wars, picked this haven and land of opportunity. Like other American dissidents I vote for the United States every day with my feet: I will never leave. On Columbus Day all who feel this way are supposed to rejoice, because Christopher Columbus beat the first path.

I cannot thank Columbus or those who sent him. Columbus and his Nina, Pinta, and Santa Maria were blown across the Atlantic by ill winds. His expedition emerged from Spain's 'final solution'--savage persecution and expulsion of its Moslem and Jewish citizens. Columbus knew, approved and benefitted from this. [We have seen the benefits given to Columbus by the Spaniards].

In early January of 1492, Spanish troops captured Alhambra, in Granada, the last Moorish bastion, the last obstacle to a new chauvinism. For seven centuries, these Moslems had lived among, shared their culture with, and traded among their Spanish neighbors. But the regime and clergy ordered them out, and their surrender was witnessed by an enthusiastic Columbus. The mariner recorded the moment for King Ferdinand in the first sentence of his 'Diary': 'I saw the Royal banner of your Highness placed on the towers of Alhambra... and I saw the Moorish King come forth and kiss the royal hands of your Highness...'

On March 31, Spain's Jews, no less integrated into commercial, governmental and cultural life than the Moslems, were handed an Edict of Expulsion ordering them out in four months.

One official suggested, 'The whole accursed race of Jews, of twenty years and upwards, might be purified by fire.' The Inquisition did force many Jews, stretched on the rack, over burning coals or tied to the stake, to pay the ultimate penalty. But Spaniards were after something financially more sound than a Nazi-style holocaust.

The wealth that slipped from tortured hands helped pay for Columbus' expedition. Sailing plans were completed when Luis de Santangel, Chancellor to the Royal Household, lent his monarch the last 17,000 florins--and by this act purchased his Jewish family's right to remain in their homeland.

Some 150,000 refugees had trudged to seaports as time ran out for the Jews on the very day before Columbus left; on the day he weighed anchor at Palos, the last band of Jewish refugees huddled at Cadiz waiting for a ship to rescue them.

The second sentence of Columbus's 'Diary' shows that the captain knew the connection between their expulsion and his departure: 'After having turned out all the Jews from all your Kingdoms and Lordships... your Highness gave orders to me that with a sufficient fleet I should go.' [Mr. Katz and the Editors of a *Picture History of the Jewish Civilization* should get together on this point.]

Along with his enormous skills, courage and ambition, Columbus carried in his heart the burning embers of hate.

On his first day in the New world, 'I took some of the natives by force.' He found the Indians 'tractable,' 'peaceable' and said that 'there is not in the world a better nation.' But his response was that they must be 'made to work... and adopt our ways' and, shipping 10 chained Arawak men and women to Spain, began the trans-Atlantic slave trade. 'From here, in the name of the Blessed Trinity, we can send all the slaves than can be sold.'

We should consider dropping Columbus Day, and perhaps selecting a second Thanksgiving. Columbus' heroism is from a flawed mold; he did not really 'discover' anything but a beach full of people who were here before him; he repaid their generosity with treachery.

Mr. Katz says that "Along with his enormous skills, courage and ambition, Columbus carried in his heart the burning embers of hate." Yet, there is no evidence that shows that Columbus did any physical or psychological harm to any Jew, or, for that matter, to any one else.

Mr. Katz further states that he "cannot thank Columbus or those who sent him." To be thankful or not is Mr. Katz's privilege, and cannot be corrected. That Columbus was 'sent' by the Spaniards is not true. Everyone knows that having failed to be subsidized in Portugal and in Spain, Columbus also set out for France to get the backing needed for his planned voyage to India, to prove that there was a route to that place by going west across the ocean.

Columbus 'took some of the natives by force." It was, therefore, a conscious act, however good or bad. How does it follow that Columbus then "repaid their generosity with treachery"? In his *Journal* of January 13, Columbus reports that there was a nation of man-eating Indians. Fifty of these, armed with bows and arrows, attacked seven Spaniards. "The Indians finding they were likely to have the worst of the affray... took to flight every one, leaving their weapons scattered here and there. The Spaniards would have killed many, but the pilot who commanded them, would not permit it." (As the *Journal* is narrated in the third person point of view, in this passage, the "pilot" in command was Columbus himself.)

If Columbus did not "discover" anything, why did he want to bring back the natives? He wanted to bring them back to show that at the end of a 3000 mile journey there was indeed a land-mass with people, and that he had discovered the way to get there so that Mr. Katz's forefathers, 'fleeing European progroms and conscriptions", by following that same route, could have found a haven in America's America, and being grateful, if not thankful to that route and its discoverer.

In the Europe of Columbus, persecution was not limited to classes of people. Nostradamus, Savonarola, Bruno, Galilei and many others, living before and after Columbus, lost their spirit if not their lives to the same blind and driving arrogance of *man*.

The content of Mr. Katz's article is bothersome because it generates feelings of anger and of reaction.

More bothersome is the fact that the editors of *The New York Times* choose, on a regular basis, to print this type of article.

What is newsworthy about Mr. Katz's article? Did he discover and reveal something new? It does not seem he did. How, then, does it fit in with the goal of the editors who claim to publish "All the News That's Fit to Print"?

After Bobadilla ordered his men to place Columbus in chains for the voyage back to Spain, Alonso de Vallejo attempted to free Columbus from those chains. But the Admiral of the Ocean Seas chose to keep them on for the duration of the voyage to Spain, further ordering that those very chains be buried along side his body upon his death.

Rabbi Miller's Columbus:

On Columbus Day 1983, Rabbi Judea B. Miller, in his article "An Exodus of Jews from Spain Included Columbus, a 'Marrano'" (*Jewish Advocate*, October 5, 1989), tells of his pride in gathering 'with congregants from Temple B'rith Kodesh at the cathedral in Seville at the tomb of Christopher Columbus. The priests and congregation listened to our prayer respectfully."

In the introductory paragraph, he states that in 1492, "the first Columbus Day coincided with the Jewish holy day of Hoshanna

Rabbah. Columbus noted this in his captain's log..." References as such by Columbus are not there, unless Columbus encoded them for the Rabbi to decipher.

"Why would American Jews gather... to honor Columbus? The reason is that Columbus was of Jewish origin and his voyage to the New World was an undertaking by Marranos, that is secret Jews. Marrano is a medieval Spanish word meaning 'swine'."

Authors as Taviani and Morison have not unearthed any documents to prove the Rabbi's conclusion.

"Though Columbus wrote profusely, he never wrote in Italian. He never uses even an Italian phrase or idiom. He always writes in perfect Spanish. He was able to appear before the Spanish throne to plead his case in fluent Spanish--without the need of an interpreter."

On various occasions, Las Casas complains about Columbus' poor Spanish. That Columbus was a foreigner to Spain is affirmed by Columbus on February 14, 1493: "He [Columbus] says further that it gave him great sorrow to think of the two sons he had left at their studies in Cordoba, who would be left orphans, without a father, or mother, in a strange land [Spain]..."

In his *Deed of Entail*, written on February 22, 1498 (see Paul Leicester Ford, *Writings of Columbus*), "...that, being born in Genoa, I came over to serve them [Highnesses] in Castile, and discovered to the west of terra firma, the Indias and islands before mentioned." "...I also enjoin Diego, or any one that may inherit the estate, to have and maintain in the city of Genoa one person of our lineage to reside there with his wife, and appoint him a sufficient revenue to enable him to live decently..." He directed that moneys be deposited in the bank of St. George of Genoa: "a noble city, and powerful by sea... [and moneys] be invested in the conquest of Jerusalem..." "Let him therefore collect and make a fund of al his wealth in St. George of Genoa, and let it multiply there till such time as it may appear to him that something of consequence may be effected as respects the project on Jerusalem..."

As is well known, on the third voyage, Bobadilla enchained Columbus and sent him back to Spain. The charges ran along Columbus' inability to govern or to administer. The real reason may have been the fact that Columbus had not discovered the gold he had been seeking. Now, Rabbi Miller gives a different reason why Columbus fell "from grace in the eyes of the Spanish monarchs..." The reason, according to the Rabbi, who puts it in the form of a question, is that the Spaniards learned that Columbus was "seeking a haven for the exiled and oppressed Jews...[as] it was apparent that he was seeking something in the new World, other than a source of revenue for the Spanish crown."

One should ask whether Rabbi Miller read the *logs* let alone other writings of Columbus. If he did, it would not have mattered. According to him, proof that Columbus was a Jew--and from Spain, not from Italy--must not be derived from "traditional documents that support Genoa as the place of Columbus' birth'; it must be derived from un-traditional documents. Alright, let's see them!

Mr. Cohen and Arawak Day:

The following article, by Richard Cohen, entitled "Columbus", appeared in *The Washington Post*, October 12, 1982, is reproduced here with little comment. What good would it do! (Apparently neither Mr. Katz, nor Mr. Cohen, nor Mr. Coen has read either Simon Wiesenthal's book or the *Pictorial History of the Jewish Civilization*):

Recently, the Japanese got themselves in a wee bit of trouble by issuing some history textbooks that did not conform to the facts. The books glossed over Japan's brutal invasion of China and the inhuman way it treated the civilian population. China yelled bloody murder and Japan had to back down. It forgot that winners, not losers, write history.

Nowhere is that clearer than in our celebration of Columbus Day, named for the man who neither discovered America nor gave it its name, and whose feat was not just the inevitable result of foresight and courage, but of advancements in navigation and ship building. What Columbus did, others would have done anyway.

But if Columbus is to be remembered, then it ought to be not only for accidentally discovering the New World but also for enslaving and murdering the Arawak Indians he met there. The Arawaks were unfortunate to have lived on the West Indian and Bahamian Islands, one of which, San Salvador, was the landfall sighted on the morning of Oct. 12.

On the island of Hispaniola, which now consists of Haiti and the Dominican Republic, Columbus set about enslaving the Arawaks and killing off any who put up the slightest protest. He sent some of them back to Spain as slaves. 'Let us in the name of the Holy Trinity go on sending all the slaves that can be sold', he wrote and kept the others on the island to dig for gold that was not there.

The story of Columbus and the Indians is an awful one. By the time Columbus finished with the Indians, there were simply none of them left. In eight years, or by the year 1500, half of the 250,000 Indians on the island had either been murdered by the Spanish under Columbus or had killed themselves out of desperation. Over on Cuba, the Indians were undergoing a similar fate. A young Spanish priest horrified at what he was seeing, wrote that in three months alone, 7,000 children died. As for Hispaniola, the Indians were gone by 1650. [Columbus was placed in chains on his third voyage, and died in oblivion in 1506. Was he also responsible for the 1982 Middle East killings?]

This is not history as I learned it. Instead, I was taught about a Columbus who was a man ahead of his time. He was brave. He was pious. He thought the world was round while others thought it was flat [Mr. Cohen apparently had not read Ceram and other similar authors of whom there are plenty. Apparently, he did not read Simon Wiesenthal's book. If he had, surely he would have made Columbus a hero]. He did not mess in slavery and genocide and he was not in the exploration biz for the bucks but so that people would someday gather around his statue, name avenues and cities after him (The District of Columbia, for instance) and hold parades in his honor. Thanks to him, this is one parade the Arawaks will miss...

No use going further. Oh virtue! why are you the attribute of *these* chosen people only?

Cohn, Cohen, Katz, the editors of *Picture History of the Jewish Civilization*, and others must have quoted directly from Columbus; yet, they draw different conclusions, making it hard for the readers to know what to make of it all.

From the *Journal* of Columbus:
Reading the *Journal*, one should be impressed by the awareness, goals and typical Renaissance purpose of this individual so reviled by the likes of the Cohens, Cerams, and the rest--a man who was the product of 1492 (and not of 1990). The Introduction speaks for itself. In the edition, *Travel & Exploration*, (Doubleday, 1948), the first paragraph is as follows:

Whereas, Most Christian, High, Excellent and Powerful Princes, King and Queen of Spain and of the Islands of the Sea, our Sovereigns, this present year 1492, after your Highness had terminated the war with the Moors reigning in Europe, the same having been brought to an end in the great city of Granada, where on the second day of January, this present year, I saw the royal banners of your Highnesses planted by force of arms upon the towers of the Alhambra, which is the fortress of that city, and saw the Moorish king come out at the gate of the city and kiss the hands of your Highnesses, and of the Prince my Sovereign; and in the present month, in consequence of the information which I had given your Highnesses respecting the countries of India and of a Prince, called the Great Can, which in our language signifies King of Kings, how, at many times, he, and his predecessors had sent to Rome soliciting instructors who might teach him our holy faith, and the holy Father had never granted his request, whereby great numbers of people were lost, believing in idolatry and doctrines of perdition. Your Highnesses, as Catholic Christians, and princes who love and promote the holy Christian faith, and are enemies of the doctrine of Mahomet, and of all idolatry and heresy, determined to send me, Christopher Columbus, to the above-mentioned countries of India, to see the said princes, people, and territories, and to learn their disposition and the proper method of converting them to our holy faith; and furthermore directed that I should not proceed by land to the East, as is customary, but by a Westerly route, in which direction we have hitherto no certain evidence that any one has gone. So after having expelled the Jews from your dominions, your

Highnesses, in the same month of January, ordered me to proceed with a sufficient armament to the said regions of India, and for that purpose granted me great favors, and ennobled me that thenceforth I might call myself Don, and the High Admiral of the Sea, and perpetual Viceroy and Governor in all the islands and continents which I might discover and acquire, or which may hereafter be discovered and acquired in the ocean, and that this dignity should be inherited by my oldest son, and thus descend from degree to degree forever. Hereupon I left the city of Granada, on Saturday, the twelfth of May, 1492, and proceeded to Palos, a seaport, where I armed three vessels, very fit for such an enterprise, and having provided myself with abundance of stores and seamen, I set sail from the port, on Friday, the third of August, half an hour before sunrise, and steered for the Canary Islands of your Highnesses which are in the said ocean, thence to take my departure and proceed till I arrive at the Indies, and perform the embassy of your Highnesses to the Princes there, and discharge the orders given me. For this purpose I determined to keep an account of the voyage, and to write down punctually every thing we performed or saw from day to day, as will hereafter appear. Moreover, Sovereign Princes, besides describing every night the occurrences of the day, and every day those of the preceding night, I intend to draw up a nautical chart, which shall contain the several parts of the ocean and land in their proper situations; and also to compose a book to represent the whole by picture with latitudes and longitudes, on all which accounts it behooves me to abstain from my sleep, and make many trials in navigation, which things will demand much labours.

Thus Columbus set forth on his voyage to discover a new route to Marco Polo's Cathay, and not, by any stretch of the imagination, to Ericson's Vinland. Nor to murder natives. Nor to expel Jews. Nor to introduce syphilis. Nor to govern as a governor. Nor to wage wars. Nor to cause death through tobacco.

That Columbus succeeded on his voyage of discovery is to his credit and to the benefits of all of us who have come to America, including forefathers of people like Ceram, Katz, Cohen, and Horsford. Yet he continues to be mistreated and misrepresented. Obviously, the chains he ordered buried with him continue to keep him bound to this day.

Fuson and Columbus:

In this rather complete book with a new translation of *The Log of Christopher Columbus* (International Marine Publishing Co., 1987), Robert H. Fuson, its author, makes many observations on the "Log" as well as on Columbus himself. His main thrust, however, is to prove the new theory that Columbus first landed in Samana Cay.

Through a certain amount of effusion, Fuson proceeds to prove the new theory that Columbus first landed in Samana and not on the other islands. While he may be right, or he may have proven beyond a doubt that Columbus first landed there, the importance of this fact is not significant. After all, no part of history to any degree was changed or affected by Columbus' first landing. His having landed on whatever island is important only in that the end proved his premise that by sailing west he would have reached land, although that island was not the land he had hoped to have reached. Any island, including Samana would have proven Columbus goal.

"Columbus discovered America at Samana Cay in the Commonwealth of the Bahamas. Although as many as nine different landfall theories have been proposed during the past 200 years, Samana Cay is revealed when one accepts the precision and integrity not only of Columbus, but also of Las Casas."

With the information being the same--that is, no new authentic documents have been found since de Lact placed the first landfall at Cat in 1625, Mr. Fuson, using his new English translation of the Log, concludes that Columbus landed in Samana. However, in 1961, Fuson placed the landfall at East Caicos. Then, in 1982, he placed it at Grand Turk. Finally in 1987, with the new translation in hand, he placed it at Samana. Scholars as Morison, Taviani, Vigneras, and many others, on the other hand, place it at Watlings. The latter draw their conclusions from Columbus' description of what he saw on that first island. He saw small bodies of water and one large one which he referred to as a *laguna* in the middle of the island. If this is true, Columbus must have landed, looked over the landscape, and taken notice of the fact that the lagoon was land-locked, meaning inside the island. Samana Cay does not have such a distinctive body of water.

However, because Columbus uses "laguna" in other occasions to refer to a semi-enclosed body of water outside the island, as observed by Fuson, which is the case for Samana, there is the possibility that Columbus may have described the latter. "There is no proof positive, but it would seem that if San Salvador [the name Columbus gave to his first landfall] had a large lake in its center, that is what Columbus would have called it [a *lago* and not a *laguna*].

"To be sure, many seekers of the first landfall have translated *laguna* as *lake*, if an interior lake supported their argument. But" continues Fuson, "what if Columbus actually meant to say *lagoon* the way he used the term on at least two other occasions, and the way it is used today? What if he meant that there was a quiet, sheltered, saltwater body, *on the coast*, about halfway along the island's length?"

It's possible that Columbus may have described a lagoon "about halfway along the island's length".

Columbus, however, could have done so only if he had stated that before landing in that particular place, he had sailed along the full length of the coastline of the island and that, having reached its outer point, he decided to double back to its center ("halfway") in that "lagoon" through which he landed. The "halfway" point would have required a conscious statement to the fact by Columbus, a statement he did not make. Had he made it, then Fuson, and some of the editors and writers for *National Geographic* (November 1986), who dedicated a great deal of space in their "Search for the True Columbus Landfall", could have come to their conclusion and therefore to their new theory. Not having doubled back, however, Columbus could not have known what the "halfway" point was other than to describe what he saw-- a body of water in the *centro*--center of the island as is justly translated--in the interior.

Although translations into English may vary, the original in Spanish has not been replaced by a new-found edition. Therefore, the original information is still the same. How can Mr. Fuson, then, draw three distinct conclusions?

Mr. Fuson, whose Army and Navy experiences bring him back to World War II, and whose academic attainments are of the best--under graduate and graduate degrees from three distinguished universities, notwithstanding the silly conflict over the meaningless landfall theory, nevertheless makes other observations which need be challenged.

Fuson's book contains a Foreword by Luis Marden, who states that "the supreme sailor was born circa 1451, by his own testimony in Genoa, one of the four maritime republics of Italy".

In Chapter Two, however, Fuson asks:

"When was Columbus born? We are not sure... Nor do we know for certain where he was born. Genoa has the edge, for Columbus said he was born there, but this is one case where his honesty may be open to question..."

In all of the documents--official or proven authentic-- Columbus claims Genoa as his birthplace. Nowhere does he, even obliquely, give any sign or hint that he may have been born elsewhere or of a different nationality. There was no reason to lie about his birthplace, nor to name another place (which he never did). Documents concerning his immediate family, including his brothers, do not show any place other than Genoa. If existing documents are not authentic, how can we impugn Columbus' integrity? More importantly, under the circumstances, why should we of any people impugn his integrity? As in law, accusations must be based on reportable evidence!

After having impugned Columbus, Mr. Fuson quotes Professor Virgil Milani as follows: "Milani... demonstrates convincingly that spelling mistakes and introduced words derive from Genoese, not from Portuguese, as many claim. This is not to say, however, that Columbus was born in Genoa, but merely into a Genoese-speaking family."

Most likely, Genovese-speaking people may be from Genova. Being from there, they may belong to some social class, albeit, the aristocracy, middle class, or perhaps to some ethnic group. Regardless, Genovese-speaking people come from Genova. Having made that probable assumption, Fuson states that "There is abundant circumstantial evidence that Columbus was of a Jewish background, at least on one side of the family. Salvador de Madariaga and Simon Wiesenthal have provided more than enough documentation to convince any objective person."

Although the books of the two authors are based on more than "circumstantial evidence" of which there is little if any, the point is that Fuson affords credibility to those works. Although that of de Madariaga can be discarded without too much difficulty, that of Wiesenthal needs to be dealt with if for no reason other than his name. (*Sails of Hope* by Wiesenthal will be treated shortly). It is important to quote more from Mr. Fuson, this time concerning a plot, on the part of Columbus' son to disprove the story that Columbus had received information on the existence of a new world from a Portuguese sailor. Supposedly, there had been correspondence between Toscanelli and Columbus that would have shown that Columbus got his inspiration from a veritable scientist and not from an unknown Portuguese peon.

On one of his more trying days of his journey, on August 9, 1492, Columbus states that in "1484, a man came to the king [of Portugal] from the island of Madeira, to beg for a caravel   to go to this land."

"I am inclined to agree with Henry Vignaud, however, that this entire correspondence was forged after the deaths of all parties concerned, in order to squelch a rumor that Columbus originally picked up on the idea of an Atlantic crossing from a dying Portuguese sailor who had already accomplished the feat. The letters were to provide a scientific justification for the undertaking, thus preserving the good name of the Discoverer... Vignaud thinks that Bartolome was the culprit, but Fernando was also capable of the ruse."

Fuson is "inclined" to agree with Vignaud, the author, who, throughout his tome--heavy in paper weight but light in content, berates Columbus, his son Fernando, and his brother Bartolome, both for the plot to deny the Portuguese on one hand, and to glorify Columbus on the other. Although Vignaud lays it on throughout, he finally concludes that even though Columbus never mentions anything either in his writings or orally with his colleagues about the plot, nevertheless, because of his silence (he never told his brother or son not to do it--therefore, he gave his tacit approval), Columbus is, at the very least, partially responsible, and therefore reprehensible. Here is some of Vignaud's language:

> **Columbus is not blameless in the matter.**--But, though this proof cannot be established, it is necessary to state that it is equally impossible to exonerate the great navigator from all complicity in a plot which had both the intention and the result of making history lie in attribut- ing to the discovery of America a character and origin dif- ferent from the true facts, and in according to the author of that discovery a credit to which he was not entitled. If Columbus refrained from taking part in the concoction of the correspondence attributed to Toscanelli, he has at least carefully hidden his obligations to the unlucky pilot, to whom in fact he owed everything. He has allowed it

to be believed, he has even taken trouble to have it believed, that his discovery was the result of a laborious working out of a scientific conception, whereas in fact it was solely due to material and practical information secretly obtained from another; and by so doing he has usurped before posterity a place to which he was not entitled. Nothing can wash his character clear from this stain; not even his many misfortunes borne with heroic fortitude, nor the greatness of the service he rendered to the world, nor yet the nobility of soul and loftiness of character he often showed under critical circumstances. There are some moral weaknesses which nothing can obliterate.

This was not, unfortunately, the only weakness from which Columbus suffered. Whatever may be the admiration felt for his great qualities, his indomitable energy, his steady perseverance in pursuing the end he had in view, his unshaken loyalty to the sovereigns who had employed him, his uprightness in all that touched the performance of his public duties, we cannot shut our eyes to certain traits in his character which reveal him in a very unfavorable light. He was violent, haughty, greedy, harsh, dissembling, and, worst of all, untruthful.

The above character description of Columbus is mild in comparison to other diatribe recurrent throughout the book. It is up to the reader who must ascertain whether, in fact, there is logical continuity between the above statement and Vignaud's following conclusion:

We must repeat again that these conclusions are largely hypothetical. Some, such as the attribution of the fraud to Bartholomew Columbus, rest only on presumption; others, on the contrary, are suggested by indications that appear to be clear enough to carry conviction. Among this number may be placed those which relieve Columbus from all material complicity in perpetrating a forgery which, moreover, appears to date after his death, and from which, in any case, he neither profited nor sought to profit.

Christopher Columbus died in 1506; his brother Bartolomeo, died in 1514. Now, at the time of Columbus' death, Fernando (the youngest of his two sons--the other being Diego)--is a probable perpetrator of the plot, according to Fuson. But Fernando was but 15 years old at that time, and the plot was concocted many years after Columbus' death, making it very difficult for Columbus to say or do anything other than to remain *tacit*--tacitness being a probable attribute of the dead. If Fernando was capable of a "ruse" in connection with his father, then documents, rather than subjective character descriptions, would be needed to corroborate the "ruse". Otherwise, *requiescat in pacem.*

It's bad enough to have Vignaud do what he does to Columbus and his entourage in this particular instance; it's worse for Fuson to implicate Fernando. And this all based on what corroborative evidence?

Shalom?

In *Sails of Hope--The Secret Mission of Christopher Columbus* (Macmillan, NY, 1973), Simon Wiesenthal maintains that Columbus, together with other Marranos or *conversos*--both of Jewish blood, planned the trip to the New World only indirectly for Spain, but directly on behalf of Jews being expelled from Spain. Columbus' wanting to be governor, furthermore, was to guarantee the viability of a Jewish state, while, at the same time, making Spain believe that he was there for Spanish interests.

On the back cover of the jacket, a quote from the Royal Edict of Expulsion is cited, giving rise and therefore reason for such a need. In the second paragraph, the following appears:

"That same night [August 2, 1492], the three sailing ships which are to carry Christopher Columbus on his voyage of discovery are anchored quietly in Palos harbor--and although they are not scheduled to embark until the following day, Columbus has ordered his crew to be on board by eleven o'clock that night. A Hebrew translator, Luis de Torres, will accompany the expedition, but strangely enough, not a single priest is included." What follows is the claim that the book is "A completely factual, exhaustively researched, radical re-interpretation of the events which led to the discovery of the new world and changed the course of history".

Wiesenthal painstakingly describes a secret plot among Jews, including Santangel and Torres, to work on behalf of Columbus' efforts to make the expedition possible. But because these people were enjoined by a secret pact, lest they be discovered and find themselves in the sight of the feared Torquemada, no trace of the plot or of the plan was either visible then or available now. If the book is "completely factual", it must have to draw the conclusions according to the facts presented. As Torres occupies so much prominence, one would expect that he be the logical link to reveal the plot. Here's *all* that Wiesenthal says:

It is interesting to speculate on the nature of the relationship between Columbus and his sponsors. Did he or did they first bring up the question of the Jewish land? How explicitly was the question treated? We can, of course, never know, but we may ponder the fact that one of the members of the expedition was an interpreter of Hebrew.

It is remarkable how little attention has been paid to this fact. To be sure, the name of Luis de Torres is usually included in accounts of Columbus's first voyage, and his role is given an "interpreter." But very few of these accounts indicate that Torres was a baptized Jew or give any inkling of the languages in which he was proficient.

From the available documents it appears that before his voyage with Columbus Luis de Torres had been interpreter of the Hebrew language in the employ of Juan Chacon, the governor of Murcia. Murcia had a large Jewish population. Torres also knew Arabic and some Chaldean. Since the expedition coincided with the expulsion of the Jews, Luis de Torres's job with the governor was obviously over. For there were no longer any Jews for whom he might have interpreted in their audiences with the governor.

Why did Columbus take an interpreter for Hebrew with him? Hebrew was not the language of any country in the known world. The only possible explanation must be that Columbus expected to be reaching countries in which Jews lived and governed.

We also know that Torres underwent baptism shortly before sailing in order to be eligible for participation in the expedition. Was Luis de Torres the only Jew or Converso in the party? The question of the number of Jews aboard Columbus's three caravels will never be fully clarified. There is no doubt that the physicians of the party, the ship's doctor, Maestre Bernal, and the surgeon, Marco, were Jews. Among the other members there are Jewish names such as Alonso de la Callo and Rodrigo Sanchez. Sanchez, who came from Segovia, was related to Luis Santangel. His official status was that of representative of the Catholic majesties. It is also known that he looked after the interests of the absent sponsors. He was one of the five Europeans who were the first to set foot on American soil. The sailor who first sighted land and who for that feat received a prize of 10,000 maravedis from Queen Isabella, is also supposed to have been a Jew. The scholar Meyer Kayserling lists a number of other names, from which he contends that about a third of the members of the expedition were Jewish. But later researchers have not corroborated Kayserling's findings.

The fact that Columbus provided himself with an interpreter of Hebrew proves that he at least hoped to encounter Hebrew-speaking people. To be sure, Luis de Torres could also offer some Arabic among his qualifications. But in Spain at that time it would have been easy enough to find an interpreter fully acquainted with Arabic from the ranks of the converted Moors. Why did Columbus hire Torres whose Arabic was somewhat scanty? Who had recommended Torres to Columbus? When did Columbus first approach Torres? It is known that in 1491 Columbus visited Murcia.

During my stay in Spain I tried to find out something more about Luis de Torres. I wondered whether there were any documents indicating how Columbus had been put in touch with Torres. The only answer I could obtain was a conjecture: No doubt Santangel or some other Converso must have proposed Torres. Columbus must have considered the composition of his party fairly early; he would have thought this out long before their majesties gave their approval to the venture in January 1492. Certainly he would have planned on having an interpreter along, for communication with people in distant lands is one of the most immediate problems faced by an explorer.

Was Luis de Torres the first European to set foot on American soil? The opinions of scholars differ. Some have inferred that the interpreter would be the first to go on land in order to communicate with the natives. We also read in Columbus' journal that as the ships approached shore, hordes of natives poured on to the beach. Columbus first mentions Torres when he speaks of sending the interpreter to talk with the chief of the natives. Remembering Marco Polo's narrative, Columbus calls this chief the Great Khan. At any rate, it is known that Torres was among the first of the Europeans to settle in America.

If the discovery of lands ruled by Jews was the common aim of Columbus, and of the Jews and the Conversos who had supported his voyage with their money and influence, the person of the interpreter would provide a key to the puzzle. Yet this crucial figure has been hitherto largely ignored by Spanish and other historians. In the *Boletin de la real academia de la historia*, in which the American scholar Alice B. Gould has summed up everything worth knowing about the members of the expedition, there is very little about Luis de Torres. Probably there is nothing more to be discovered about him in the archives. We do know, however, that Columbus sent him, together with Rodrigo de Xeres on shore to communicate with the natives. And so we can conclude that after the landfall in America the first words addressed to the natives were words of Hebrew.

Wiesenthal mentions Luis de Torres only one more time, in connection with tobacco: "... one of the "blessing" the expedition brought back for the rest of the world was connected with Luis de Torres, the interpreter. After the landfall Columbus had sent Rodrigo de Xeres and Luis de Torres to visit the ruler of the island. They returned bringing rolled up, half-burned weeds that the natives called *tobaccos.*"

Thus, Torres introduced tobacco to Europe--a "blessing". If one were to follow on Mr. Katz, however, Columbus would be responsible for the death, throughout the world, of all those who have died from smoking, and those yet to come. The observation is beside the point. The need is to show the basis, in terms of traditional documents, for Mr.Wiesenthal's declarations.

Mr. Wiesenthal dedicates many pages on the birth place of Columbus, noting that of the many nations claiming it, Spain, Portugal and Italy have the best possibilities. Because he is not convinced about the veracity of the documents, claiming Genova as Columbus' birth place, he analyzes all possibilities. Although he tends to believe that Columbus was born near a little town by the name Genoa in Majorca, rather than near Genoa, Italy--because there is no conclusive evidence in his opinion, nevertheless he arrives at one conclusion: no matter where he may have been born, Columbus was of Jewish blood. Furthermore, the woman that bore him, as well as those he either married or had sexual contact, were also Jewish, be they the Fontanarosa in Italy or the Perestrello in Portugal.

Wiesenthal makes many other qualified claims: "Meanwhile Columbus was going all about the country increasing the number of his acquaintances, meeting more and more Jews and Conversos, and expatiating on his plans. He kept his ears well cocked to his surroundings and was fully conscious of the hatred for the Jews and the consequences this might have. It seems evident that he found a hearing among Jews and Conversos. Unfortunately," Wiesenthal then adds, "we have no records of just whom Columbus met and when."

In 1494, Count Giovanni dei Borromei, confessed "before history the fact that Cristobal Colon is of Majorcan and not of Ligurian descent..." Wiesenthal then adds that whereas this document "would support the idea that Columbus came from Majorca... Spanish scholars... are highly skeptical." Meaning, that the document went the way of the false Vinland Map.

Though there are no records, one is made to believe that the motor behind the life of Columbus and the voyage of discovery he undertook were made possible by Jews and Jews only, and at great peril to themselves.

"Why should Santangel [a Jew] have taken the enormous risk of offering to finance the expedition himself? What if Columbus did not return from the perils of the ocean sea, or if, even more awkwardly, he came home empty-handed? Under those circumstances Santangel could hardly have appealed to the Crown to repay his advance. He would not only lose his money but would have to swallow reproaches for having advised the queen to take a worthless adventurer into the royal service."

In talking about the role of Torres, Wiesenthal states that the "scholar" Kayserling concluded that one third of Columbus' crew was Jewish. In the same paragraph, however, Wiesenthal also states that "researchers have not corroborated Kayserling's findings." A rather exhaustive and conclusive list of the crew can be found in Fuson's book which shows no such "third". So, why does Wiesenthal consider Kayserling a "scholar" rather than a scoundrel?

As for the emphasis placed on Torres as the interpreter of Hebrew in the absence of a priest, it would seem that most Europeans of that time believed in a linguistic theory that God gave humanity the first language through Hebrew. That single language then turned into the Babylonian metaphor. So, in their eyes, it was still possible to find part if not all of the remnants of the Hebrew-speaking lost tribes. On not finding *none*, let alone seeing how useless Hebrew and Spanish proved to be on the first encounter with the natives, Columbus and his followers must have had to conclude that those other primitive people may have gotten their language from another god.

As for the fact that Columbus was steeped in the Old Testament and that he brought with him his ardent, but secret, Jewish identity wherever he went, it is interesting to note that in all of the sightings in the new world, he gave names from his contemporaries and mainly from the New Testament. Here, if Columbus had had any secret mission, and wanted to express a message, he could have done it without much risk by naming at least an island, or river, or port after some personage from the Old Testament or even name his children from the Talmud.

Mr. Wiesenthal would be correct were he to conclude that all 15th century Europeans were of Jewish background. Jesus Christ was a Jew, and so was his God. Furthermore, the Apostles were Jews, and the highly revered Mary. In praying to all those individuals and deities--all of Jewish origin--Columbus was therefore Jewish. Likewise, one can say that Lincoln is Jewish; his name is Abraham.

Fortunately, if Columbus were Jewish, it would not change anything. It certainly would add to the list of great Jewish achievers--both men and women, and Columbus would continue to be hated or admired according to one's prejudice.

As can be seen, there are no new documents to warrant a revision of *columbiana*. However, Wiesenthal's revisionism would lead to the terrible conclusion of treachery--the worst sin any man could commit: that of forsaking one's people for personal and egotistical gains. Certainly, if Columbus had been Jewish, and he having denied it or hidden it, he would generate, in the undersigned, scorn for his person notwithstanding his achievements.

Wiesenthal and his followers have created a horrible dilemma for Columbus: knowingly he deceived either the Spaniards or his own people. Were this true, no amount of rationalization about the *good* end justifying the *bad* means could save Columbus from a charge of treachery.

If claims cannot be substantiated through traditional means-- from authenticated documents as well as from the writings of the authors themselves, then charges or claims based on rumors should not be made unless new evidence is uncovered and published.

In his book, *Documents on Columbus's Early Life*, Morison gives a transcription of a Deposition of 31 October 1470, done at the office of Notary Nicolo Raggio, in the City of Genoa document 170, with the signatures of three witnesses, stating that "Christofforus Columbo, son of Demenico, over 19 years old, in the presence, and by authority, advice, and consent of the said Domenico, his father present and approving..." The document needs no comment. What can be added is the fact that Domenico, the father, at one time held a public office in the city of Genoa--a position that would not likely have gone to a Genoese of Jewish background. By law, Jews were prohibited from holding public office of any kind.

In our case, one must conclude that, somehow, Mr. Wiesenthal has gotten hold of the "large wooden barrel" that Columbus threw overboard on February 4, 1493, and he is keeping it a secret. Fearing destruction, death and doom, in his last moment of life amidst a terrible hurricane, Wiesenthal would want us to believe that Columbus wanted to tell the world he was a Marrano working to establish a Jewish state under the pretext of working for Spain.

In *The Daily Free Press* (March 21, 1990), Adrienne Brodsky gives a profile of Boston University Professor of English, Barbara Helfgott Hyett, a poet and an authority on the Holocaust. Brodsky says that the professor "decided to write on Columbus becuase she 'was flattened after the Holocaust book [I wanted] to find ... somebody happy and upbeat' to write about." Having read Columbus' "complete journal of his life", Professor Hyett then traveled "to Spain, Portugal and the Canary Islands to do research for her book." While there, "she discovered that Columbus was Jewish."

In contrast to the Holocaust, not to mention Torquemada's Inquisition, almost anything or anyone would be "happy and upbeat". In the case of Columbus, he was morose and somber, always with a chip on his shoulder. On the other hand, he was courageous, and his feats speak for themselves. In this we can share in Professor Hyett's uplifting enthusiasm. Her conclusion that "Columbus was Jewish" needs corroboration, however. And should, as a result, be proven that Columbus was of Jewish ancestry from Spain, Portugal or the Canary Islands--and not from Italy--then we should all be willing to revise history and to accept the new findings.

In view of what Columbus accomplished, he is certainly above ethnic or national claims. He was neither somber nor great because he was Italian; he was great for what he did under the flagship of Spain: greater because he never realized that in his voyages to find wealth, he discovered a road of hope for all those who, thereafter, have come to the Americas.

***

Results

The Age of Exploration and, therefore, of Discovery, coincides with the beginning of what has come to be known as the Renaissance. The period goes from the 11th to the 17th century, and is generally considered the greatest intellectual revolution the world has known.

During this time, the Italians, who were recognized as Genovese, Pisans, Amalfitans, etc., were unique in that they were among the first to make discoveries about the physical world--through exploration, and about the spiritual world--through their humanistic studies. While they showed the world how to follow in their footsteps, ironically, they were also the first to be outdone, both to their detriment and that of their native land. It may be said that the Italians, who had no business venturing out on the open seas, did so at the expense of Italy and on behalf of nations as Portugal, Spain, France, and England--nations that became rich and powerful, thanks to the explorers and navigators from Amalfi, Pisa, Genoa, Venice, Vicenza, Perugia, and Florence.

The Middle Ages went from about 500 AD--the fall of the Roman Empire, to about 1000 AD--the birth of the Renaissance, the latter coinciding with the birth of city states generally known as the republics of Amalfi, Pisa, Genova, and Venice.

During this time, the Europeans believed that beyond the pillars of Hercules--that is, beyond the Strait of Gibraltar, the open waters of the Atlantic were infested with monsters and giants. Since they also believed that the earth was flat, they imagined huge water falls dooming any expedition. These beliefs caused the Portuguese, Spaniards, French, English, Dutch and Norwegians to stay close to shore. When the Italians proved that there were neither monsters nor precipitous water falls, the peoples of those nations broke out into the oceans, and colonized the vast lands of Africa and of the Americas.

Few know, however, that Amalfi, aside from being one of the first maritime power with a republican type of government, made three important contributions to the art of navigation and of government:

1) Flavio Biondo introduced the compass.

2) The *Tabula de Amalpha* became an international code for maritime activities.

3) The *Consuetudines Civitatis Amalfie* introduced a manner of governing through popular representation which gave rise to the various forms of modern democracy.

Pisa, meanwhile, had also given the *Carte Pisane*, which provided a network of lines representing half winds; these were used extensively throughout the open seas.

The history of the Age of Discovery is mainly Italian, accomplished by individuals who had no business venturing beyond the Mediterranean Sea. Yet, they did. In so doing, they worked on behalf of others and gained very little if anything for themselves other than the contempt of their contemporaries and of their future *American* progenies.

The driving force behind the Age of discovery was the recurrent desire to acquire knowledge about Asia. The goal of the Italian city states and of other European nations was to reach the East--that is, China and India--and to establish communication and commercial routes with them. The Europeans were aware of Orientals with their refined and opulent wealth as they were aware of the Mongolian hordes with their specter of destruction.

The first European to travel to Asia was Giovanni dal Piano dei Carpini, a Franciscan from the region of Perugia. On a mission to Germany in 1221, he founded the convent of Metz. In 1245, Pope Innocent IV sent him on a mission to the Khan of Tartary to protest the Mongols' invasions of Christian lands. After about a year of travels through Poland, Russia and Central Asia, he reached Karakorum in Mongolia. This was in 1246. His trip lasted about two years. Although the message he brought back to the Pope had little consequence, his report of the Tartars made a tremendous impact on all Europeans. His history of the Tartars, *Historia Mongolorum*, represented the first, and now the oldest description of Central Asia. The entire history, however, was finally published in 1839.

Carpini's reports on the Tartars surely reached the ears of Marco Polo in Venice. Together with his father Niccolo, and his uncle Matteo, Marco journeyed to China on a trip that took him some 24 years--from 1271 to 1295. He was the first to return from thee and to recount all he had seen and done. His book, *The Book of Marco Polo*, was written while in jail, for he had been captured by the Genovese, in the battle of Curzolari in 1298. Actually, Marco dictated his adventures to Rustichello da Pisa, who transcribed it into French and published it under the title, *Livre des Merveilles du Monde*.

The book was immediately translated into Latin as well as into various European languages. Although the original manuscript was lost, a definitive edition was made and published under the title, *Il Milione*--The Million. Why the new title?

Because the ever-so-popular book was not believed (the descriptions seemed so exaggerated), the story goes that the readers quickly called it the book of a million lies, from *Marco il milione*; hence, the new title, *Il Milione*.

But, in spite of this negative evaluation, the book nevertheless incited the imaginations of the Europeans. Discredited though he was, Marco Polo's book nevertheless continued to be read and printed.

By discrediting Marco Polo, the Europeans sought to bring credit onto themselves. However, once the path had been discovered and shown, there was little they could do other than to discover variants of the same routes to lands and to nations he had so accurately and expertly described. Fortunately, some believed he was telling the truth. (Columbus, for one, carried the book of the "million lies" wherever he went, especially on his voyages to the New World.)

Fate would have it that Marco Polo, (captured by the Genovese, arch rivals of the Venetians), ended up in jail where he dictated his memoirs--the book that gave the Europeans the single most important impetus for their future explorations and consequent discoveries. Were it not for that book, Europeans would not have known gun powder, nor of its use for land and sea warfare. The book also brought about the invention of rockets and grenade launchers and guns which soon became routine both for the Italians, who invented them (pistol from Pistoia), and for the other Europeans, who used them to perfection.

Carpini and Polo showed Europeans how to reach China by land routes, first by Carpini and then by Polo, the Europeans were not satisfied for the simple reason that commerce by land was not profitable. They sought, therefore, less expensive sea routes. The nations that more specifically sought these routes were Spain and Portugal, located there where the pillars of Hercules had been and were still dominating. To discover those routes, and eventually to secure them, the two nations hired Italian sailors and explorers and placed them in charge of the various expeditions.

It should be of no surprise, therefore, to find an Italian by the name of Lancelotto Malocello discovering, in 1270, the Fortunate or Canary Islands off the coast of West Africa. Ironically, Malocello rediscovered the island, for it had been colonized by the Romans. (With the fall of the Empire, traces of this island had all been lost).

Likewise, the Vivaldi brothers worked for Portugal. For 10 years, from 1281 to 1291, they sailed along the coast of Africa hoping to reach India. According to two texts, Ugolino and Guido Vivaldi sailed to the Canary Islands, to Senegal and to Abyssinia, and to Aksum, the ancient capital of Ethiopia. Though no one knows exactly what happened to them, their navigations and explorations, however, were well known--especially their routes around Africa in their attempt to reach India.

In 1455, a Venetian by the name of Alvise Cadamosto, and a Genovese by the name of Antoniotto Usodimare, while working for Prince Henry of Portugal, discovered the Senegal and Gambia rivers, as well as the Cape Verde Islands off the west coast of Africa. Alvise Cadamosto (Ca da Mosto), returned to Venice in 1463, where he had military and naval charges. He told about his voyages along the coasts of Africa and elsewhere. Eventually, his reports were printed and published in Vicenza in the *Book of the First Navigation by Ocean to the Land of the Blacks of Lower Ethiopia.*

Although Italian navigators and explorers made their knowledge known to the world, still there remained the open ocean to be explored. But the fear of dragons and of precipitous water falls contained the courage of the sea-faring Europeans; it also kept their ships close to shore.

Aside from the Italian navigators in the service of Portugal, others acted as consultants to Prince Henry himself and to his admirals as well. One such individual was Paolo dal Pozzo Toscanelli, a scientist and cartographer from Florence.

Having studied the book of Marco Polo, and having collected all of the possible information on voyagers and expeditions, Toscanelli--

a mathematician who gave geometry lessons to Brunelleschi--also sent a letter to F. Martines in which he explained that the Orient could be reached by sailing west on the Atlantic Ocean. Toscanelli drew a map and, together with other scientific information, sent it to the Portuguese Court. The information, however, must have made little impact at the Court--later, Columbus was to have made the same impact. Nevertheless, the Portuguese preferred to sail along the coast of Africa.

Much as he had done with the book of Marco Polo, Columbus paid attention to the ideas of Toscanelli, which further ignited his desire to cross the vast ocean. Cristoforo Colombo, a little known Genovese sailor, traveled everywhere to get help for an expedition that would have taken him to Marco Polo's China by the route indicated by Paolo Toscanelli. Wherever he went, though, he met with resistance and scorn. The Europeans did not dare believe possible a voyage by Columbus. The earth, for them, was not yet round, and the oceans were filled with monsters and giants.

In 1492, finally, Christopher Columbus made the Europeans almost believe that the earth was round and not flat, when he returned to Spain with specimens of live "Indians" and of other things.

What is strange about Columbus' fateful voyage, and the subsequent three, is that in spite of his having proven the earth was round and void of monsters and of precipitous water falls, still no other European dared cross that Ocean for a good five years after Columbus' first voyage. Such was their courage and daring.

In his lifetime, Columbus, who was born and grew up in Genova--as witnessed by the testimony written in his own hand, which has still be proven a forgery--made his four trips of over 3000 miles each, on uncharted waters, and without ever missing the bull's eye. The Spaniards, on the other hand, for whom he worked, weren't as interested in charting the oceans. Their obsessions was finding gold. When Columbus failed on his mission to find enough of the yellow metal, he was taken prisoner by Bobadilla, chained to the ship, and sent back to Spain. Thus, for the first time, the Spaniards were forced to sail the ocean by themselves.

Although there are many maps that show the four voyages of columbus, one of the best is that drawn by Mr. Hale of England. What these maps generally fail to show, however, is that during his fourth voyage, Columbus had explored the lands of Panama, looking for a waterway or land route that would have taken him to the unknown Pacific, and ultimately to Marco Polo's Cathay.

What is an important, and at the same time an interesting aside, is the fact that upon his return from the first voyage of 1492, Columbus made his first stop on one of the islands of the Azores, which were under Portuguese dominion. According to Samuel Eliot Morison, part of Columbus' crew was jailed by the Island's Captain, who was doubtless the first European to learn about the route to a "New World". What is more unusual is that in his last leg toward Spain, Columbus landed in Portuguese waters, his ship having had to anchor off of Belem, Lisbon. What this means is that though the Portuguese had learned of the successful voyage, still they were not convinced that the earth was round. Even after Columbus' fourth voyage, no one dared cross the ocean, except for other Italian navigators.

In 1497, five years after the first voyage of columbus, England began to take notice. Forced to take action, England hired Giovanni Caboto, an Italian from Genova and Venice respectively, and placed him in command of an expedition to the "New World". Together with his son Sebastian, credited with having turned a weak British fleet into the most powerful of its day, the two Italians did for England what columbus had done for Spain, with the difference that whereas England praised and admired the two Italians, Spain did nothing but discredit the man responsible for its future power. Of greater importance may be the fact that the two Italians proved to the English that out there in the Ocean, there were no monsters or precipitous water falls--that the earth was *finally* round.

The irony of Cabot's trip is that Giovanni, not Columbus--and no one else, was the first to set foot on North American soil. More ironic is the fact that upon doing so, Giovanni also planted two flags: the English, representing England, and the Venetian, representing his beloved republic of Venice.

Thus, an Italian gave to England what no Englishman had been able to give. Caboto opened a continent and established a British fleet through which England gained its hegemony. And Italy?

Italy, on the other hand, lost the Caboto to the Cabots and to the Lodges. And, the fact that an Italian flag was planted in the soil of the new world has lost all significance for modern Americans.

Giovanni Caboto returned to England with reports and specimens similar to those of Columbus. Still the English and other Europeans did not know that the lands claimed by Columbus for Spain and by Caboto for England were those of the New World. For the Europeans, those lands and its *Indians* had not existed neither in their literature nor in popular legends nor in sagas; for, no one--*but on one-* *-had* reported on them or brought back specimens of any kind, especially living ones, before the two Italian explorers.

Not to be outdone by Spain and by England--the feats of Columbus and of Caboto had become well known--Portugal finally decided to enter the race across the Atlantic Ocean in quest for a route to the west that would reach Asia. Portugal did so by employing yet another Italian--this one a Florentine by the fateful name of Americo Vespucci.

After having explored the coasts of South and of North America, and after having studied the American Indians and probably compared them with the Chinese described in Marco Polo's book, Vespucci concluded that the land masses were not part of China or of India. They were the lands of a New World--*Mundus novus.*

Having brought this information back, the Europeans had to believe, once and for all, that the Earth was round and the Ocean navigable.

More important to Italy, a German cartographer named the New world, *America*, after Americo Vespucci. All the while, Columbus languished in Spain in complete oblivion. On his death, no obituary appeared any place.

That is not all.

France, which had looked on with a certain amount of disinterest, could not wait any longer. Even this country, with so many ports on the Atlantic Ocean, was to gain its territories in the New World through the services of an Italian. He was Giovanni da Verrazzano, the Florentine navigator at the services of the French Monarch.

In 1424, Verrazzano explored the coasts of North America, discovering Narragansett Bay, the Hudson Bay and River, and the site of present-day New York City. On returning, after his two voyages, he wrote a very important book, *On Navigation and Voyages*, the contents of which he delivered in 1524 to Francis I of France.

The important feats of having discovered land and water routes completed, there remained only the circumnavigation of the globe. This was done by the Spaniards under the leader of Ferdinand Magellan, a Portuguese at the service of Charles V. Magellan left Spain in 1519 on his very famous journey of circumnavigation. Bad luck would have him killed on the island of Matcan in April 1521, thus robbing him the glory for having completed a journey which would have clinched, once and for all, the earth's sphericity.

Only one, of the five ships that had begun the voyage, was now returning. On board was Antonio Pigafetta, a scribe from Vicenza, one who did more than just note the daily activities of the mariners. It was his book on the circumnavigation that dissolved European ignorance. For Italy, it meant another name to a long list of men and women that had brought glory to nations whose people often ungratefully diminished rather than appreciated those heroic feats.

In summary, the Italians made possible the age of Exploration and of Discovery. More important, they made the following land masses available:

1) Practically all of South America and much of North America for Spain.

2) The entire area of present-day Brazil, together with the vast lands of Africa, including the Canary and Cape Verde Islands for Portugal.

3) Good part of present-day Canada and of the United States, including lands deep in the Congo for France.

4) Finally, they made available the land of present-day United States, first for England, and then for the rest of the world.

These countries have derived great and unmatched wealth and power. Compare the influence these countries continue to have on those land masses, and one is hard put to understand the treatment the Italians have and continue to receive.

The Italians have shown the way. Yet, they are last--even ridiculed. Let's look at their fate:

Giovanni Carpini, who first went to Mongolia, is hardly mentioned in history books.

Marco Polo ended up in jail. His book came to be known as *The Million*, to signify that it contained that many lies. Yet, every European tried to match his matchless feats. Luckily today, some 600 years later, scholars are admitting that the one million lies were a fabrication of the general and deep ignorance and close-mindedness of the European themselves.

Lancelotto Malocello discovered the Canary Islands, which the Romans had colonized and the Europeans lost. Who knows the name Malocello?

325--To America and Around the World

For ten years the Vivaldi brothers from Genova sailed for Portugal around the coasts of Africa, finally to lose their lives at sea or in some unexplored land.

Cadamosto and Usodimare discovered, among other places, the Cape Verde Islands for Portugal. Where are they recognized?

Columbus was jailed, ridiculed, and disgraced. He died in complete oblivion. No man yet has done for the world what he did. But he continues to be denigrated.

In 1978, James Carter, President of the United States of America, changed Columbus Day from the 12th to the 9th of October, proclaiming the 9th of October also Leif Erickson Day, on behalf of an individual whose dates of birth and of death are not known, a man who never brought back to Europe one single specimen of any kind.

Giovanni and Sebastiano Caboto have become the Cabots and the Lodges. They were the luckiest in the world because their children have thrived, thanks to the great work and courage of these Italian forefathers.

Giovanni da Verrazzano was massacred in Spain. Yet, he had discovered the Hudson River and the Hudson Bay. But it took a massive protest on the part of hundreds of thousands of Italian Americans to have his name share in the honor of the bridge, *The Verrazzano Narrows Bridge*.

Antonio Pigafetta lives only in his book.

And the Italian Americans? They are for the most part ignorant of the contributions of their forefathers, which is the biggest sin of them all.

The Age of Exploration and of Discovery! It was accomplished by Italians to be enjoyed by others who have been as ungrateful as the Spaniards were cruel to the one and only Admiral of the Ocean Seas.

Pigafetta ironically speaks of the "Ysole de li ladroni"--the islands of thieves.

And Vespucci lives in the name of *America*!

Thanks be to God.

Amerigo Vespucci
(Unknown artist)

America

Bibliography

Books

1. Bradford, Ernle. *Christopher Columbus*. The Viking Press. New York, 1973

2. Cameron, Ian. *Magellan and the First Circumnavigation of the World*. Saturday Review Press. New York. 1973

3. Ceram, C.W. *The First Americans*. Harcourt, Grace Jovanovich. Orlando, Florida. 1971

4. *Columbus and Related Family Papers*. Richard L. Garver; Donald C. Henderson. The Pennsylvania State University Press. Studies No. 37. 1974

5. *Columbus*. Selected Papers on Columbus and his Times. Griffon House. Whitestone N.Y. 1989

6. Columbus, Christopher. *Travel & Explorations*. Doubleday. New York, 1948

7. Fuson, Robert H. *The Log of Christopher Columbus*. International Marine Publishing Co. 1987

8. Ford, Leicester Paul. *Writings of Columbus*. New York, 1892

9. Giardini, Cesare. *The Life & Times of Columbus*. Curtis Books. New York, 1967

10. *Glorious Age of Exploration*. The Encyclopedia of Discovery and Exploration. Doubleday. New York. 1971

11. Granzotto, Gianni. *Cristoforo Colombo*. Arnoldo Mondadori. Milano, 1984

12. Hale, John, R. *Age of Exploration*. Time Inc. New York, 1967

13. Hall, Robert. *The Kensington Stone Is Genuine*. 1982

14. *Journal (The) of the First Voyage of Christopher Columbus*. Translated by Clements S. Markham. Hakluyt Society. London. 1893

15. *Many Nations--One Nation*. Noble & Noble. New York, 1974

16. *Picture History of Jewish Civilization*. Massada Press. Israel, 1970

17. Robbin, Irving. *Explorations and Discoveries*. Grosser & Dunlap. 1961

18. Morison, Samuel. *Admiral of the Ocean Seas*. Little Brown. Boston. 1942

19. Morison, Samuel. *Christopher Columbus, Mariner*. Mentor Books. New York, 1942

20. Paolucci, Anne. *Cipango!*. Griffon House. New York. 1985

21. Pigafetta, Giovanni. *Voyage Around the World*. Translated by John Pinkerton. London, 1812

22. Polo, Marco. *Book of Ser Marco Polo*. London, Murray. 1875

23. Ridley, Jasper. *Garibaldi*. Viking Press. Minneapolis. 1974

24. *Tabula de Amalpha*. Di Mauro Editore. 1965

25. Verrazzano, Giovanni. *On Navigation and Voyages*

26. Wiesenthal, Simon. *Sails of Hope--The Secret Mission of Christopher Columbus*. Macmillan. NY. 1973

329--To America and Around the World

Newspaper, Magazines, Visuals

American Heritage
Boston Globe
Boston Herald
Harvard Magazine
Jewish Advocate
Italy-Italy
L'Italo Americano
National Geographic
New Haven Register, The
Newsweek
New York Times, The
Progresso Italo Americano
Readers' Digest
Righteous Enemy
Saturday Evening Post
Science Digest
Sons of Italy Times
Time
Washington Newsletter

Index